Joomla! 1.5 SEO

Improve the search engine friendliness of your web site

Herbert-Jan van Dinther

BIRMINGHAM - MUMBAI

Joomla! 1.5 SEO

First published: October 2009

Production Reference: 1011009

Published by Packt Publishing Ltd.
32 Lincoln Road
Olton
Birmingham, B27 6PA, UK.

ISBN 978-1-847198-16-7

www.packtpub.com

Cover Image by Ed Maclean (edmaclean@gmail.com)

Credits

Author

Herbert-Jan van Dinther

Reviewers

Jose Argudo Blanco

Niko Kotiniemi

Acquisition Editor

David Barnes

Development Editor

Dhiraj Chandiramani

Technical Editors

Gaurav Datar

Dhwani Devater

Copy Editor

Sanchari Mukherjee

Indexers

Rekha Nair

Hemangini Bari

Editorial Team Leader

Gagandeep Singh

Project Team Leader

Lata Basantani

Project Coordinator

Rajashree Hamine

Proofreader

Lesley Harrison

Graphics

Nilesh R. Mohite

Production Coordinators

Dolly Dasilva

Adline Swetha Jesuthas

Cover Work

Dolly Dasilva

About the Author

Herbert-Jan van Dinther was born in September 1959 in Heusden, the Netherlands. He first came in contact with computers during his study at the Fontys Hogeshool in Eindhoven. He is currently working as an ICT Manager and owns a small part-time company named Web site Builder and SEO Consultant that focuses on Joomla! and WordPress. He holds a Bachelor's degree in Business Economics.

His first web site was built with Microsoft FrontPage in 1999 and he introduced the "new" Google search engine to a lot of people at that time. Google now has a market share in search of up to 98 percent in the Netherlands. He wanted his and his customers' sites to rank well in the search engines and his quest and passion for SEO knowledge has not left him since that first site.

Later he came across the NetworkDNA methodology to structure computer network documentation , which was created by Don Krause. Don Krause introduced him to Mambo — the content management system that later became Joomla!. To promote the methodology in the Netherlands, a web site based on Joomla! is now ranking high in the Dutch search engines.

Joomla! is now one of his biggest passions and sharing his SEO knowledge about Joomla! has resulted in several web sites and blogs on that topic. He also published the *Little Joomla SEO Book,* a free PDF file about Joomla! 1.0 SEO. Currently, he is working on a new web site `http://www.herbertjanvandinther.com` to show how powerful and easy Joomla! is for building your own site.

I want to thank all the people at Packt who helped me to create this book and promote the Joomla! content management system and show people how they can improve their sites. They showed me how to improve my writing and gave some excellent advice and contributions to make this book a better read.

I also want to thank my wife and children for the patience and time they gave me to accomplish the large undertaking of writing this book.

About the Reviewers

Jose Argudo Blanco is a web developer from Valencia, Spain. After finishing his studies he started working for a software company, always working with PHP — a language he learned to love. Now, after six years, he is confident in his experience and has started to work as a freelancer in an attempt to give his personal vision to the projects he undertakes.

Working with Joomla!, CodeIgniter, CakePHP, JQuery and other known open source technologies and frameworks, he expects to build stable and reliable applications that reflect his desire of making better web experiences.

He has also worked as reviewer for the book *Magento – Beginners Guide* and hopes to continue working with Magento-related projects.

> To my girlfriend Silvia, without her support I couldn't have reached this long.

Niko Kotiniemi is a web developer and web/mobile technology enthusiast living in Jyväskylä, in central Finland. He has worked on developing and maintaining web sites professionally as a freelancer for over three years. Lately he has also reviewed four Joomla! books for Packt Publishing:

- *Joomla! E-Commerce with VirtueMart*, Suhreed Sarkar, Packt Publishing
- *Joomla! Accessibility*, Joshue O Connor, Packt Publishing
- *Joomla! Cash*, Brandon Dawson, Tom Canavan, Packt Publishing
- *Joomla! 1.5 Template Design*, Tessa Blakeley Silver, Packt Publishing

Niko Kotiniemi is currently employed as a web designer at the Guidance and Counseling Services for Adults — National Coordination Project (www.opinovi.fi). Over the past few years he has been employed by the Federation of Special Service and Clerical employees, ERTO (www.erto.fi) — a labor union whose members, among others, include those that work in the IT-service industry in the private sector.

He continues his lifetime computer hobby by studying a Bachelor's degree in Software and Telecommunication Engineering at the Jyväskylä University of Applied Sciences, JAMK. In his spare time he enjoys outdoor activities, developing his web site (www.aktiivi.com), spending time with his family and friends, or delving into that next ultimate solution or API that will allow applications and web sites to interlink and share information.

Table of Contents

Preface	**1**
Chapter 1: Developing your SEO and Keyword Strategy	**7**
Setting up your SEO strategy	**8**
Solving basic Joomla! 1.5 SEO problems	9
Global configuration meta tag settings	11
PDF, Print, and E-mail icons	11
Meta generator tag	12
Why do you need to do keyword research?	13
How to do basic keyword research	14
The tools of the trade	**15**
Free tools	15
Google's Adwords	16
Wordtracker	19
SEO Book Keyword Tool	21
Commercial tools	22
Keyword Elite	22
iBusinessPromoter	24
KeywordDiscovery and SEO toolkit	27
Choosing the right key words	**28**
Building your keyword list	33
Setting up your baseline statistics	34
Summary	**40**
Chapter 2: Optimizing Site Structure	**43**
Optimizing your site structure for SEO	**43**
Using sections and categories to create structure	44
Sections and categories	44
Grouping related topics together	45
Putting your keywords to work	46
Create a better-optimized structure with keywords	48
How will a better structure affect your rankings	48

Improving your site's usability for users and search engines	49
Showing your site structure at a glance	49
Small and fast improvements for usability	49
Placing uncategorized articles	50
Improve your menu structure for SEO	51
Create a better structure with menus	51
Restructuring your menu items	52
How to use separators and submenus for SEO	55
Why a sitemap component is essential for search engines	56
Why you should use a sitemap.xml file	56
Installing and configuring a sitemap component	57
Installing and using Xmap sitemap component	57
Submitting your sitemap to search engines	63
Verifying your site with Google	63
Verifying your site with Yahoo!	65
Verifying your site with Bing	66
Using the robots.txt file to guide Search Engine Robots	66
Putting the robots to work	67
Improving the Joomla! robots.txt file	67
Summary	**70**
Chapter 3: Improve Joomla! SEO with the Joomlatwork SEF Patch	**71**
Downloading and installing the Joomlatwork patch	**72**
Getting hold of the patch	72
Installing the patch	73
Make your titles more keyword rich	**74**
Create keyword-rich HTML titles for menus	77
Create keyword-rich HTML titles for pages	79
How to use the new Joomlatwork fields	80
Making better use of the HTML title	80
Improve your pages' metadata	**82**
Why does metadata matter? How does Google use it?	84
Using the description tag effectively	84
Using the keywords tag effectively	85
How to avoid duplicate meta tag descriptions and keywords	85
Control how search engines index your site	**86**
Control all search engines with the Robots meta tag	86
Google settings	87
Upgrade, uninstall, or modify the patch	**88**
Some other changes from the patch	**88**
Generator Meta name	88
Copyright	89
The Joomlatwork SEF component	**89**
Summary	**90**

Chapter 4: How to Write Keyword-rich Articles	**91**
Importance of writing with keywords	**91**
Choosing your keywords	91
Choosing the topics to write about	92
Finding the keywords to target	92
How do Google and Yahoo! show your keywords	93
Writing with keywords in mind	**95**
Putting structure into your pages	95
Getting the best placements for your keywords	95
Optimizing your articles	**96**
Start writing naturally	97
How to write better titles	97
Getting more keywords into your title	98
Making sure you stay focused	99
Keyword density—what is it and why bother?	100
Using headlines in the best way	**100**
How to make your articles scanable	101
Getting keywords into headers and paragraphs	102
Using the metadata fields to your advantage	**103**
Writing good meta tag descriptions	104
How to use the Keywords field	104
Putting it all together	106
Summary	**108**
Chapter 5: Joomla! Blogging and RSS Feeds	**109**
How is blogging good for SEO?	**110**
Creating fresh content	110
Google and blog indexing	110
Setting up Joomla! as a blog	**111**
How to structure your blog section	111
Choosing your blog categories	112
Stay focused and limit yourself	113
Creating a blog menu	114
Why use a Full Text instead of Intro Text feed	116
Separator and blog categories	116
Commenting anyone?	**117**
Why comments are important	118
Interaction with your visitors	118
Installation and configuration of the Disqus plugin	118
Setting up your commenting service on Disqus	119
Limitations of Disqus	122
Putting your RSS Feeds to work	123

Using Google's FeedBurner for SEO	**125**
Choosing your FeedBurner options for optimal results	127
Replacing your RSS Feed with the FeedBurner feed	131
How to claim your blog on Technorati	**132**
Using separate blog components	**134**
MyBlog—a commercial blogging component	135
Summary	**138**
Chapter 6: Create Search Engine Friendly URLs with sh404SEF	**139**
What are the best SEF URLs?	**140**
Available choices for SEF components	**141**
Why you should choose sh404SEF	**142**
How to get hold of sh404SEF	**142**
Installation and basic configuration	143
Looking for the optimal basic configuration options	144
Setting up the plugin	147
How about the 404 page	148
Looking at advanced configuration settings	**150**
Taking care of extended basics	154
How to optimize your plugins	154
Extra components, SEF, and other plugins	155
Language setting and SEF	156
Getting advanced, are you?	**157**
Cache management	158
Advanced component configuration	158
By component settings	161
Using the best Meta/SEO option settings	162
Security 404, and advanced	164
How to change your Home page Meta settings	**164**
Putting meta tags on Non-SEF components	165
Taking it one step further—special URLs	167
Solving and preventing possible problems	**168**
Summary	**170**
Chapter 7: The Importance of Good SEO Joomla! Templates	**171**
Finding the right template for your site	**171**
What to look for in SEO templates	**172**
Why validation matters	**175**
Why you should look at code positioning	175
Leave your tables behind	176
Choosing between free and commercial templates	**177**
Another problem with free templates	179

Why go for commercial templates?	179
What does usability have to do with SEO	**181**
How to make your site sticky	182
Headlines and typography	182
Going for fixed or fluid?	**183**
Display font changes for bigger or smaller text	185
Why use fast templates	185
Summary	**187**
Chapter 8: Why Speed is Important in SEO	**189**
Finding your slowdowns	**189**
Using OctaGate for insight	190
YSlow is what you need	192
Using the cache function of Joomla!	**195**
Set the caching for your modules	196
Optimize your server settings	196
Caching outside Joomla!	197
Optimizing CSS and Javascript	**197**
Looking at drawbacks and warnings	199
Optimizing your CSS files	200
Combining CSS files	202
Doing easy file path optimization	203
Looking for errors in log files	**204**
Improving your images	**204**
Resizing your images	205
Using the right program for the job	205
Naming your files with keywords in mind	208
Using the on page size parameters	208
Using Caption, Alt, and Title	209
Summary	**210**
Chapter 9: Tracking and Tracing to Improve Your Web Site	**211**
Looking at your options	**212**
Using your own separate AWStats	214
Getting your statistics for free	216
The Alexa web site information	216
Getting free site analysis from StatCounter and Google Analytics	218
Looking at your StatCounter stats	219
Don't count your own visits	221
Looking at StatCounter information and graphs	222
How to analyze Google Analytics	226
Filtering out your static IP address visits	228
Excluding your visits from a IP dynamic address	228

Getting the big picture of traffic	229
What to look for by numbers	231
Learning more of you traffic sources	234
Reading more about your Keywords	235
Structure and content analysis	236
How to select a different time span	237
Summary	**239**
Chapter 10: How to get Incoming Links	**241**
Do you want to use paid incoming links?	**241**
Helping people helps you with link building	**242**
Commenting done the right way	**243**
Finding places to comment	244
Looking back at Alexa	246
Creating your own linking empire	**247**
Google Sites	248
Blogger	249
Squidoo	250
HubPages	251
WordPress	252
Blogging on WordPress and your ranking	253
Digging deeper into WORDPRESS.COM blogs	254
Using free blogging services	255
How to minimize your blog writing time	**255**
Using your best content for link building	256
Writing articles for links	256
Learning how to ask for a link	**257**
Knowing what to include in your link request	259
Summary	**260**
Appendix A: A Joomla! Case Study in SEO	**263**
Choosing the niche	**264**
Picking a domain name	264
Setting up the Joomla! 1.5 base installation	**265**
Installing the SEF patch and sh404SEF component	265
Installing a good Joomla! SEO template	267
Naming the sections and categories	**269**
Building the menus	**270**
The main menu	272
Using images in blog layout	274
Installing and configuring a sitemap	**275**
Writing the content	**276**
Using 404 to guide visitors	276
Using the HTML title and meta tags	277

Fast and furious, or slow going   279
Using Google Webmaster tools   **279**
Set your preferred URL   280
Google's help on meta tag errors   280
Analyze results, rinse, and repeat.   281
Rounding it all up   **284**

Appendix B: Joomla! robots.txt and .htaccess   **285**
Making sense of robots.txt   **285**
Setting your rules for robots   285
Standard Joomla! robots.txt   286
Improving the standard for image searchers   287
A complete example   287
Learn to love your .htaccess file   **288**
The basics   288
The good and the bad   289
Solving the most common problems   289
Some common problems   289
.htaccess extras   290
Final thoughts on 301 redirects   291
Redirection to a new domain   291
Working examples for your site   292
Standard Joomla! .htaccess   292
FollowSymLinks set Off   294
FollowSymLinks set Off RewriteBase On   295
Basic sh404SEF SEF basic .htaccess standard   296

Index   **299**

Preface

Many people are building web sites with Joomla! because it is an easy-to-use-and understand content management system. The fact that it is free is also a factor that makes Joomla! one of the most popular systems that you can use to build your own web site.

It is only after your Joomla! site is built that you wonder why there are such less number of visitors and why you don't rank as highly in the search engines as you thought you would. At that moment you start investigating different sources and possibilities to improve your rankings and get more visitors. Joomla! SEO will help you attract those visitors and improve the way you rank in search engines by giving you the techniques and knowledge to help you achieve your goals.

What this book covers

Chapter 1 will give you an overview of what we will cover in this book, and get you started with the foundations of your SEO strategy by creating your keyword list. Besides that you will set up a baseline to monitor your progress, using some statistical tools.

Chapter 2 helps you understand and implement the best way to structure your content for better search engine results as well as giving your visitors a better experience. We also look at files such as `sitemap.xml` and `robots.txt` to guide Search Engine Robots. You will also improve on your menu structure so that it reflects your new web site structure.

Chapter 3 covers the installation and use of the Joomlatwork SEF patch, which essentially gives you even more power to optimize your Joomla! site by enhancing some core Joomla! items. You will see what improvements are made and how you can benefit the most from these changes. We also look at some of the basics of meta tags.

Chapter 4 covers content ideas, deciding which keywords to target, and the importance of structure in the content of your pages. You will also learn about keyword placement, how to enhance your titles, and the use of headers and paragraphs. You will read more about the meta tags description and keywords, along with the importance, and proper use of those fields.

Chapter 5 helps you set up a blog within Joomla! and shows you the external tools that you need to use to get the most out of your blogging efforts. You will read more about the importance of blogging and commenting systems, along with how to implement solutions that make Joomla! an even better blogging tool.

Chapter 6 covers the installation and configuration of sh404SEF — the best component for creating search engine friendly URLs in Joomla!. You will learn about the basic and advanced configuration settings of this component, and how you can use it to your advantage. We will also look at possible errors that may arise and how to fix them.

Chapter 7 covers Joomla! templates and their influence on your web site. You will learn what makes an SEO template a good one and how to find one that fits your needs. We also look at the choice between free and commercial templates, along with the need for code validation and source optimization.

Chapter 8 discusses all the possibilities for improving the speed of your web site. Speed is a necessity for users and Search Engine Robots. You will learn about the built-in cache system, and learn how to find possible delays and how to correct them. You will see the effects of image optimization and the best way to use images in your pages.

Chapter 9 covers the need for and use of statistics programs to track your visitors and progress. You will look at the data provided by such programs and learn how to interpret them. StatCounter and Google Analytics are described to give you an insight into the way you can use the data collected from your site, in order to gain even better rankings, and to improve the conversion rate of your site.

Chapter 10 covers several different ways to get more incoming links, from commenting on other sites to blogging on other platforms. Building incoming links is time consuming, but if you do it the right way it is a very good way to boost your web site's rankings.

Appendix A covers a complete case study of creating a web site in Joomla! and how it evolves. It takes you from choosing a domain name to structuring the site for best performance. You see what benefits and problems are involved in finding the right template, as well as the installation of components, and how to get into the search engines. We also touch on the use of Google webmaster tools.

Appendix B covers Joomla! `robots.txt` and `.htaccess` files. Especially the later can cause big problems for a Joomla! webmaster if it is configured the wrong way. There is an explanation of the different options within `.htaccess` and `robots.txt`. You get real life examples that can help you solve common issues to prevent error 500 pages on your site.

What you need for this book

This book describes how to improve a Joomla! 1.5 web site for search engine rankings. You need to have a Joomla! 1.5 web site installed and hosted on a publicly accessible server where internet users can have free access to it.

You need to know how to install Joomla! components and you need to have access to the administration panel on a super administrator level to make some changes in the configuration of your web site.

You also need to have access to the root of your Joomla! installation, preferably using FTP to install the SEF patch and to change your `robots.txt` and `.htaccess` files.

Who this book is for

This book is written for anyone using Joomla! — ranging from owners of business sites, to web site developers and personal web site owners. Any Joomla! web site owner who wants to sell products or services, or send out a message to the world will find that getting better rankings in the search engines will help them reach their goal.

Some prior knowledge of Joomla! is expected, but no prior knowledge of search engine optimization is needed for this book. The reader will get a deeper level of knowledge on how to make their web site rank better and attract more visitors to their site.

Conventions

In this book, you will find a number of styles of text that distinguish between different kinds of information. Here are some examples of these styles, and an explanation of their meaning.

Code words in text are shown as follows: "If you don't use the second option you would have an extra `/index.php/` in the URL."

New terms and **important words** are shown in bold. Words that you see on the screen, in menus or dialog boxes for example, appear in our text like this: "If you look at the configuration panel, there is a small section called **SEO Settings**".

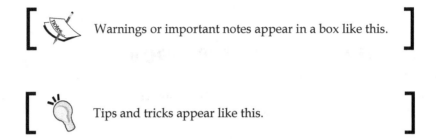

Warnings or important notes appear in a box like this.

Tips and tricks appear like this.

Reader feedback

Feedback from our readers is always welcome. Let us know what you think about this book—what you liked or may have disliked. Reader feedback is important for us to develop titles that you really get the most out of.

To send us general feedback, simply drop an email to `feedback@packtpub.com`, and mention the book title in the subject of your message.

If there is a book that you need and would like to see us publish, please send us a note in the **SUGGEST A TITLE** form on `www.packtpub.com` or email `suggest@packtpub.com`.

If there is a topic that you have expertise in and you are interested in either writing or contributing to a book, see our author guide on `www.packtpub.com/authors`.

Customer support

Now that you are the proud owner of a Packt book, we have a number of things to help you to get the most from your purchase.

Errata

Although we have taken every care to ensure the accuracy of our contents, mistakes do happen. If you find a mistake in one of our books—maybe a mistake in text or code—we would be grateful if you would report this to us. By doing so, you can save other readers from frustration, and help us to improve subsequent versions of this book. If you find any errata, please report them by visiting http://www.packtpub.com/support, selecting your book, clicking on the **let us know** link, and entering the details of your errata. Once your errata are verified, your submission will be accepted and the errata added to any list of existing errata. Any existing errata can be viewed by selecting your title from http://www.packtpub.com/support.

Piracy

Piracy of copyright material on the Internet is an ongoing problem across all media. At Packt, we take the protection of our copyright and licenses very seriously. If you come across any illegal copies of our works in any form on the Internet, please provide us with the location address or web site name immediately so that we can pursue a remedy.

Please contact us at copyright@packtpub.com with a link to the suspected pirated material.

We appreciate your help in protecting our authors, and our ability to bring you valuable content.

Questions

You can contact us at questions@packtpub.com if you are having a problem with any aspect of the book, and we will do our best to address it.

1
Developing your SEO and Keyword Strategy

Joomla! SEO is not as difficult as some people will try to tell you. Most of the things you will see and learn in this book, could have been accomplished just by using your common sense. However, there are some things that are a bit more technical and there are some topics that you should start with, before progressing to the geeky nerdy stuff.

Here are some challenges that lie ahead of you and that you will have tackled by the end of this book:

- Choosing and using the right words for your web site: This includes how to choose the right keywords and work them into your site structure.

- Improve the default SEO setup of Joomla!: This includes configuring SEO settings using patches and special components, and how to choose or alter your template parameters.

- Create search-friendly content: This includes using the right keywords in the right places, producing search-targeted pages. Using Joomla! with a blog section is a great way to get more pages into the search engines index.

- Formatting content for users and search engines: This includes how to choose and use the right-link text and how to improve that by making good use of headings and meta tags.

- Keep track of your progress: Using tracking tools and implementing them in Joomla!, along with analyzing the results will help you gain more insight on how to improve your site further.

- How to promote your site: This includes how you can get more inbound links, which will drive traffic to your site and improve its search ranking.

Each of the points we just discussed will improve the chances of your site getting noticed more often on search engines, thus bringing more visitors to your site. That is your goal and you can take action right now by setting up your SEO strategy.

At the end of this chapter you will have your very own SEO and keyword strategy ready to work for you, and you will be ready for the next step.

Setting up your SEO strategy

As I mentioned earlier you have to do some work on your Joomla! site to improve its ranking, but where do you start? Baby steps will not take you where you want to go. You really need some kind of a game plan to help you out.

First you need to make some basic improvements to your Joomla! web site to eliminate some of the basic flaws in SEO for Joomla 1.5. We will then dive into keyword research, which is an essential part of your SEO process. Without targeting the keywords that people are actually searching for, you cannot take the next step.

This is when you build your SEO strategy. You cannot do everything at once when you want to get your site up in the search engines. You have to choose where you are going to spend your time and optimization efforts. By the end, you should have done most of the things we will talk about in this book, and you might have chosen to leave certain aspects of the process out of your strategy.

Create a small list of what you intend to do first, second, and so on. Here is a list to give you some idea:

- Brainstorm and get relevant keywords
- Set up the **Joomla! SEO** basics and global configuration settings
- Install the **Joomlatwork SEF** patch
- Install and configure **sh404SEF**
- Optimize robots.txt and .htaccess
- Install a counter and analytics tool
- Structure or restructure the site based on keywords
- Write and rewrite the content of the pages
- Optimize your images and page loading speed
- Start building incoming links

The technical requirements can be implemented very fast, and getting it to work will just take a few hours. The brainstorming and keyword research takes a lot more time and effort. However, you need to know which way to go with your web site, so keywords are essential.

For your site it could be that you already optimized a lot of things and you just have to move articles and categories around to improve the usability and theme of the site. You might feel that you have enough content and you can start building incoming links.

The order in which you do things is all up to you. My suggestion is to start with the technical improvements such as the SEF patch and an SEF component. This way you can make sure that your new URLs are working and picking up the rankings you already have. Once you have those elements in place, you can start the fun work—improving you titles, meta descriptions, content, and lots more.

At the end of this chapter you will have figured out a good game plan for your SEO. Also once you have finished reading this book, you will have covered the most important aspects of improving your web site—to have a better visibility in the search engines.

You can add some extra things to your SEO strategy such as the use of AdWords or affiliate promotion, but these topics are not covered in this book. They will cost you money and you might not want to do any advertisement. If you get this advertisement stuff wrong, it might cost you a lot of money, so I will leave that part to the specialists in this field. In this book, we will focus on getting the best organic search results possible for your Joomla! based web site.

Solving basic Joomla! 1.5 SEO problems

If you look at Joomla! 1.5, you will see that there are just a few settings in the administrator control panel under **Global Configuration** for SEO and meta tags. The right setup of these options is one of the tasks you have to do right at the beginning.

If you look at the configuration panel, there is a small section called **SEO Settings** as shown in the following screenshot:

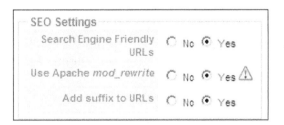

URLs without activating the first option will show as
`http://www.cblandscapegardening.com/index.php?option=com_content&view=article&id=6&Itemid=6.`

But with the first option set to SEF URLs active it changes to `http://www.cblandscapegardening.com/services.html`.

This URL is also based on the other two options, which are active as shown in the previous screenshot. The option **Use Apache mod_rewrite** means that you are on a Linux or Unix based hosting platform and that you have the rights to access `.htaccess` file. If you don't use the second option, you would have an extra `/index.php/` in the URL. You really shouldn't use that option if your Joomla! site is on a Windows server or on your local PC, as it will break the URL to your pages and will produce **error 500** page as the server doesn't know what to do with the `.htaccess` file.

The third option just adds the `.html` extension to the URL, thus making it look like a static web site. Using the `.html` extension is beneficial as people and search engines know that they are directed to a real content page and not a directory.

If this is all so great, what problems could there possibly be? It is possible to have different URLs to the same article if you have more than one link to it through several menu items. If you create a menu item, the title of that item will become the URL pointing to the item. Joomla! uses the title-alias field to create the URL.

This becomes a problem if you link categories in one menu item to the section in which that category is in another menu item. This is because you create multiple links under different URLs to the same page. If you want to blog with Joomla!, this is something that is very likely to happen.

Also, look at the following URL: `/landscaping/8-landscape-gardens/8-outdoor-patios.html`. You can see that the `/section/` name, categories with ID number, and the page title with the ID number are included. The ID number is used to make sure that you don't get URLs that are the same, and thus only one page can be reached. You don't want numbers in your URL for two reasons. First, it can confuse your visitors as they might expect an article about eight different outdoor patios. The second reason is that you want the URL to be as clear and as short as possible and numbers don't really work that well unless you really have an article about eight outdoor patios. Also, the creation of more menu links will lead to a duplicate content issue — something that most content management systems have, but it is better to avoid.

I will show you how to change your site setup to overcome and prevent these kind of problems. I will give you some information on the new `rel="canonical"` option to give the search engines your preferred URL when we look into the SEF components. I will also show you whether "nofollow" options are still valid if we look at the SEF patch and content creation. Both these options have a new or improved benefit for SEO.

Global configuration meta tag settings

If you use the **Metadata Settings** under **Global Configuration** fields, you are placing the same description and keywords on every menu item that is not pointing to a specific article.

So, with every menu item you create in your Joomla! web site, you create duplicate descriptions and keyword meta tags, something the search engines don't like. These duplicate descriptions appear in the result pages—something that you probably want to avoid. You want the right descriptions and keywords to be indexed.

Clear the fields in **Global Configuration | Site**. Do not use the Global Meta Tags at all! I will show you how to create a better meta tag description and set of meta keywords later on, but for now, please let Google and other search engines pick their own snippets to show in the search engine result pages.

PDF, Print, and E-mail icons

Although it is a nice idea to give your visitors the option to view and print your content in a PDF or print format, it provides extra food for the search engines. With Joomla! 1.0.x you would find a lot of PDF pages in the Google result pages.

With Joomla! 1.5 there are some simple options you can configure to prevent this from happening. Just select **Content | Article Manager | Parameter** and Joomla! will open an overlay screen. Here you can scroll down and disable **Icons, PDF Icon,** and **Print Icon** by selecting **Hide** then click on **Save** and you are done.

Meta generator tag

Joomla!, just like WordPress, inserts an HTML tag that says:

```
<meta name="generator" content="Joomla! 1.5 - Open Source Content
Management" />
```

This is of course a nice way to show that you use Joomla!, to the people who view the source code. However, from an SEO point of view, this information has nothing to do with the content of your pages, and it adds an extra line to your page size. This can also be a nice indicator for hackers to know the version of Joomla! you are using.

The good thing is that all these issues can be solved with minimal effort by changing some settings and using some extra components and patches.

Why do you need to do keyword research?

Keyword research is essential for optimization, and if done the right way, you may even find some gold mines you can work with in your niche market.

First things first, I am going to tell you why you need to do it. It is actually quite simple — you need to know what your potential visitors/customers are looking for. You need to find the words and phrases that your potential customers use when they use a search engine. Of course there is more to it than that — you also want to know how much competition is there for those words, so you can estimate your chances of ranking well.

Let's start by simply looking at what you already know about your site topic. You already know a lot about your current customers, but do you know what people are looking for on the Internet that you could possibly sell to them? It is a bit like fishing — you first have to know what kind of fish you want to catch, and the bait you need to use in order to catch them. The tools with which you catch the fish aren't that important. At the end only the result counts — eating fish!

Keyword research is simply finding the right bait to draw your potential customers to your site. You already know some of the keywords people are searching for. You know your business and the terminology that comes with it and its importance.

This is where most web site owners, just like you, are making an incorrect assumption. The terminology used by you is most likely not what people are searching for. For example, you might think that "harden off" is what people are looking for, but in fact it is "how to get my indoor plants into my garden". You know you have to "harden off" those plants before taking them outside, but you can also see that "harden off" is not included in the search.

People are looking for an answer to a problem they have. It is up to you to provide the answer to their questions. If you do, they will love you for it and hopefully do business with you.

But wait, there is more!

By carrying out keyword research you will not only find the most profitable terms you want for a rank, but also the way your site should be structured/restructured. Another reason is that picking the right targeted keywords and optimizing those terms will improve your revenues. Whether you are selling digital products, information, or services such as landscape gardening.

An old study from Cornell University shows that the first result on the Google search's result page will get more than 50 percent of the clicks. Second gets about 15 percent, and the third gets around 10 percent, the rest goes in smaller portions of max five percent and down to the other competitors.

This is why you want to make sure you are ranking higher than your competitors. It can also give you a traffic boost if you start ranking—number one for more specific searches instead of focusing on more generic terms. Ranking on generic terms such as "cars" is a lot more difficult to do than ranking for a more specific term such as "hybrid performance cars".

Wouldn't it be nice to have your site in the top three? Having your pages further down from the initial search results will give you a lot less traffic, and hence fewer potential customers. If you start ranking better in the search results, you also need to try and draw people to click on your site link. Once we get into the meta tags issue and how to write for better results, I will give you some pointers on how to do this. Keep those results in mind and think about your web site as we go into the hard labor of researching keywords for a landscape gardening site and of course, for your web site.

How to do basic keyword research

Keyword research is not that difficult to do, it is just a matter of using the right tools and using your common sense. You must keep in mind that during this research you will come across loads and loads of keywords and phrases you might want to use.

Create a list of all the keywords that are used in your web site's topic area. Write them down. You are going to work with these later on in this chapter. Put them in a spreadsheet, a word document, or a text file. It doesn't matter how you write them, but just do it!

Personally, I prefer Microsoft Excel as I can easily structure and restructure some content afterwards, and it can import .csv files produced by some of the keyword tools that we will use. But if you can work better with another program, maybe even a Mindscape map, please use that. It is all about getting the job done.

There are a few other things you need, well actually two things:

- A pad of Post-it notes (if you want, get some different colors)
- A marker for writing down some keywords (not too thin)

You will need to use these for structuring your web site based on the main keywords you will find. Once the basic list is ready, you will start building a new one, based on your findings from the keyword tools we will use. One word of caution though—restrain yourself from putting too many keywords and key phrases in the second list. We will draw topics to create articles that will be put into the site structure that is based on the first list.

You have to make sure that at the end of this process you have a list that you can really work with. Remind yourself that only you can decide whether or not you are able to write good articles and content for those words. This last advice is essential for building a site that attracts lots of visitors in the long run.

Even with a massive list of keywords, you have to provide quality content on the subject of your site. Having a good list of keywords and phrases just helps you to attract search engines and get good rankings for your pages, but at the end of the day it is the visitor who decides if your site is good enough.

If he/she thinks it is not, in the end the search engines will leave, as the bounce rate of your site will be too high. We will get deeper into the signs of problems like a high bounce rate in the Analytics part of the book.

The tools of the trade

There are mainly two types of tools—free and commercial. We will first discuss the free tools.

Free tools

Let's start out simple, by going to **Google's AdWords** tool.

Google's Adwords

This tool is available at `https://adwords.google.com/select/KeywordToolExternal`. It is a great tool to use—just check if your results are for the right language and country, and then fill in your keywords. You can find those options and alter them by using the screen just above the input table. Then type the characters shown to you and hit **Get keyword ideas** and look how Google gives you information about:

- Keywords
- Advertising competition
- Approximate search volume (previous month)
- Approximate average search volume

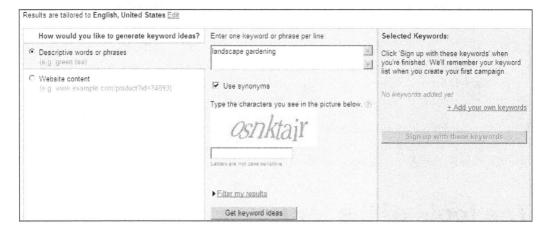

After you run the tool, take a closer look at the screen, click on the small drop-down button, and select **Show All**.

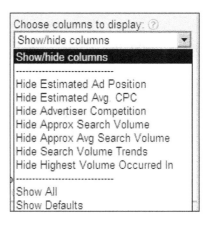

You now have more information than in the default screen. One thing that stands out for the targeted terms are the trends. You can clearly see that April and May have the largest search volume, which is not surprising considering that these are the months when people want to start working on their garden. What is also nice to see is that **landscape gardening** has a lot more searches than **garden landscaping**.

For your site topic you can now start adding terms to your list. Don't forget the keywords that will bring you local results. In case of landscape gardening, "Los Banos" should be included in the terms to target. Using your village location in the keywords and phrases, you are going to target direct traffic that will convert better than just the general keywords.

If you are going to use the location item, make sure to include the surrounding villages and try to get traffic from those places as well. There are some easy ways to do this, which I will show you once we get to the writing section.

As you can see in the picture, selecting the **Approx Avg Search Volume** as the basic sorting field will show you how large the number will be of your potential visitors.

If you are targeting a special niche and want to get some revenue through **Google AdSense** you can also see the average price that AdWords users will have to pay per click. If you are not targeting a niche, it will give you some indication of how difficult it will be to rank well. The higher the price for a keyword or phrase, the more likely it is that you have many competitors.

We will be looking at those competing numbers later.

Keywords	Estimated Ad Position ⑦	Estimated Avg. CPC ⑦	Advertiser Competition ⑦	Approx Search Volume: December ⑦	▼Approx Avg Search Volume ⑦	Search Volume Trends (Nov 2007 - Oct 2008) ⑦	Highest Volume Occurred In	Match Type: ⑦ Broad ▼
Keywords related to term(s) entered - sort by relevance ⑦								
landscape garden	1 - 3	€1.13		49,500	74,000		May	Add ⌄
garden landscaping	1 - 3	€0.80		27,100	27,100		Jul	Add ⌄
gardening landscaping	1 - 3	€1.20		8,100	8,100		May	Add ⌄
garden and landscape	1 - 3	€0.93		6,600	6,600		May	Add ⌄
landscape gardening	1 - 3	€0.94		8,100	6,600		May	Add ⌄
garden and landscaping	1 - 3	€0.78		4,400	4,400		Apr	Add ⌄
garden landscape design	1 - 3	€0.99		3,600	3,600		May	Add ⌄
garden & landscape	1 - 3	€0.05		Not enough data	2,400	No data	No data	Add ⌄

Once you have selected these keywords, click on **Add**, make sure you scroll down the page as it holds some great findings for you—the **Additional keywords to be considered** field! You might notice that in the first results you did not find the term **landscape garden**. However, once we go down to the additional keywords section you can see that **landscape contractors** is popping up and so is **gardeners**, but that is a more generic search and much more difficult to rank for. Go through your **Additional keywords to be considered** list and click on **Add**, if you think you have found a relevant term to consider. It should give you some new ideas to work with. It will also give you an insight on how Google thinks these terms are related.

Once you get into structuring your web site for optimal results, you are going to use this knowledge to your advantage. Remember to do several keyword searches with this tool, in the same session you can also build your basic keyword list very quickly.

After adding your most important keyword phrases, click on **Get more related keywords**. Google will insert all the keywords and phrases you selected into the search field, saving you lot of time as you will not be required to type them again. Plus, it gives you new ideas instantly—isn't that great!

Additional keywords to consider - sort by relevance							Add all 114 » Download all keywords: text, .csv (for excel), .csv	
garden	1 - 3	€1.01		24,900,000	24,900,000		Jul	Add
gardens	1 - 3	€1.15		5,000,000	5,000,000		Jul	Add
plants	1 - 3	€0.72		6,120,000	5,000,000		May	Add
landscape	1 - 3	€1.18		2,740,000	2,740,000		Apr	Add
landscaping	1 - 3	€1.07		1,500,000	1,830,000		Apr	Add
gardening	1 - 3	€0.88		1,500,000	1,500,000		May	Add
landscape supplies	1 - 3	€1.02		165,000	246,000		May	Add
landscape design	1 - 3	€1.68		165,000	201,000		Apr	Add
garden design	1 - 3	€0.85		135,000	135,000		May	Add
landscape contractors	1 - 3	€1.77		40,500	135,000		Aug	Add
landscape lighting	1 - 3	€3.87		165,000	135,000		May	Add
gardeners	1 - 3	€1.64		110,000	110,000		May	Add
japanese garden	1 - 3	€0.51		110,000	110,000		Jul	Add
landscapers	1 - 3	€1.19		74,000	110,000		Jun	Add
landscape architect	1 - 3	€1.37		110,000	90,500		Oct	Add
landscape architecture	1 - 3	€1.32		110,000	90,500		Oct	Add
landscaping ideas	1 - 3	€0.51		49,500	74,000		Apr	Add
retaining walls	1 - 3	€0.95		74,000	74,000		Apr	Add
garden english	1 - 3	€0.68		49,500	49,500		May	Add
landscape architects	1 - 3	€1.00		60,500	49,500		Oct	Add
landscape designers	1 - 3	€1.41		60,500	49,500		Apr	Add
landscape jobs	1 - 3	€1.47		74,000	49,500		Oct	Add
landscaper	1 - 3	€1.22		49,500	49,500		Apr	Add

I told you earlier that I like Excel for importing `.csv` files. This Google tool has a sidebar using which you can build your keyword file to import from. Once you are done with adding keywords, use the export function to download your keyword file. You can import the keywords and sort them later. I would also encourage you to take a screenshot of the list of keywords you find.

The list is built from a large number of searches, ordered by frequency, but after the import you loose this sorting as it is then sorted alphabetically. By using the screenshot you can sort it again based on the numbers in the screenshot.

Wordtracker

Another great tool is the free version of Wordtracker, but that will give you a maximum of 100 results. It is not my favorite tool, but it shows you some extra information on the search topics such as daily search indication. It is available at `http://freekeywords.wordtracker.com/`.

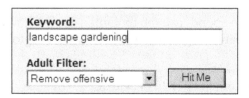

In the Wordtracker tool you fill in the keyword or phrase that you want to investigate. If you are building a site that is more focused on adult entertainment you can remove the adult content filter, but for most of us it is best kept active. The results presented in the following screenshot are daily search numbers, instead of the monthly figures used by Google's keyword tool.

landscape gardening	
29 searches (top 100 only)	
Searches	**Keyword**
15	landscape gardening
3	landscape gardening in japan
2	landscape gardening in america
2	winter gardening and landscape maintenance
1	computer aided design and landscape gardening
1	gardening landscape designs
1	gardening landscape templates
1	landscape gardening history
1	park landscape gardening inc
1	tulsa gardening landscape service
1	what are the different steps in landscape gardening
29	total searches

Wordtracker offers paid services as well. The above mentioned free tools are limited in the number of results that they are allowed to pull from the Wordtracker database. On the Wordtracker site the service is promoted as a subscription with which you will be able to:

- Optimize your web site content by using the most popular keywords for your products and services
- Generate thousands of relevant keywords to improve your organic and PPC search campaigns
- Research online markets, find niche opportunities

Of course this comes at a price, 59 USD per month or 329 USD per year at the time I am writing this. You can get started with a 7-day trial to check if it works for you.

If you have the money to spend, use the tool intensively for a month, as it is the number one choice of search engine optimizers across the globe.

 Check out http://www.wordtracker.com/academy page to learn more about keyword research.

SEO Book Keyword Tool

Another tool that uses the Wordtracker database might give you some better ideas, as it also shows Google, Yahoo!, and MSN (Live) daily estimates for searches. This tool is called **SEO Book Keyword Tool** and is available at `http://tools.seobook.com/keyword-tools/seobook/`.

After you have typed the term you want to research, make sure you click on the **Submit** button. A simple *Enter* will not start the process of finding the keywords, you have to click on **Submit**.

Once the information is processed you will see the following screen. In the field to the right you can click on other tools that will show you the results instantly. The one you should try for sure is Google's search-based keyword tool. This is a new tool that has a slightly different approach than the AdWords tool. You have to keep in mind that the date used is limited to the previous month(s), and hence it will change as trends and seasons change.

For the landscape gardening site this is really important, as it will be for any season-influenced results. Therefore, make sure to use every tool available to get the overall picture.

In the SEO Book Keyword Tool you also have the possibility to **export to CSV**. However, you get all the terms and you cannot preselect the ones you like.

WordTracker	WordTracker count	Google daily est	Yahoo! daily est	MSN daily est	Overall daily est	Yahoo! Suggest	G Trends	Google T E	G Suggest	G SB-KW	G Syn~	AdWords Keyword Tool	G Insights	Quintura	KW Discove
landscape gardening	16	20	6	2	28	Y! Sug 2	G Trends	G traf est	G Sugg	G SB-KW	Goog ~	AdWords KW	G Ins	Quin	KD
landscape gardening in japan	4	5	1	1	7	Y! Sug 2	G Trends	G traf est	G Sugg	G SB-KW	Goog ~	AdWords KW	G Ins	Quin	KD
landscape gardening in america	3	4	1	0	5	Y! Sug 2	G Trends	G traf est	G Sugg	G SB-KW	Goog ~	AdWords KW	G Ins	Quin	KD
winter gardening and landscape maintenance	3	4	1	0	5	Y! Sug 2	G Trends	G traf est	G Sugg	G SB-KW	Goog ~	AdWords KW	G Ins	Quin	KD
computer aided design and landscape gardening	2	3	1	0	4	Y! Sug 2	G Trends	G traf est	G Sugg	G SB-KW	Goog ~	AdWords KW	G Ins	Quin	KD
gardening landscape designs	2	3	1	0	4	Y! Sug 2	G Trends	G traf est	G Sugg	G SB-KW	Goog ~	AdWords KW	G Ins	Quin	KD

Commercial tools

Apart from the subscription-based Wordtracker, the tools mentioned earlier are free to use. There are some commercial tools for keyword research, which we will now discuss.

Keyword Elite

Keyword Elite is a piece of software that will cost you about 176 USD, but you get a great tool for that price. It is available at `http://www.keywordelite.com`

With Keyword Elite you can easily research all your keywords with one program and it will dish out the best phrases you could possibly want. Uncovering search terms that you probably would not have found quickly without the tool. It's easy to use, once you get the hang of it, and it is well worth the trouble of learning. The documentation is very clear, so you can get started right away.

You can start with the keyword list building process and choose from which sources the list should extract the keyword phrases.

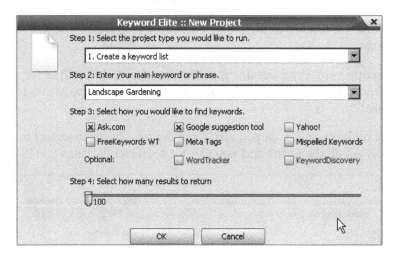

Once the initial search is done, you can start refining the results by selecting the field, which is capable of either eliminating some terms or refining per search engine. Of course, some sorting options for alphabetical order and even the number of words in the search phrase are available.

The best keywords are not only specific, but you also get the **Parent Keyword**, which gives you some idea for category names in your Joomla! site.

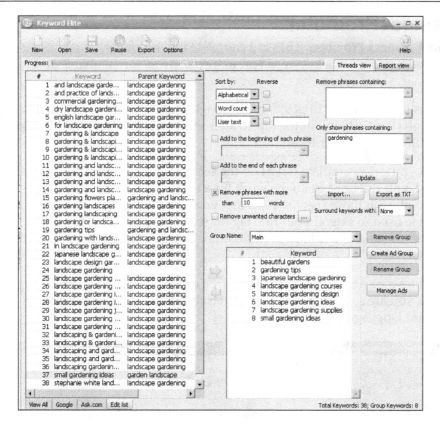

What I really like about Keyword Elite is that it is fast and easy. If you have an account on commercial sites such as Wordtracker or KeywordDiscovery, you can use them right from this tool.

Under the **Preferences** option you can also set the Google and Yahoo! region to get the keywords from — the standard setting is the US.

The thing I don't like about it is the fact that it is not so easy to see the number of searches per day or month or the number of competitors on a certain term.

iBusinessPromoter

Internet Business Promoter (IBP) is a complete tool for doing
SEO research and it has a keyword research option too. It is available at
http://www.ibusinesspromoter.com/.

IBP claims to get you top 10 positions in Google and it delivers just that. I have
several web sites that rank in the top 10 after implementing some of the tips and
changes IBP suggested for those sites.

Although you get a complete report on the sections of your web site that need to be
optimized, you still need to do the work for a Joomla! site. Here this book will help
you by pointing at those specific tasks that you might need to address. For example,
the possible need to extend your title tag for search engines where you don't want to
change the title on the article page itself. More on this is available in Chapter 3 and
Chapter 4.

IBP provides a nice tool for keyword research and helps you gain more insight in the
fields that you are searching for. IBP also has the ability to get keywords for other
regions and languages.

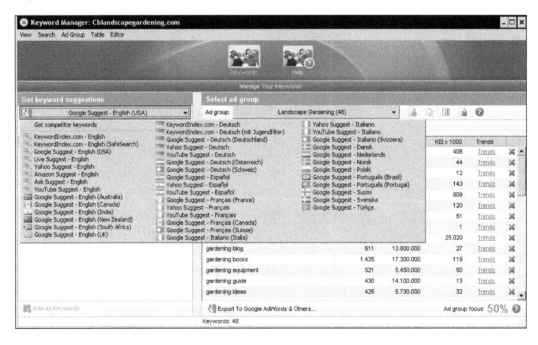

Once you have set the regions you want the results for, you get a list of possible keywords along with both the number of searches that are done per month and the number of pages you are competing against. This is followed by a number called **KEI x 1000**. **Keyword Effectiveness Index (KEI)** is calculated as (Number of searches per month^2)/Number of competing sites. The higher the KEI the better, but you need to look at the real competition and decide if the keyword is really the one you want to go after.

In the following screenshot you can see that the first two keywords have an extremely high KEI value, but if you look at the terms you know that they are too generic to focus on for you to realistically get a high ranking. Keep in mind the goal of your web site and think about how well these terms will work for reaching that goal.

Select ad group

Ad group: Landscape Gardening (48)

Switch To Editor   Refine   Get Searches, Results & KEI

Keyword	Searches	Results	KEI x 1000	Trends
gardening	38.225	58.400.000	25.020	Trends
landscaping	23.086	37.500.000	14.212	Trends
landscaping materials	9.684	39.200.000	2.392	Trends
organic gardening	8.637	19.200.000	3.885	Trends
gardening tips	4.454	9.170.000	2.163	Trends
landscaping services	2.530	60.100.000	107	Trends
gardening tools	2.168	81.800.000	57	Trends
koi fish	1.862	1.240.000	2.796	Trends
landscaping ideas	1.715	15.700.000	187	Trends
gardening books	1.435	17.300.000	119	Trends
landscaping design	1.432	35.100.000	58	Trends
japanese garden	1.200	44.700.000	32	Trends
flower gardening	1.194	2.340.000	609	Trends
home gardening	1.075	15.400.000	75	Trends
water gardening	1.002	142.000.000	7	Trends
landscaping company	979	35.000.000	27	Trends
garden landscaping	741	4.560.000	120	Trends
gardening magazine	696	13.100.000	37	Trends
backyard landscaping	651	1.040.000	408	Trends
garden ponds	651	8.360.000	51	Trends
gardening information	640	27.500.000	15	Trends
landscaping software	623	923.000	421	Trends
gardening blog	611	13.800.000	27	Trends
landscape gardening	583	948.000	359	Trends

You can click on **Trends** shown in the previous screenshot and view the trends on **Google Trends**. This is really beneficial. You can see when to add new content to your site to gain momentum as the market is waking up after the winter season.

As I mentioned before, IBP is an optimization tool that will help you to get higher positions. It does that by analyzing the top 10 competitors for a large number of items like phrases used in the title, the domain name, meta descriptions, meta keywords, images, loading time, and lots more.

The report that is created gives a comparison of your site to the competition. It shows you where you need to change things, including some tips on how and what to change. It is up to you to make those changes. Once you are done, run the report again and see if your site has a higher score now, and thus chance of improving in ranking for the keywords of your choice.

The initial score for the landscape gardening site is shown in the following screenshot. You can see that we need to do some work on this site for it to rank well.

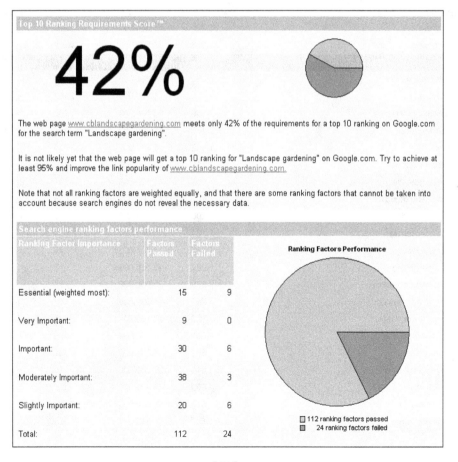

Top 10 Ranking Requirements Score™

42%

The web page www.cblandscapegardening.com meets only 42% of the requirements for a top 10 ranking on Google.com for the search term "Landscape gardening".

It is not likely yet that the web page will get a top 10 ranking for "Landscape gardening" on Google.com. Try to achieve at least 95% and improve the link popularity of www.cblandscapegardening.com.

Note that not all ranking factors are weighted equally, and that there are some ranking factors that cannot be taken into account because search engines do not reveal the necessary data.

Search engine ranking factors performance

Ranking Factor Importance	Factors Passed	Factors Failed
Essential (weighted most):	15	9
Very Important:	9	0
Important:	30	6
Moderately Important:	38	3
Slightly Important:	20	6
Total:	112	24

Ranking Factors Performance

☐ 112 ranking factors passed
☐ 24 ranking factors failed

There are many other tools and sites that can help you with your keyword research, but the above tools we just discussed are the ones I found best and easiest to work with. Let's now look at the last commercial tool.

KeywordDiscovery and SEO toolkit

It draws results from several search engines, but still I have not seen it pull up any new findings. Visit http://www.keyworddiscovery.com/search.html.

The following screenshot shows results of the free version. They also have a paid subscription-based model and software that starts at 69.95 USD per month. With that subscription you get more results and you can see the past 12 months of trends for the searches of the keyword. In the case of landscape gardening you should see a decline towards the winter season and some growth in the spring.

Enter Keyword: Landscape gardening Search	
Query: **Landscape gardening**	
Results 1 - 38 of 37 Page: 1 2 3 4 5 6 7 8 9 10	
Search Term	**Total ?**
landscape gardening	31
landscape gardening lichfield	15
landscape gardening jobs	9
free landscape gardening ideas	6
landscape gardening overview	5
definition of landscape gardening	5
supplement to landscape gardening in japan by condor 1912	4
copy of landscape gardening seminar	3
steps in giving a seminar about landscape gardening	3
gardening landscape	3
landscape gardening ayrshire	3
what is landscape gardening	3
pricing landscape gardening jobs up	3
craft projects with landscape timbers -gardening	2
gardening and landscape books	2
landscape and gardening supplies	2
landscape gardening courses north west	2
landscape, gardening	2
landscape gardening ideas	2
landscape gardening jobs in east sussex	2

You can purchase the SEO Toolkit that extends beyond the keyword research and is a more complete SEO tool such as IBP from **Trellian**, the owner of **KeywordDiscovery**. It has been around for a long time, so it must be worth the money, but in this case I am not speaking from experience.

Looking at these three tools I can say that if you just want to do basic research on keywords, you should use Keyword Elite as it is really focused on delivering a great set of parent keywords and very specific search terms that fall under those keywords. IBP. However, goes beyond keyword suggestions and gives you a complete tool to optimize your site from beginning to end. You can use KeywordDiscovery to verify whether you are on the right track with the keywords you selected, but you should rely on it for that.

Choosing the right key words

Once you have done your research, it is time to sort all the words and phrases you selected.

You will find a truckload of data that you need to organize and arrange into some useful information. Start by categorizing the words accordingly as you know your web site topic best, and create some nice **Keyword packages**. By keyword packages, I mean the list of related keywords that you build. These packages contain the keywords you selected as the main keywords and the search terms related to them.

For example, for a Joomla! web site, you could have main keywords be Joomla! themes, Joomla! components, Joomla! plugins, and so on. Under Joomla! themes you can have the search terms, free Joomla! themes, magazine style Joomla! themes, and Joomla! SEO themes.

If you have imported the list of keywords into an Excel spreadsheet, you can sort most of the terms easily. But you need to do more with this keyword list. Yes, you have built your basic list already, if you followed the steps above and did it for several of your web site keywords.

Now you are getting into the fun part of choosing the right words to target, by using search engines such as **Google**, **Ask**, and **Yahoo!** Who would know better than the sites in which you want to improve your rankings? We will start with ask.com, make sure you use the site's USA version as some of the local ones don't support the options we want to use.

Once you have the site open, type in the keyword you want to check, in our case study example that would be **Landscape Gardening**. Type slowly and you will see with each character you type, the list of **Search Suggestions** will change and reflect terms that ask.com thinks are related. Write down the words that you want to use from your keyword list, and start sorting those terms.

On the search results page there is a column that says **Related Searches** also. In that column you will see some topic related terms you might want to use later.

> Related Searches
> Free **Landscape** Design
> Design a **Garden** Free Online
> **Garden** and **Landscaping** Ideas
> **Garden Landscape** Software
> **Landscape Design Gardening**
> **Landscape** Plans
> **Landscaping** a Front Garden
> **Landscaping** Yards
> **Landscaping** Ideas
> Rock Retaining Walls
> **Landscape** Plant Guide
> Country French Gardens

But there is a hidden treasure for you on that site as well—click on the **Q&A** tab which is in beta, but works fine for your purpose.

Look at the questions asked and their answers. If you have done the first section of this chapter right, you will find several of the keywords from your list in these questions.

Use the answers to your benefit when you start to write your content.

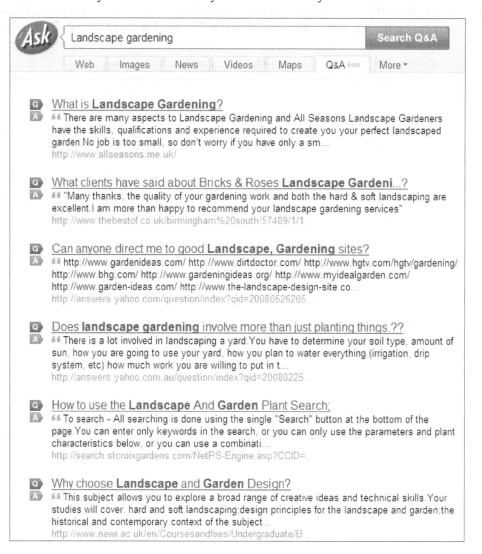

Ok, we are done with `ask.com`, so let's move on to `yahoo.com`.

Here you do the same exercise and you see the same thing happening. Don't forget to use the up and down pointers to see more.

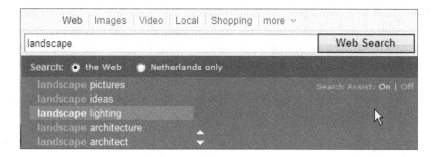

Go to the results page and you will see why you really want to check these engines to get more grip on the sorting of your topics.

Just look at the wealth of topics and concepts that Yahoo! offers. You can really get into sorting your keywords with this kind of help.

Next stop: Google.

Again you will get a drop-down box with the related search terms:

But Google gives you just a little bit more to use. Did you notice the numbers to the right of each search term? Here you can see how difficult it is going to be if you try to rank with those keywords. The numbers reflect the competing results Google has found for you. Remember, I told you we would get into the competing numbers? This is where you can see those numbers right away. As you can see in the previous screenshot that the term **landscape** has **160,000,000** results, in the following screenshot you see that **landscape gardening ideas** has only **288,000** results.

Now search for your keywords and get back to your keyword list and check how many searches are done with the terms you picked. But even without a lot of searches, you should quickly get an idea of how to use this extra information for your site. For best results, choose words and phrases that are most likely to have a lot of searches and have less competition.

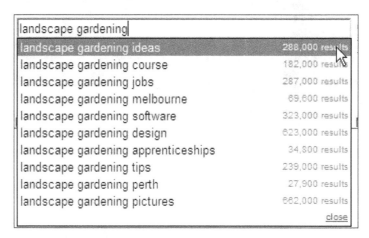

If you are lucky enough to have a broad topic, you will see that Google gives you related searches on your topic at the bottom of the results page.

Searches related to: **landscape**

| landscape **company** | **yard** landscape | landscape **jobs** | **garden** landscape |
| landscape **architect** | landscape **planning** | landscape **bricks** | **landscaping pictures** |

You are going to use this information later for structuring/restructuring your web site. Write them down on a separate page or spreadsheet, so you don't lose it in the crowd of keywords in your list. Use them again for moving the keywords you have found into topical clusters.

Still not sure how to find the right words?

Here is a simple idea to get you going. Go to a library and find a book about the topic of your web site. You may also visit amazon.com for the same purpose. In this case study, it would be about gardening, landscape gardening, and koi fish. Check the layout of the book and of course the table of content, which will give you some clue about how to structure your keywords.

On amazon.com you might want to check if there are any books that you can **LOOK INSIDE** They mostly show you the Table of Content, Excerpt, and the Index. Those items should also give you an idea on what terms to put together. You can do one more thing; go to http://www.wiki.org and search for your main topic. You might find some nicely structured pages on it that will point you in new directions to explore. One word of advice: stick to the subject or you may easily get lost or sidetracked on Wiki.

Building your keyword list

Once you are finished with your research, create a smaller list by reviewing the results you found and put them in an Excel sheet. How did you do? I hope you are learning a lot and still have fun doing it. It has been hard work, but you will see how you are going to use your list and several topics in this book, I promise. Following is the list of keywords for our case study:

- Landscape gardening
- Ideas
- Tips
- Designs
- Jobs
- Architects
- Software
- Plants
- Water features
- Gardener
- Lightning

- Supplies
- Retaining walls
- Designers
- Japanese garden
- English garden
- Gardeners
- Garden
- Patio
- Deck
- Greenhouses

Setting up your baseline statistics

Now you need to do something else before you start using your keywords list. You need to know the performance of your site in traffic and its search engine ratings. You should really know how visitors come to your web site and you need to measure and analyze that traffic. You should install these trackers before you start optimizing your site, because you want to make sure:

- You don't lose traffic after your efforts
- You can see how optimization works to your benefit (no better incentive to keep working on SEO than that)

Therefore, you should use two separate analytic services, so that you can compare results. And make sure you aren't measuring the wrong statistics. The one I always start with is www.statcounter.com. This is because the graphs and numbers are clear and easy to understand, and also you can use it as a hidden counter (many others need an image of some sort), and you can block your own visits from showing up in the results. To get started, go to www.statcounter.com and register for a new account, don't worry, it's free.

Log in to the site, create a new project, and then fill out the form shown in the following screenshot:

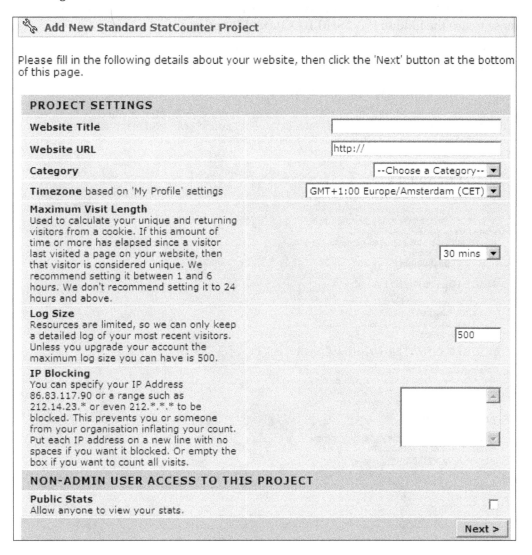

Use the **Next** option to get to the next screen (shown in the following screenshot) and choose the counter option. I have activated **BUTTON ONLY** option on the site, but that is just for showing you what counter I use. In your case it might make more sense to use the hidden **INVISIBLE COUNTER** option.

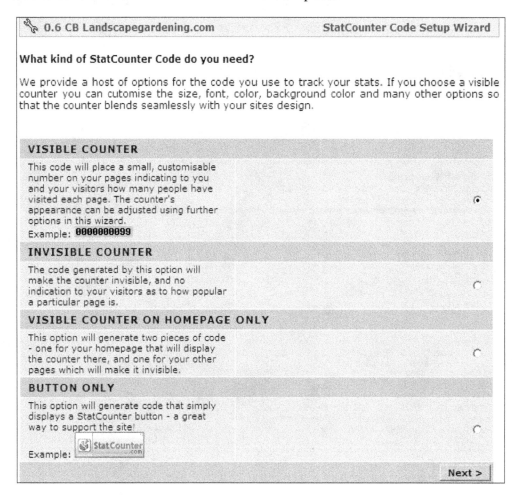

Next is the **Installation Options** screen, shown in the following screenshot. Leave this as default, as you will use the basic code on your site.

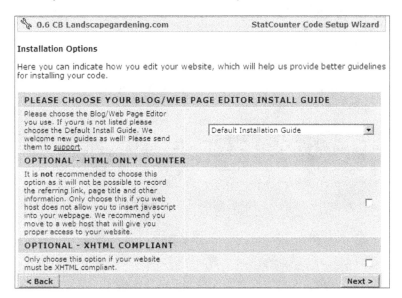

Now you need to copy the code, so just click on it to select the entire code and copy it to the clipboard of your computer. You will get an email from StatCounter which will contain the code as well.

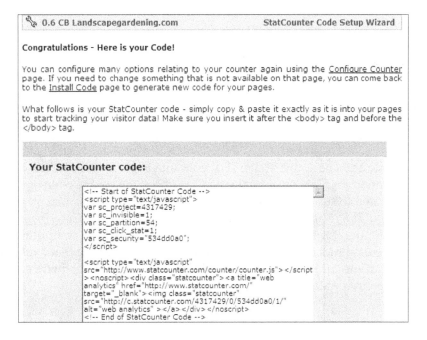

Now you need to get the code into your Joomla! site. Most people will copy the code into the template's HTML code just before the `</body>` tag. But you don't do this because you want to make sure the code will still work if you change templates or use a different template for another section. You want to set and forget the options to make sure you see all visitor stats all the time.

So how to do that? Joomla! makes it so simple for you. Log in to your admin panel choose the menu item extension and then module manager, and click on the **New** button in the right side top menu.

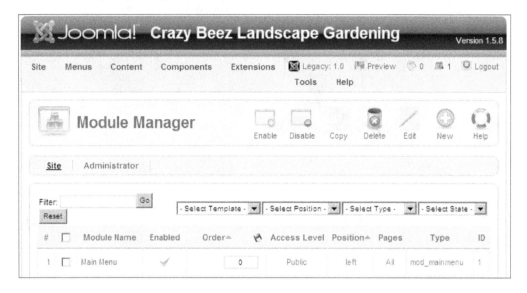

Then select **Custom HTML** from the list, and paste the StatCounter code into the field below the setting that says **Custom Output**.

Don't save the module yet, we have to give it a place and set the **Show Title** option to **No**. I always set the module to **left** in the **Position** menu. You can pick a spot to your liking, but the left side menu is mostly the closest to the `</body>` code.

Save the module and check the frontend of your site to see if it shows up. If you use the invisible option for StatCounter, you need to check the source code of the page that was generated to see if it is really active. Once you have done that, go back to StatCounter, find the record of your visit, and create a **Blocking Cookie** under the **CONFIGURE** option for the counter. Now, your visits from that computer will not be registered anymore. The blocking cookie is a small text file that contains the information StatCounter looks for if you visit the site. If it is there, then your visits are not recorded in the statistics of your site.

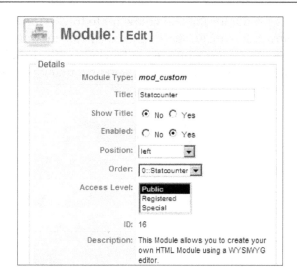

I told you we are going to use two trackers, the second one is being **Google Analytics**. If you don't have a Gmail account yet, go get one, log in, and activate the **Analytics** function. You will be using more features of Google for your SEO, so you really need to get an account from www.googlemail.com — it's free.

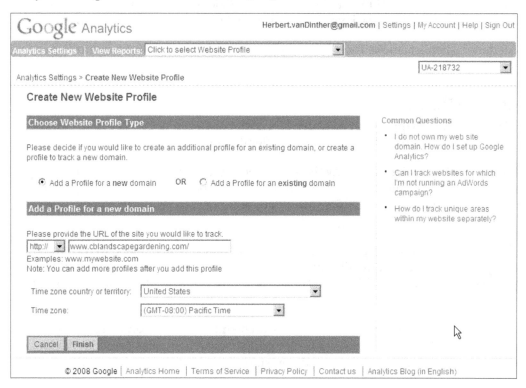

Create a new web site profile for the site you want to track. Copy the new analytics code and paste it below the StatCounter code in the same module, or create a new one the same way as earlier. Once you are ready, click on the **Edit** button and in the top right corner of that screen it will show a small icon that you have to click on to check if the code is implemented the right way.

Now you should see the following screen:

See the small line where it says **Waiting for Data.** That means you can come back tomorrow to see if anything has been recorded. Google updates the data every 24 hours so you cannot track your visitors in real time as StatCounter does.

All done? Then lets move forward and start with the use of your keyword list.

Summary

We started this chapter with a small overview about what we will cover in this book and some of the topics that need special attention on your Joomla! site.

We also looked at the options available for setting up your SEO strategy by pointing to the technical improvements such as patches, SEF components along with `robots.txt`, and `.htaccess` file. After that, you can start working on your content like title and content rewriting, and link building.

You saw how you can improve the basic Joomla! SEO settings like URL rewriting, and you can read about the PDF and Print icons problem. You learned about the problems you may face if you don't clear the global meta tag description, and how to fix those problems.

You read about the need for keyword research and how to do keyword research with some paid tools and some free tools that popular search engines provide. We looked at some of the commercial tools, and you started to build your keyword list.

Besides the keyword and SEO strategy you have also installed one or two traffic analysis tools in your site that we will look at in more detail later. These tools will show you the progress you make while optimizing your search engine. At the end of the optimization process, you can use the information provided by these tools to improve your site even further.

This chapter provided you with some basic knowledge about the direction your site should be going in, looking at the keywords and search terms that you want to rank for. With the list of your keywords and search terms ready you can now move forward and improve your SEO capabilities to use those keywords in an effective way.

2
Optimizing Site Structure

You probably started your Joomla! site to get your message on the Internet. It doesn't matter if that message is a service you want to provide, if you want you can sell products, or inform people about your passion.

What matters is that you want people to see your message. One of the key elements you need to consider for that to happen is the way you structure your site for SEO.

Upon building your site, did you think about the structure for the content and how you can provide the information to your visitors from a clear point of view?

Joomla! forces you into structuring your content with its Section and Category structure.

Optimizing your site structure for SEO

In this chapter, I will show you how to use that structure to create a better flow through your site, as this will be beneficial for SEO. I will also show you how to make sure the Robots can find all the pages you want them to find.

You will learn about the following topics:

- Using sections and categories to create structure
- Creating better usability for users and search engines
- Improving your menu structure for SEO
- Why a sitemap component is essential for search engines
- Submitting your sitemap to search engines
- Using the `robots.txt` file to guide Search Engine Robots

At this point you are going to use the information you gathered in the previous chapter to structure or restructure your current site setup so that both visitors and Search Engine Robots will have a better understanding of your web site.

Using sections and categories to create structure

As you know, Joomla! uses sections and categories to hold your articles and most people will tell you that it is rather inflexible. However, it is a great feature for Search Engine Optimization because you are forced to structure your content into clearly-defined subjects.

Sections and categories

Sections are created using the Section Manager and are created using the most relevant keywords that we find. The title of the section is also the alias that is used in the SEF component. I use sections to keep my content organized in a structured manner, but I keep them out of the URL as I like the shorter URL that is created by using just the categories. You will read more about this in Chapter 6.

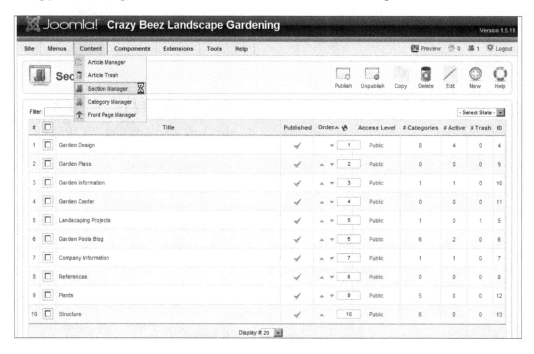

Categories are my most important features, so those need to be really full with the keywords we have found. During the set up of those categories you need to focus on the keywords and keyword phrases you have selected.

Categories, of course, are created and handled by the **Category Manager**.

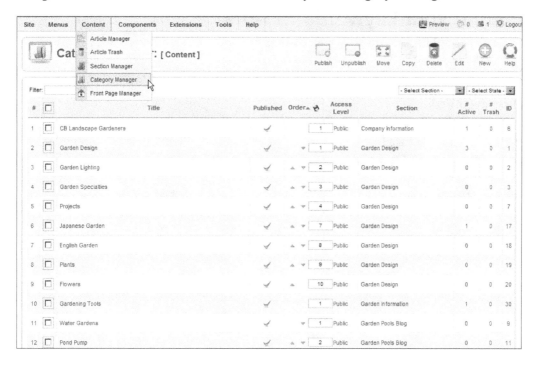

Grouping related topics together

To build your site in the right way for search engines, you have to cluster the topics of your site into related pieces.

This will also provide a better way for you to organize the content, and will help your readers reach their goal in a quick and easy manner.

For example, a gardening site could be built on a wireframe of the following sections, which could be reflected in the menu item that you create:

- **Garden Design**
- **Garden Plans**
- **Garden Information**
- **Garden Center**

- **Landscaping Projects**
- **Company Information**
- **Garden Pools Blog**

Putting your keywords to work

You have to set up the categories including the keywords you want to target, and also make sure the category names are not too long.

The following screenshot shows how the **Garden Pools Blog** section is organized into categories:

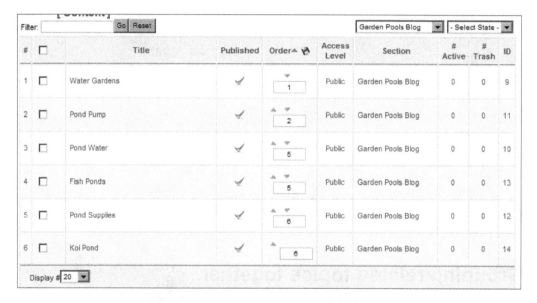

As you can see, you now have used several of the keywords found while working through Chapter 1 and have added some that were found in further keyword research in the titles of the categories. Just as a reminder, here are the main keywords that we initially found:

- Landscape Gardening
- Ideas
- Tips
- Designs
- Jobs
- Architects

- Software
- Plants
- Water features
- Gardener
- Lightning
- Supplies
- retaining walls
- designers
- Japanese garden
- English garden
- Gardeners
- Garden
- Patio
- Deck
- Greenhouses

You can also see that the phrases used to name each section are in line with the subject of that section.

Naming the sections and categories in this fashion provides you with keyword-rich titles and URLs.

To use your own keyword list, I suggest using Excel or any other spreadsheet software to filter out the main topics of your site. The filters you use are your choice — they could be the words and phrases that have little competition. Or you could focus on the most searched items and not look at the competition. What works best for my sites is filtering and sorting the keywords that have the highest relevance to the topic of the web site, combined with key phrases with lesser competition than the highest topical searches, but still having a good amount of searches.

When sorting those keywords and phrases, it sometimes works a lot better if you use post-it memos in different colors to create a framework. Write the first keyword in one color and then write the other keywords in different colors.

Just stick them on a door or whiteboard and start moving the keywords around until you have a framework for your web site.

Once you are done with the framework, you should still have some great keywords left. Use that list later when you start writing your articles, which should of course be in the right categories.

Create a better-optimized structure with keywords

If you place your keywords in the order that you think they are related, you are one step further along in your Search Engine Optimization efforts.

You see, what you just did is called **Latent Semantic Indexing (LSI)** and is used by search engines to determine the topic of a web site.

If the Search Engine Robot finds those keywords on your site, your site is going to be recognized as being based on a certain topic, well organized, and thus ready to get higher rankings because of its relevance to that topic.

Putting your keywords together in this manner also has two great benefits for your web site:

- Better usability
- Better ranking possibilities

The first benefit is that your visitors are able to go to the topic of their choice very quickly and they will be able to navigate through your web site with greater ease. That should also result in a better click-through rate. It is also a good indication for Google that they presented the right search results.

How will a better structure affect your rankings

I should give you a short explanation on the subject of better ranking possibilities. You see, you already chose the right keywords and looked at the competition for those keywords and phrases.

You may have noticed that there is a lot of competition trying very hard to rank for those words. Now you have an advantage over people who are targeting only those hard-to-reach keywords.

Choosing and using the correct related terms and phrases will lift your site up into the search engine results pages for those difficult-to-compete keywords as well.

The package of keywords you have chosen for your site will contain a lot of information about the main topic of your site. The search engines will, after some time, start to rank you for some of those main keywords as well.

Improving your site's usability for users and search engines

Now you have created this greatly improved structure on the backend, and it's time to make sure it is also reflected on the frontend where your visitors will see it.

Showing your site structure at a glance

Besides writing quality content, one of the best things you can do for your web site is to make sure, that your site visitors can navigate through your site as easily as possible.

If you have never heard about Steve Krug and his book *"Don't make me think"* (available at online stores such as Amazon or your local book store under ISBN Number 978-0789723109), then this is your chance to learn by reading one of the best books on usability. I can also say that this is a book that you really have to read to get more insight and ideas about how to improve you site from a visitor's point of view.

The improvements you are going to make to your site now with the menus will most certainly improve its usability for your visitors, but there is still more that can be done.

Small and fast improvements for usability

You can make the following improvements right away without too much effort:

- **Make your articles easy to read and scan by using headers and sub headers**:

  This can be done by breaking long text into smaller parts and adding sublines and headlines as introductions to new paragraphs. We will learn more about this in Chapter 4.

- **Use images that provide more insight in to the subject of your articles**:

  Using related images means that you break long text by adding pictures, but those should reflect the topic of your articles. For example, if you write about tigers, place images of tigers in that article. Using images in this manner will draw your visitors into reading the article.

- **Look at modules that you have placed on your web site**:

    The questions you need to ask are: Do you really need the modules? Do they add extra functionality for your visitors? Looking at modules is really about how you want your web site to be seen. For example, for a community site, the number of online users is an indication of the activity on that site. The online user module is not something you want on your business site, as you don't want to distract your visitors from the introduction of the services you provide. If you are the only one who logs in, why have the login module? Use the Administrator panel instead. If you don't really act on or update your polls, what is the point of having a polls module on your site? These are the questions you need to ask yourself and act on them to "unclutter" your site.

- **Change your module placement**:

    This means that you need to think about the most important aspects of your site. You have to make sure that the most important menu items and modules reflect the main topic of your site. For example, if you have a menu containing links to general information about your site such as contact info, directions, a sitemap, and so on, then does that need to be at the top of your sidebar? Wouldn't it be much better if the menu, with the links to the services you sell, were the one in the most prominent position? Make sure the most relevant menus and menu items are in the best place to show off the topic of your site. If you use AdSense ads to monetize your site, you want to place them in the best position on your site to make money. Think about it that way for any module position changes you want to make. Placing your modules in the right position can make the difference between a new or a lost customer.

Placing uncategorized articles

You can also have uncategorized pages in Joomla! 1.5, and you are going to build some of those as well, because you need some pages outside the structure of your site. Pages inside a category have the advantage of getting the category keywords in the URL. At the bottom of the page you get the "next" and "previous" links for pages included in that category. These last options can be of benefit for your readers.

Pages in the uncategorized section will be, for example, your disclaimer and privacy statement. You can use the uncategorized section to contain other pages—such as contact details, or directions to your store. These pages are not in the main categories of your site structure. Non-category pages will not have any section and/or category keywords in the URL. If you are working with advertising services such as AdWords, you might use such pages for highly-focused landing pages. Personally, I prefer using the pages in a keyword-rich category.

The pages such as disclaimer and privacy statement will get a special code to keep them out of the search engine indexes, as they are mandatory for any web site, but should not get too much emphasis even thought they are linked to on every web page of your site.

To ensure this, we go to the **Metadata Information** screen and put in the **Robots** field the line **noindex, nofollow**. This means the search engines should not include that page in their index, that is, their robots should neither follow the link to that page nor follow any links on the page.

Improve your menu structure for SEO

The same way that improved with your backend structure, you now have to make improvements to the frontend. But there are some things to consider while creating an even better experience for your visitors.

Create a better structure with menus

A basic startup Joomla! site builder will put up menu links to the sections that are created because those are the main topics of the web site.

Your site might be built in just the same way. This means that you have one, or maybe two menus with all the links to your content.

Within the Joomla! menu items you can choose how sections are shown:

- Using a blog-like layout that will show the content of your articles all on one page
- In an article list that will show your article titles in a long list that people can click through

You can use links to navigate through different sections of your web site. However, this should be done only if you have a very large web site with lots of different topics. If not, go for links to categories. As an example, if you wanted to build a large web site about Joomla! and WordPress, then you could create categories such as templates and themes, along with category plugins and installation. If you were to use the category "plugins" and you only used categories in the URL, then which system does this refer to? Adding the section title to the URL will prevent that problem as it would create links such as /joomla/plugins/ and /wordpress/plugins/.

If you put your site content in menu links to categories you might end up with a long list of categories in one menu.

Having a long single list of categories is not a good thing, neither for your visitors nor for Search Engine Optimization.

It dilutes the focus of your visitors and doesn't tell the Search Engine Robots what your main topics are—for example, the **Main Menu** from the landscape gardening site.

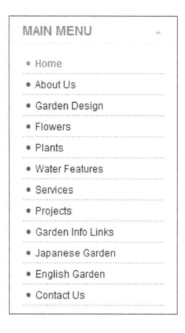

It looks just fine and it will grow over time to be a longer list. If you look more closely, you see that the subjects are not in a really nice layout and structure. Information is scattered in the menu and topics are not really grouped together.

Restructuring your menu items

You can do a much better job if you split this information into separate menus. Separate menus give you the possibility to improve the usability of your site for your visitors, but are also helpful from an SEO point of view. By combining the different topics on your site's information, you can create more focused menus based on overviews on different topics. Using and creating menu modules in this way you will be able to to have them appear to your visitor when he/she clicks on a specific topic, and to hide them where you don't want to show them. Imagine a water garden's menu with topics for those who are really interested. You could set the module to be shown if a person clicks on that topic.

If you use a menu item like Suckerfisch, which creates CSS-based drop-down menus, you can create those structures within that system. The restructuring process will then be more focused on sorting the menus into submenu items than new separate menu modules. The showing or not showing of specialized topical navigation menus is still a valid choice in that case. Go to the **Menu Manager** and create menus that reflect the main keywords as you used in the sections. You can create a separate menu for each section and again use your keyword list for naming these menus.

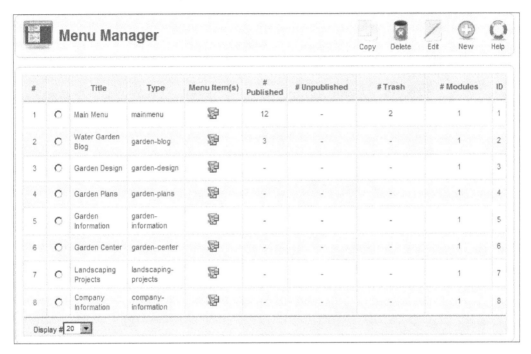

Go back to your **Main Menu** and click on the menu items you want to group together. Joomla! has a function in the **Menu Item Manager** called **Move**. With this option you can move the menu items in one single action to the new menu of your choice.

If your web site is cluttered with a long menu, but you are already ranking on nice keywords, you can still move the menu items without any problems. The links will not change if you move them.

If you are done with moving the category menu items, you can end up with something like this:

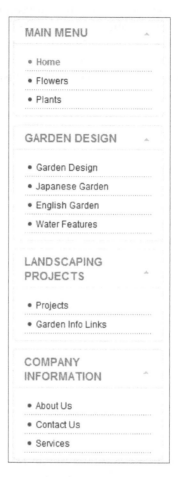

You may also end up with the menu showing a drop-down list, as shown in the next screenshot. However, that possibility has to be built into your template. If it is implemented, make sure it uses CSS classes to accomplish this, and not JavaScript or Flash movies because they are not as easy for Search Engine Robots to read. In fact, JavaScript-based menus are not read by search engines at all. One way to overcome this is to make sure your menus are also reflected in the sitemap. This way the path to the pages is guaranteed to be visible and crawable.

How to use separators and submenus for SEO

If you would still like to keep all the links in one menu, you should place separators in between categories, and move each category title so that it is below one of the separators.

That way, you can create nice submenus and also group the topics together.

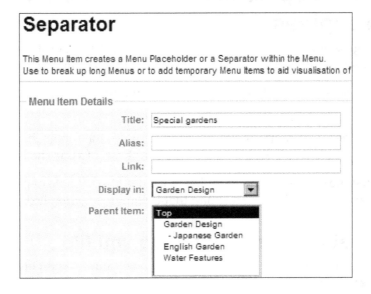

The following is an example of such a separator — **Special gardens**. The two categories **Japanese Garden** and **English Garden** are placed as submenu items:

As you can see, the structure of the web site is now much clearer for both visitors and Search Engine Robots. The menu titles now lay more emphasis on the main topics and keywords of your site and the categories are nicely grouped together for fast scanning by your visitors.

Why a sitemap component is essential for search engines

Sitemaps are great for your users. If you have done a good job, or if you have structured or restructured your menus, it will show in your sitemap.

Users like sitemaps to navigate through your site and find the topics of their interest more quickly.

For search engines, a sitemap is now essential! It guides the robots through your site and the sitemap structure will show where the emphasis of your site is.

Make sure that the sitemap component being used is also capable of creating a file called sitemap.xml based on the sitemap that is shown on your site.

Why you should use a sitemap.xml file

Robots can be guided to the most important terms and information on your web site through the sitemap.xml file.

For Search Engine Robots such as the Googlebot, sitemaps are the food they like — an overview of the whole site on one page.

But the main reason why you should have the `sitemap.xml` file is that you can use it to provide the search engines with the preferred URL that points to your articles.

In combination with the `sh404sef` component, which you will read about later, a sitemap is the best possible solution to prevent duplicate content issues.

If you are pointing to the same article on your site with different URLs, you are able to tell the search engines, using the `sitemap.xml` file, which URLs they should use.

Installing and configuring a sitemap component

As I said in the previous paragraph, Search Engine Robots like sitemaps. Sitemaps will give them a single page with all the links that should index. For Search Engine Robots, a sitemap is really important because they then know what to find and where.

It is a great way to show the robots what is important and what is not. Within the sitemap file, the system will give a priority value to the pages, which are the most important—such as the new pages or articles.

Creating a sitemap for a static web site is really a tremendous job. However, for Joomla! it is a simple task that is done for you automatically if you use a sitemap component.

The best one I know for Joomla! 1.5 at this moment is Xmap.

Installing and using Xmap sitemap component

You can download Xmap from `http://joomla.vargas.co.cr/`, where you can also download some extensions that will create parts of the sitemap for extensions such as Virtuemart and MyBlog.

You can also download it from `http://extensions.joomla.org/extensions/site-management/site-map`.

Another sitemap component that does a great job is Joomap, but this component includes some hidden advertisement links that could harm your search engine efforts. It creates and includes links in the source code to non-related sites, which you should avoid. Therefore, my choice is to use Xmap!

After downloading Xmap, install it like a normal component.

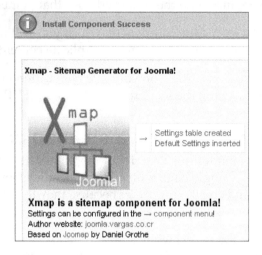

Configuring Xmap

Go to the Component and open it to see the administrative overview, which is pretty simple to look at.

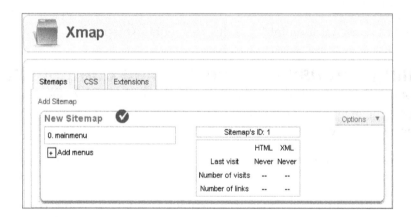

So, first let's go through the **Options**.

Under **Preferences** you will find the most important information, such as the location of the XML sitemap.

Here you can set the options for what to include in the menu and what to exclude, organized in a very simple manner.

Other preference options

Other options are to show the menu titles (**Show Menu Titles**), and if you want to include a link to the author (**Include link to author**), which refers to a link to the Vargas site, not the author of the articles. For now, leave the menu titles active, but from an SEO point of view don't include the link to the author. However, if you want to show some appreciation for the author's work, leave the link active.

- **Number of Columns**: This option is used in the layout of the sitemap. For a smaller site keep this to **1**. However, as the site grows and the page becomes too long, you can update it according to your needs.

  It is always nice to show your visitors if a link in the sitemap is going to take them to another site, which is why the image file is there. You can change the image to your liking as well.

- **Excluding Menu IDs**: This is a way in which you can lose links to the pages such as privacy statements and other mandatory pages that you need to link to, but don't want to show it on your sitemap. Remember, you are going to submit the sitemap information to the search engines, so make sure it has the relevant links and pages.

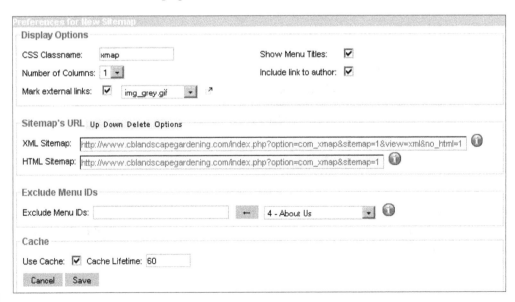

- **Cache Lifetime**: This is the time between rebuilds of the sitemap once it is accessed. Of course, this is dependent on the frequency with which new content is placed on the site. Leaving this to the default value works for standard Joomla! sites, and needs to be changed only if you notice that it takes too long for updates to get into the map.

- **SET Default**: This option means going back to the default setting. This option doesn't ask for a confirmation, so be careful, and only select it if you are sure you want to reset your options, especially if you have made a lot of changes to your preferences.

- **Copy**: This option will create a second instance of the sitemap, which you can and should use if your web site grows so large that the sitemap itself is getting very large. It is important for you to know that Google doesn't like pages that have more than 100 links on it. You can prevent this by having different sitemaps for the different menus on your site, if it gets really big.

- **Delete and Clean** cache speak for themselves.

Adding menus to the sitemap

Adding menus to the sitemap is done by clicking on the **+** sign. It shows a drop-down list through which you can select the menus you want to include in the sitemap.

After you click on **Save**, you are done with the configuration. The component doesn't close automatically nor does it say it's done, you just see that the menus are now included.

Linking to the sitemap

The next step is to create a link to the sitemap component in your menu. Click on create a new menu item and choose Xmap. It should be in your content selection list.

Go to the page through that menu link and check whether it fits in your site. Xmap takes some of the template CSS, so it should blend with the rest of your site.

If you have some special components installed such as Virtuemart, MyBlog, or RSGallery2, download the extension that you can install into Xmap so that it will create sitemap links for the content from those components as well.

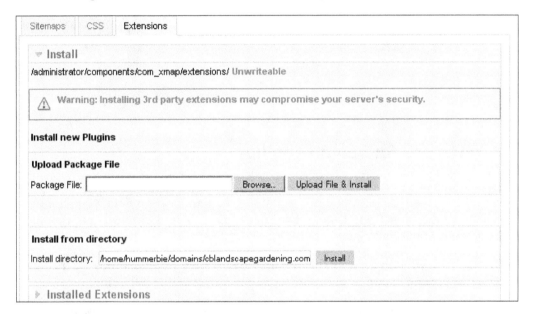

If you installed an extra extension, make sure you go back to the **Extensions** tab, choose **Installed Extensions**, and see if there is an extra options field.

Here you can see the options for Virtuemart, where you can set some information on the **Category Change frequency** and **Product Priority** that is referred inside the sitemap.xml file.

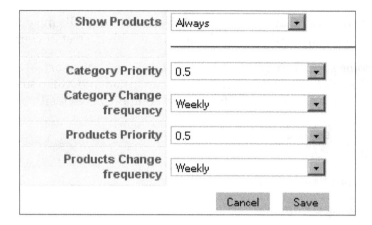

XML sitemaps for search engines

As you looked at the preferences of Xmap, you saw the link to the sitemap.xml file.

Hovering over the **Info** button at the end of the sitemap location field, you should see some text that says **Copy link and submit to Google and Yahoo**. Go to that link and see what is included.

I will show you what to do with this link in the next paragraph and how to include this in your robots.txt file. The sitemaps.org indicates the following:

> *Sitemaps are an easy way for webmasters to inform search engines about pages on their sites that are available for crawling.*

But there is more to it than that. A sitemap also includes a date, time, and weight factor, as search engines would like to know what pages are new and are more important than the others.

You can read more about those items and functions on the http://www.sitemaps.org web site.

The sitemap.xml standard is one that has been agreed to by all major search engines, so be sure to include one on your site.

Submitting your sitemap to search engines

Now you are ready to submit the link to the search engines, which you can do by logging in to their webmaster administration panels.

For Google go to webmaster tools using the **About** link on the Google site and logging in — `http://www.google.com/webmasters/`.

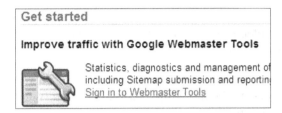

Add a new web site through your dashboard and go through the steps shown in the next screenshot:

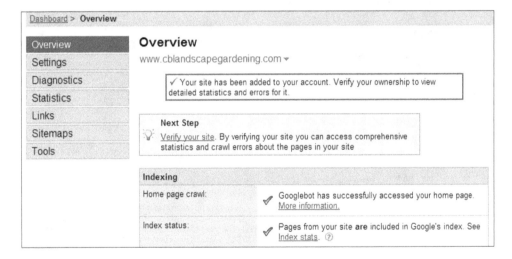

Verifying your site with Google

Verifying your site has to be done, so that Google will show the information only to you and not your competitors.

Google offers two options to verify your site ownership.

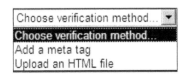

Please go for the HTML file option, as this has two advantages:

- Your verification is not template dependent
- The HTML file doesn't interfere with your XHTML validation code, unlike the verify meta tag

It is also a lot easier if you need to verify a number of sites as you just need to upload the file to the root directory of your Joomla! installation.

After you make your selection, Google will give you some instructions on how to create and name your HTML file.

Like I said, this file can be used for all the web sites that you want to verify with Google webmaster tools, as the file name is unique to you (which is why I am not showing the name in this book.).

Uploading and verification

After uploading the file click on **Verify**.

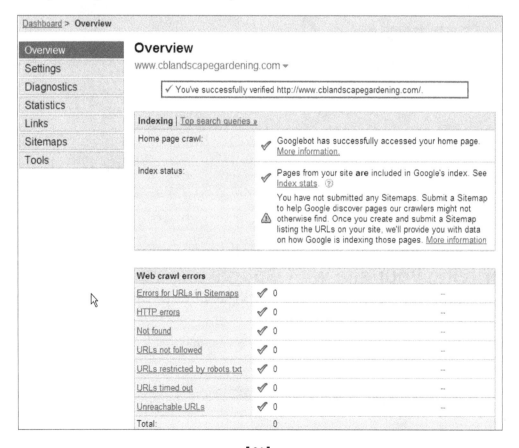

If the site is verified, you can see a lot of information that Google has on your site already.

You can look through that information and see what is going on with your site from Google's perspective.

Your sitemap.xml in Google

As you want to tell Google about your sitemap file, go to the menu option.

Copy and paste the `sitemap.xml` link from Xmap and submit the sitemap.

Now, Google will tell you the status of your submission, which is currently **Pending**. This means comeback later to check if it is ok.

Crawling and checking the file takes some time, so go on to the next search engine and come back later.

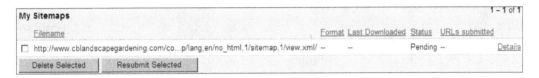

Verifying your site with Yahoo!

You can find the webmaster tool from Yahoo! at `http://siteexplorer.search.yahoo.com/`

Here you also need to have a login id, this time with a Yahoo! account (also free)

After logging in, choose **Add My Site**.

With Yahoo! you also need to verify your web site ownership. Here the same applies as with Google, that is, instead of the meta tags choose the HTML file to verify.

You also need to upload the verification HTML file, but this one differs per web site.

Here, verification also takes time, so once you click the validate link after uploading the file you'll have to wait a while—come back tomorrow!

Verifying your site with Bing

Verification of bing.com is done through either a meta tag or .xml file, I don't have to tell you which one to choose.

This .xml file also needs to be uploaded to the root of your Joomla! installation.

With Bing, authentication is really fast, you can go to your site listing and see what bing.com already knows.

As a result of your actions, the main search engines know about your sitemap.xml file or the equivalent from Xmap and you can start monitoring your site's indexing through the control panels.

The rest of the search engines will know the link to your sitemap.xml file after their spiders have crawled your robots.txt file.

Your sitemap.xml in Bing

Bing also has a place for webmasters: http://www.bing.com/webmaster. Of course you need a login id here as well, this time with a live account (also free). Once logged in you can add a site and sitemap link at the same time.

Site	
Web address:	
Sitemap address:	
	(Optional, if you already have a sitemap.)

Contact information
If you would like Live Search to contact you if we encounter specific issues with your site, enter your email below. (optional)

Webmaster e-mail:	
	☑ Sign me up for a periodic news update for webmasters.

Submit

Using the robots.txt file to guide Search Engine Robots

The robots.txt file is one of the files most people pay little or no attention to, but it is a really important file for your Search Engine Optimization efforts.

Putting the robots to work

Search Engine Robots use this file to check whether they are allowed to go into specific directories or not.

You can guide the robots with simple terms like `Allow:` and `Disallow:`.

You can even create rules for specific Search Engine Robots to follow.

All Search Engine Robots (web site crawlers) have their own names:

- Googlebot (Google)
- Yahoo slurp (Yahoo)
- MSNBot (Microsoft Live and MSN)
- Teoma (Ask.com and others)

There are lots more, but these spiders will show up more frequently than others.

Improving the Joomla! robots.txt file

Now you have your sitemap and the link to the XML version.

You need to inform the search engines that you have this file for their robots to crawl.

There are two ways to do this, and I suggest you use both. Firstly the inclusion into the Joomla! `robots.txt` file, and secondly, using the webmaster tools from the search engines to provide and check them.

The Joomla! robots.txt file

The first one is the simplest to include in your `robots.txt` file. Using `robots.txt`, the standard for Search Engine Robots, you can direct them to or away from certain parts of your web site.

The following is the content of the standard `robots.txt` that is in the root of your Joomla! installation:

```
User-agent: *
Disallow: /administrator/
Disallow: /cache/
Disallow: /components/
Disallow: /images/
Disallow: /includes/
Disallow: /installation/
```

```
Disallow: /language/
Disallow: /libraries/
Disallow: /media/
Disallow: /modules/
Disallow: /plugins/
Disallow: /templates/
Disallow: /tmp/
Disallow: /xmlrpc/
```

`User-agent:` * means that this file and the following statements are meant for all Search Engine Robots. `Disallow:` means that they should not crawl and index information in that directory or file.

If you want to create a special rule for a single Search Engine Robot; for example if you want only the Googlebot to index your images, you can add a line to give it special permissions.

```
User-agent: Googlebot
Allow: /images/
```

Putting the sitemap link in robots.txt

You should add an extra line to this file to include the link to `sitemap.xml` so that the robots can find them.

```
Sitemap: <sitemap location>
```

In my case it would be the following statement:

```
Sitemap: http://www.cblandscapegardening.com/component/option,com_
xmap/lang,en/no_html,1/sitemap,1/view,xml/
```

If you include your own sitemap link you have to make sure it is in one line!

Search engine webmaster tools

The second option mentioned tells the search engines where to find the sitemap by pointing them towards the XML version of your sitemap. For Google it means adding the sitemap into the Webmaster Central.

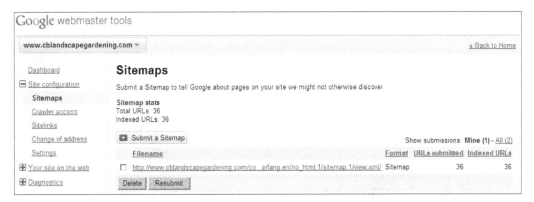

Yahoo! and Microsoft's Bing both have similar tools under `http://siteexplorer. search.yahoo.com` and `http://www.bing.com/webmaster`. For both you need to have a free user or email account for that specific search engine to use those tools.

Summary

In this chapter you have seen how the structure of your web site has an impact on your rankings. And you have seen how to communicate and guide the search engines with the `sitemap.xml` and `robots.txt` file. In the `robots.txt` file there is a lot of extra information in the appendix and for basic use the information provided in this chapter is enough. We also covered:

- Using sections and categories, to create a structure by using the keywords you want to target, to make sure your site topic is clear.

- To create better usability for users and search engines make it clear to the users and search engine spider, what your site is about.

- Improve your menu structure for SEO by carefully structuring or restructuring your menus, again using your main keywords.

- Why a sitemap component is essential for search engines and how you can use the Xmap component. One of the best features of the sitemap component is that new pages and articles are included in the file automatically so it is a real "set and forget" system. The search engines make sure that the Search Engine Robots will pick up the new content on a regular basis.

- Submitting your sitemap to search engines and making sure it is correct and validated.

- Using the `robots.txt` file to guide Search Engine Robots to the correct URLs and allow or disallow access to your web site's file structure.

3
Improve Joomla! SEO with the Joomlatwork SEF Patch

Joomla! 1.5 has some great Search Engine Optimization options already in place, but still there are some things that can be improved. Installing the Joomlatwork SEF patch will give you those improvements.

In this chapter you will learn the following skills:

- Downloading and installing the Joomlatwork SEF patch
- Making your titles more keyword rich
- Improving the metadata of your pages
- Controlling how search engines index your site
- How to upgrade, uninstall, or modify the patch

At the end of this chapter you will be able to see the SEO improvements this patch brings and how you can use the patch to your advantage.

Downloading and installing the Joomlatwork patch

What is the Joomlatwork patch anyways? The Joomlatwork SEF patch consists of a number of files that replace the original Joomla! files. These files will provide you with a lot more features to optimize your web site for better search engine visibility and performance. The Joomlatwork SEF patch will overwrite some of your core Joomla! files. This means some of the files from your default Joomla! installation will be replaced by files that are altered to make the improvements you want.

I normally would not encourage you to use a patch, as patching core files creates problems if you want to update to the next Joomla! version. For this patch, I am making an exception because it brings a lot of improvements to Joomla! from a Search Engine Optimization point of view.

It is fine to use this patch. After a Joomla! update the guys at Joomlatwork will have the patch updated to the latest version in two or three weeks or sometimes even sooner. This means you don't have to worry about using an insecure version for too long after a new release. Is there an alternative for this SEF patch? Yes, and we will look at that option in Chapter 6. However, this option will take a lot more time to implement and manage than the SEF patch. Other SEF components now offer meta tag management options, but a lot of work is needed to manage and get the similar options you get from the SEF patch.

Getting hold of the patch

Getting hold of the latest version of the patched files is simple. Go to `http://www.joomlatwork.com` and find the **DOWNLOADS** section.

From the **DOWNLOADS** section choose the directory **Joomla 1.5x SEF patch**, from which you can choose the version for your Joomla! installation.

[Make sure you use the correct version of the patch for your Joomla! site.]

If you don't know which version of Joomla! you are currently running, go to the **Help** menu and click on **System Info**. There you can see the version you are using.

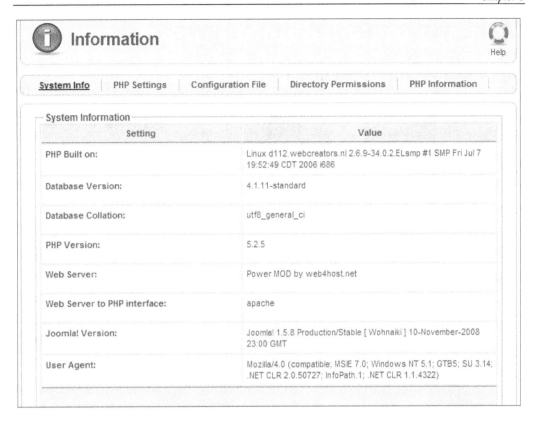

Installing the patch

Download the Joomla 1.5 SEF patch for your system and unpack it to your local drive.

Installation is really simple. Just upload the files using FTP to your Joomla 1.5 installation root directory. This is the directory where you installed Joomla!.

Make sure you copy the directory structure from the unpacked (unzipped) patch.

Using an FTP upload with the same account as you used for the initial install will provide the right security in place to overwrite the default files.

Name ▲	Size	Type
administrator		File Folder
components		File Folder
includes		File Folder
libraries		File Folder
metaconfig.xml	2 KB	XML Document
robots.txt	1 KB	Text Document

Make your titles more keyword rich

After installation you have to change the global configuration.

The following screenshot shows the familiar Joomla! default configuration page:

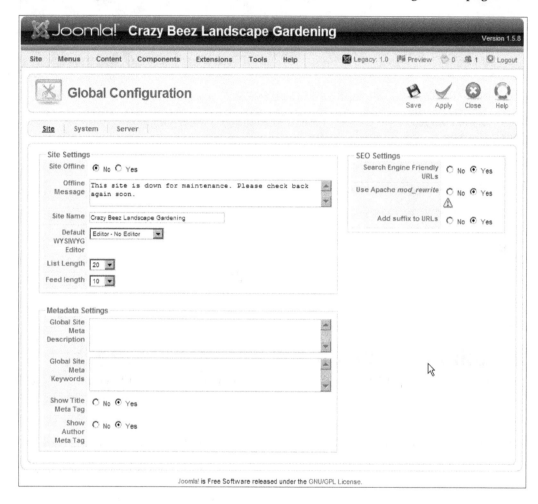

Take a look at the **Global Configuration** after the patch is installed. One thing that stands out is the new **SEO** tab.

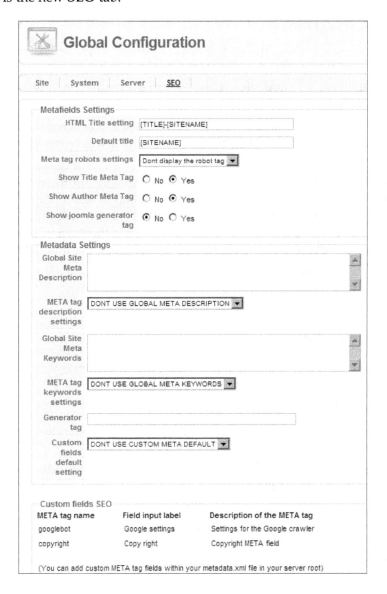

One of the new additions is the **Metafields Settings** tab that contains several items. The following list explains options under **Metafields Settings**:

- **HTML Title setting**

    This field must be filled. You can use [TITLE] to display the article or menu title that you supplied when you created the article content.

    You might want to add site's name— with the hyphen in between ([TITLE]-[SITENAME]).

    If you choose both, make sure your standard site title is not too long. Search engines don't show very lengthy page titles, so it will be cut off after a certain number of characters.

    Google, Bing, Yahoo!, and Ask use different lengths for the number of characters that they will show in the search engine result pages. Therefore, it would be a good practice to keep your title below the shortest length permitted by the major search engines. Here is a short list of the major search engines and the number of characters they show in the title field:

    ◦ Google 66 characters

    ◦ Yahoo! 72 characters

    ◦ Bing 66 characters

    ◦ Ask 67 characters

    I always use the [TITLE] field only, but I can understand you might want to use the [SITENAME] option to get some branding in the title.

- **Default title**

    Default title means that the [TITLE] of the site is used if there is no other title defined.

    However, you could also use this field for separately branding the site title. Simply change the [SITENAME] according to your own choice. The [] is used to get parameters from the configuration file.

    For example, you could set the title to [TITLE] – **Gardening Ideas**, which could give you an HTML title in the search engines such as **How to build a pond – Gardening Ideas**.

Create keyword-rich HTML titles for menus

In the **Menu Item** there is a field called **Title** and you have the option to **Show** it or **Hide** it. From the menu bar in your administrator panel, choose **Menu**, then select **Main Menu**, and click on the menu link you had created earlier from the **Menu Items**. After that select the option **Parameters (System)** on the right side of your screen as shown in next screenshot.

The title shown in the screenshot is on the page that is created by that menu item, so if you use a table or a blog layout, you will see that title on the screen.

But the title shown in you browser's title bar is the one that search engines will pick up and display on their results pages.

If you have a menu item called "landscape garden" then that is displayed as the **HTML Title** of your page. You may want to use a longer title for SEO, but you don't want a long title in your menu.

For example, in this menu item you want to set the **HTML Title** to **Landscape Garden Design services and realization**

The same goes for your content articles, although there you have more space to work with.

Let's look at some of the changes created by the patch:

- The possibility to use different HTML titles for menu and content items
- Meta tags such as description and keywords for menu items

If you create links to menus without the patch, you have very little control over the metadata such as description and keywords for that item.

However, the link does show up in Google and other search engines, so do you want more control over it than just the **Page Title**.

The field **Page Title** is not the HTML title, which is shown in your browser's title field.

The title shows up on the **Menu Item** page if you have selected **Yes** in the **Show Page Title** option.

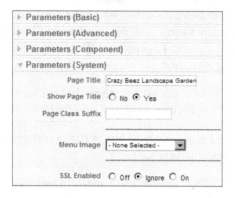

You can see in the following screenshot that after the SEF patch implementation there is a new item called **MENU item meta data**, which you can now use as described.

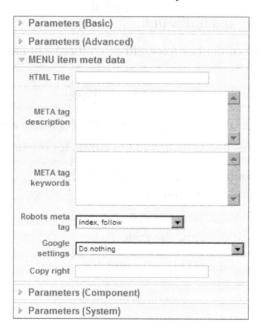

Once you have the extra **MENU item meta data tab** you can add your own **HTML Title**, your **META tag description**, and **META tag keywords**.

You can also use the simple **Robots meta tag** drop-down menu to get values such as **index, follow, index, nofollow, noindex, follow**, and **noindex, nofollow**. These options are explained in the Appendix.

The other **Google settings** that you can use are, for example, **noarchive** to prevent search engines from saving cached copy of the page in their cache.

Cache means that a copy of the page is stored on the search engine servers until it is refreshed. The frequency for updating depends on the timeframe set by the site, or by the time elapsed between two article appearances.

The more you write, the better the chance your ranking will improve.

Create keyword-rich HTML titles for pages

As we saw earlier, not only menu items are affected by the patch, the fields related to the content of the articles are also affected.

Although there was a **Metadata Information** tab present, it now contains some extra fields that are basically the same as you have read before.

Please keep in mind that these items are what you need to get your site in better shape for search engines.

How to use the new Joomlatwork fields

The fields added to both menu and content pages are:

- **HTML Title**
- **Google Settings**
- **Copy right**

The only changed field is the **Robots meta tag** field.

Making better use of the HTML title

This is very important for getting better rankings; you can improve your ranking a lot simply by changing the keywords used.

What is the HTML title? The HTML title is the text that is shown at the top of the browser window of the Internet Explorer.

But it is also the title that Google and other search engines use in their index, and is shown on the search result pages.

Without the patch, this title is the one you give to your menu item or your article in Joomla!

For example, in the following article, the title is **How to build a pond**.

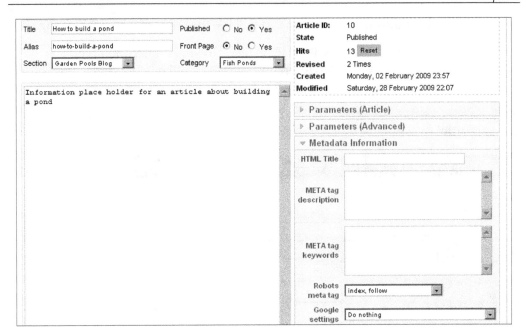

If you want to include extra keywords or completely change the title for the search engines then you can use the **HTML Title** field.

In the following screenshot, I changed the **HTML Title** to **How to build a great pond in your landscape garden.**

I also added the **Meta tag description** and **Meta tag keywords**.

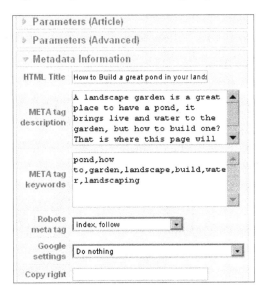

If you look at the following screenshot you will see the effect of this small change.

The page is the same and starts with a short title. However, the content for search engines is now better optimized with more keywords, and a better description of the page's content.

You can also see that the title in the Internet Explorer's title bar is now different from the page title.

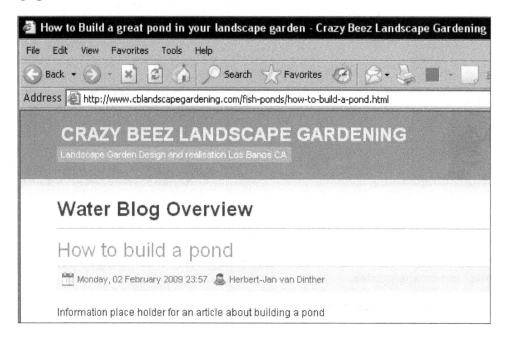

In the next chapter, we will look at how to write keyword-rich articles. You will also get some tips on how to write effective titles.

Improve your pages' metadata

The patch also gives you extra configuration settings for metadata. Optimal configuration of these settings is one of the key factors in further improving your site for SEO. The metadata of your pages is the data that is not shown in the content of the page itself. Metadata records are created for search engines to get more information about the page, such as who created the page, the title of the page, and more importantly, a short description of the content of the page that can be shown on the search engine result pages. Using these options in the correct way helps you to rank a lot better in most search engines.

Therefore, let's start with these settings and take action to put them right. Let's start by looking at the changes and options that are now available in the **Global Configuration** screen.

```
Metafields Settings
              HTML Title setting   [TITLE] - [SITENAME]
                  Default title    [SITENAME]
        Meta tag robots settings   Dont display the robot tag  [v]
            Show Title Meta Tag    O No  (•) Yes
          Show Author Meta Tag     (•) No  O Yes
        Show joomla generator      (•) No  O Yes
                           tag
```

- **Meta tag robots settings**

  This setting is used to tell the Search Engine Robots if they should index and follow the content of the article, or web site. By default Joomla! will tell the Search Engine Robots to index, follow every page, but you don't need to do that. Search engine spiders see the exception rather than the rule, and will index pages and follow links unless they are told otherwise, so just use those fields for special pages. Leave this field as it is, but keep in mind that you will be able to use this setting on page by page basis if you need to.

- **Show Title Meta Tag**

  This field should always be set to **Yes** so that you can change the title specifically for the search engines. With the parameter set to **No**, the **HTML Title** is not shown in every article and menu link. You can see how this affects the page meta tags fields later on.

- **Show Author Meta Tag**

  If you have a web site that is created by different authors, or you use Joomla! for blogging with different authors, you should set this to **Yes**. If you or the web site owner is the only one who writes articles, this is not really necessary.

- **Show joomla generator tag**

  As you read before, it is best not to show the generator tag, so set it to **No**. The removal of the generator tag can also be done using an option in the sh404SEF component. Another option is to hack the Joomla! core files, which I don't recommend, as you need to keep track of every hack you make because you will need to do them again after each core update.

As for the other metadata settings, my suggestion is not to use them, as it will only provide duplicate content to the site.

Why does metadata matter? How does Google use it?

Metadata is one of the areas where you can make a better site then your competitors.

There is a lot of discussion about metadata and whether or not you should use them, but in my opinion it is definitely worth the time you spend on them.

If you look at the search result pages from Google, you will see a **snippet** below the title of each page in the list of results.

Google creates these snippets from the content of your page unless you have provided a short, but most likely description for that page. This description is what you have written into the **META tag description** fields.

Using the description tag effectively

Based on what you just read, you can imagine that you have some influence on what is shown by the search engines.

Using a description is a great way to get people to click on your link that is shown. All you have to do is write a good short summary of the content of your page and make sure that your keywords are there.

Look at the description as a short advertisement for you page, and write keeping the potential visitors in mind.

For example, "building a pond in your landscape garden is not that difficult if you follow the right steps to make it, and choose the best place within your garden, read more here..."

You don't have a lot of space to write this description, as Google will limit the length to about 165 characters in two lines.

In the above example, you will find keywords relevant to the site, such as pond, landscape, garden, and building. If those words are also used in the title, Google will show them in bold if they are used in the search term.

Try it yourself, run a search and look at what is below the link you are most likely to click on. You will see that it's going to be the best description that catches your click.

Using the keywords tag effectively

Some webmasters and SEO specialists still use the keywords tag to stuff all the keywords they can find into that field. It is a great way to make sure that your rankings will drop like flies. Don't do that!

What you should do is, look at the content of your page/articles and choose somewhere between four to maximum ten keywords that you want to include in that field. You can write them as keywords or keyword phrases of two or three words, and separate them with a comma. You can write each word once and don't separate them with commas. It does not make a difference for the search engines because they use them as indicators for the content relevance only.

And here is the catch that most are still missing, make sure those words are used in your content! If the word is not there, don't use it!

How to avoid duplicate meta tag descriptions and keywords

Search engines don't like duplicate content, so you want to minimize any possibility to have duplicate content on your site.

Similar to the menu items issue mentioned before, Joomla! articles in which you did not fill the meta tag fields such as **META tag description** and **META tag keywords** could end up having duplicate content issues. You should always use the **META tag description** and **META tag keywords** fields on the pages you write.

If you haven't filled those fields, the default Joomla! installation will put the descriptions from the **Global Configuration** in each and every page you have created.

Of course it is best to use those fields in every article you create on your site, but sometimes you forget. The Joomla! SEF patch will prevent the **Global Configuration** fields from being attached to the content pages. In the normal Joomla! installation the Global **META tag description** and **META tag keywords** are used if there is no metadata article created. The SEF patch will prevent this from happening and will not show any metadata if you did not put it there.

> Normal installation: Global metadata is present on every page, unless the metadata fields are used.
>
> Patched installation: Global metadata is present only on the front page and not on the pages that follow, unless written in the metadata fields.

Control how search engines index your site

There are several other options build into the SEF patch, which you can use to guide the search engines and tell them what to do with your pages.

In the previous chapter, you also read about the `robots.txt` file. With this patch you get control over spiders and indexing on the page level.

Control all search engines with the Robots meta tag

The **Robots meta tag** is there to guide the Search Engine Robots to navigate through your site, telling them they should index the pages.

In the standard Joomla! **Robots meta tag** you have to write the terms yourself. However, with the patch you can use the drop-down box, which should make it easier for you to quickly change the settings.

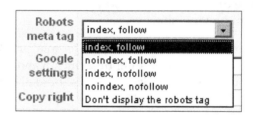

If you don't specify that you want to use this field, it is not shown and the robots will use their default, which is **index, follow**.

So your pages will be indexed and the links on the page will be followed.

For pages such as privacy statements, disclaimers, and site rules you can use the **noindex, nofollow** option, as you don't really want them in the search engine results.

Links to these pages will be shown on every page of your site. However, they are not as important as the link to your home page, so take them out of the index with the **noindex, nofollow** option.

Google settings

The new field **Google settings** give you more control over how Google handles your article pages.

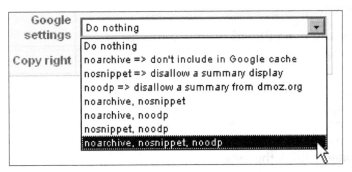

My suggestion is to leave them set to the standard option, **Do nothing**. The only cases where you should use these options are when you find that you are wrongly affected by the **Open Directory Project (ODP)** description for your site (**noodp**), or if your have some copyright concerns about a specific page (**noarchive**). For example, if the description of your link on dmoz.org web site would conflict with the actual content of your site, then you should use the **noodp** option. If you have copyrighted content that you don't want to show up in the cache function that Google provides; for example, an article that should only be visible to logged in users you use the **noarchive** function.

In some special cases, where you want to change the way search engines handle your pages, you should use these fields in the way they are intended:

- **noarchive**: This means that you don't want Google to cache the page's content on its servers. Mostly this is done for content that you want to get indexed, but is changed frequently. With this option set, Google will not show a previous version from its own servers.
- **nosnippet**: This tells Google that it should not create and use its own summary, or any other summary to display in the result pages.
- **noodp**: This one is used because you have no control on how the ODP (http://www.dmoz.org/) editors will describe your web site in their directory. This description was used by Google and other search engines, but now it is less important than it was some years ago. You can use this option to tell the search engines not to use the description that is given to your site if it is added to the ODP

The other options in the drop-down box are combinations of the options we have just covered. If you want to use these options, make sure you understand the effects they might have on your rankings.

Upgrade, uninstall, or modify the patch

You might have some concerns about using this patch. I can imagine that you want those concerns to be addressed, so here are some of the issues you may encounter, and their solutions.

- **What if you don't like it? Simply uninstall it:**

   The version 1.5.8 of the Joomlatwork SEF patch also provides an undo package that contains the original files for the version you are running. To completely remove this patch you can simply download the undo file, unzip it, and upload it in the same way you did for installation files. It could not be easier than this, to reverse the work done. But I can tell from experience that you don't want to undo this patch, and as you learn about its benefits you will come to think the same way.

- **What if I want to upgrade Joomla!:**

   You should not only want to upgrade Joomla!, you sometimes have to upgrade Joomla! to get access to new functions, or for security. If you are going to upgrade, hold on until the patch is updated, and then do your upgrade directly followed by the SEF patch upgrade. I can tell you from experience that you will see the difference if you upgrade without the patch. Your site will run without problems after the Joomla! upgrade. However, you will notice the difference after a few days, once the number of visitors' to your site starts dropping.

Some other changes from the patch

The most important changes done by the patch are mentioned in the previous paragraphs, but there are two other items that I would like to mention.

Generator Meta name

Joomla! is a content management system that places a small line in the source code of each page:

```
<meta name="generator" content="Joomla! 1.5 - Open Source Content
Management" />
```

Now, this line simply promotes Joomla! 1.5 if a visitor of your site looks at the source code to see what system you are using, as they may be keen to use the same system.

However, this same line is also visible to people who are looking for sites to hack.

It also adds an extra line to your page and this line is not really needed, so you should remove it. The patch will remove this line for you.

For your Search Engine Optimization efforts you want the cleanest code possible, so I remove the extra line of code from my sites.

Copyright

The **Copyright** field adds another meta tag line to your source code that contains the copy right information you add in that field.

If you have a web site where several people write articles, you could use this field to show the copyright for that user, for that year.

For example, if the article is written by Herbert-Jan van Dinther, you can fill this field with "Herbert-Jan van Dinther — 2009".

If you are the only editor, you don't need this field, so remove it — again cleaning up the source code.

The Joomlatwork SEF component

Besides the files from the patch that you downloaded previously, Joomlatwork.com also has a real component that you can install. The component basically does the same things as the downloaded patch, but gives you some extra options.

The following is a short overview of things that are different from the patch:

- You can install it like any other component, so no FTP uploads required
- The component is Joomla! version independent, it uses .xml files to overwrite the Joomla! default settings
- It gives you an overview of all the **META tag description** and **META tag keywords** from the content of your articles and menu items, so now you can see where you have to do some work
- It gives you keyword suggestions based on the content of your articles, which you can simply click on to activate
- Assign meta tags and descriptions to component's URLs, which is useful if a component doesn't provide that functionality by itself.

To get this component you have to buy the rights for support for six months at a very reasonable price of 14 Euro and download the component (at the time of writing).

The support also includes fast updates for new Joomla! versions, if there were any major changes that affected the component.

Please note that the price mentioned above is for a single domain/web site, and for additional sites you need to purchase additional licenses.

If you want to know more about the component, you can go to `http://www.joomlatwork.com` and check for the information.

For most people the SEF patch will do fine, and its combination with the sh404SEF component will add some extra functionality.

You will read more about the sh404SEF component in Chapter 6.

Summary

The Joomlatwork SEF patch offers more than just a few SEF tweaks. It gives you more control over your site, and the ability to work on your site's Search Engine Optimization at the content level.

It gives you the following:

- Meta tag fields for menu entries
- A separate HTML title for menu and article entries
- Fixes for the duplicate meta tag descriptions and keywords from the Global Configuration
- Removes the generator meta name
- Makes it easier to work with the Google settings and Robots options
- Gives you copy right code on individual article pages

For me these are the most important aspects to use and work with this patch, and I think you will find them really useful as well.

I hope that these features will get into the Joomla! core in one of its future versions.

4
How to Write Keyword-rich Articles

Writing good quality content is the best way to improve your site for the search engines, and to attract inbound links and targeted visitors to your site. In this chapter we will learn:

- How can you improve the ranking of your web site in the search engine result pages
- How can you write articles that will really get you the visitors you want

Importance of writing with keywords

First of all, Google and other search engines will index your articles and look for relevance of the search term used in their site in the content of your article. One of the things they will scan and index your articles for is the keywords, or search words, which are used by the searcher. The searcher is, of course, your potential visitor and you want that visitor to get to your web site. This means you should give that visitor a reason to visit your site right there on the search result page. Later in this chapter we will look at the titles and meta tags. , and you will learn about the options you should set to display the right kind of information to your prospective visitors.

Choosing your keywords

When it comes to keywords, you have to go back to your keywords list and look at the keywords that are being frequently searched for. You have to use words from the list you created in Chapter 1. Those words will bring you the most relevant traffic, and you should write your articles around them. By now, you probably know these keywords better than your potential visitor and you also know the combination of words that he/she is most likely to search for.

In the keyword list that you have composed, there should be some real gold nuggets that you can use. The best choices are the ones with a lot of searches and low competition.

Choosing the topics to write about

Looking at the keywords you have selected, it is time to choose the topic of your article. The topic must specify the problem you are going to solve and how you can solve it. One thing you must remember when you write the article is that the searcher is looking for either:

- A solution for his/her problem
- A way to learn more about the topic of his/her interest
- Some information on a service or product
- A place to buy a specific product or service.

One or more of these interests of your potential visitor needs to be covered by the topic of your article.

Finding the keywords to target

Depending on the interest of your intended visitor, you will have to use different keywords to target them. These keywords should be reflected in the content of the article and the content of the article should help your visitors to reach their goal.

For example, if they want information about "digital photography", you need to have those two keywords in place. If he/she is having a problem with photographs, you should include keywords such as "How to solve the problem with your digital photos". This way you will have included the basic keywords digital, photo, solve, and problem. The "How to" part is to tell the visitor that he/she is going to find the answer to the problem on your site.

If the visitor wants to buy a digital camera, he/she will look for specifications, reviews, and price information. In that case you can include keywords such as the brand, the type of camera, review, comparison, and technical data. You could also have a header stating: "Is the new Sony A350 worth it's price, read our review, and compare the specifications."

How do Google and Yahoo! show your keywords

You should do a search on Google or Yahoo! and check how the keywords of your search result are displayed. This simple exercise can help to get more insight on where your keywords will show on the results pages. I searched for landscape gardening in order to show you what to look for. You should do the same for your topic and the keywords of your site so that you can see how your competition is doing.

In the following screenshot you see the results of a Google search for landscape gardening. The main thing that stands out is the fact that the keywords you searched for are shown in bold. One other thing that is also obvious is that the search keywords are in the title, in the snippet, and if possible in the URL of the page as well.

Looking at the following screenshot, you will notice that Yahoo! also shows the keywords in bold, but it puts more weight on the URL than on the snippet. For Yahoo! it seems that the title and the URL are the most important factors.

What we see on both the search engines is that your keywords need to be in:

- The HTML title—the title index of the search engines
- The snippet—most likely to be the meta tag description
- The URL of the page

I will show you some other places that you can use to build the relevance of your keyword in the page, but those are not directly shown in the results. They play a big role in getting higher positions in the search results. Here the key to be remembered is the relevance part.

Writing with keywords in mind

Once you start writing, make sure you have the list of the keywords you want to use, next to your PC. Don't have them on your screen—print them out or write them down. This is because you need to be able to write the content of your page without having to switch back and forth from one application to another to view the list. Get those keywords into your head and start writing your article. You will see how it will flow into your content without much effort.

Putting structure into your pages

One thing that I always struggle with is the structure of my content. By structure I mean the way in which content is placed on the page, does it have a natural flow, or is it jumping around and changing focus all the time. It is important for your visitors to have some sense regarding where the article is heading and how it can help them.

I learned a nice trick that you too can use:

- Write the most important subject of your topic first
- Add the sub-topics below the main ones
- Fill in the content

This way you have the main content in place and you can move the subjects around, within the topic, to give it the structure you are looking for. It is like cooking—first make sure you have all the ingredients (the subjects), do your preparations such as cutting and slicing the ingredients (writing the content), and then start cooking. At the end it all comes together in the dish you made.

After you are done with writing, check if the framework of your page is still correct. If not, copy and paste it into shape. Now here is the big difference, if you get the order of putting the ingredients wrong the dish is messed up, while writing the content you can rescue the dish by changing the order to provide a better structure.

Getting the best placements for your keywords

You have seen how Google and Yahoo! show your keywords. If you have a closer look, you will see that your keywords should be in place first. You should place them in title, meta tag description and keywords, and of course in the content of your article.

One of the best places to have your keywords in your article is the first paragraph. Make sure to use your keywords in the first 100 to 200 words of this paragraph. If you can get them into the first two or three sentences, that is even better. Also the last paragraph should contain the keywords but your content needs to be on topic. In this paragraph your keywords should be in the last sentence.

You see how things keep coming back. It is not just the single simple placement of your keywords, but the whole package that makes it possible to outperform your competition.

So to sum it all up, your keywords need to be in:

- Article title
- HTML title
- First paragraph
- Last paragraph
- Meta tag description
- Meta tag keywords

Optimizing your articles

After the first few pages of this chapter, let's get into the real mood of things, it's now time to work on your site. Armed with the list of places to put your keywords in, improve your pages.

I will take you through a sample article and show you how to change the most important items on every page. For this, I will show you an example of how a page changes from flat content to an optimized and scanable page.

Writing content can be a long process once you start putting the content into your Joomla! site, even if you prepared your content before you logged in to your site. In the standard setup of Joomla! you have a limited session time for working on the content and hitting the **Save** or **Apply** button. You would not be the first one to lose all your hard work because Joomla! ended your session. To prevent that you have to change the value of the **Session Settings** in the **Global Configuration**. Choose the **System** tab and on the right side of your screen you will see the **Session Settings**. Change the value to something that fits your writing time. I have set it to **60** minutes as I tend to write long articles.

Start writing naturally

When you start writing your article, just do it in a natural way, write like you would normally do. Focus on what you want to tell your visitor as if you were talking to that visitor in person. Changing the way you write is something you shouldn't do, keep your own tone because that is what your visitors are used to.

What you can do is pick a content page from your site that doesn't get many visitors from the search engines, but you feel is a sample of your quality of writing and should deserve more attention.

The first thing you should do is look at the title of that page and analyze the following:

- Does the title contain the right keyword?
- Is the title catchy enough for a searcher to click on?
- Is your page scanable?
- How frequently did you use your keyword? In the title you should use the keyword once or twice, not more than that.
- Does the article fit the overall topic of your site?
- Did you use the meta tag description?
- Did you fill in the meta tag keywords field?

How to write better titles

Titles are the most important aspect of your content for search engines. In 2007, `seomoz.org` publicized an article on Google's search engine ranking factors, the article is still a great resource if you want to know more about SEO factors. You can find it at `http://www.seomoz.org/article/search-ranking-factors`.

37 of the world's best search engine optimization specialists worked together on this piece of information, and the number one factor for good rankings was, and still is, keyword use in the title tag! Simply rewriting the title of your page can help you to get better rankings.

If you started with a title such as "Japanese Garden" it would be in competition with about 21,000,000 hits on Google. If your article is about the design of Japanese Gardens, and you add the keyword "design" to the title, it is:

- More on topic and relevant to the search results
- In a much better position to compete

Changing your title from "Japanese Gardens" to "Japanese Garden design" will get you in competition with 735,000 competitors. Those are numbers that you can handle to start with and try to rank better.

Getting more keywords into your title

Now it's time to look at what your article is about—did you write about the design of Japanese Gardens in general, or about the structure of the Japanese Garden, or maybe even a specific garden in a museum in Tokyo. The article I am writing about contains a lot of information about the use of garden elements such as stones, water, and plants.

The title could now be changed to "Choosing design elements for your Japanese Garden" or "Japanese garden design—choosing the best elements and structure". In these titles you have the main keywords "Japanese Garden" along with additional keywords such as design, elements, and structure. So now you have a lot more possible keywords to rank for, than just "Japanese Garden".

The best part of this title rewriting for your web site is that you get more visitors who have found your site on the topics related to Japanese Gardens. In the long run, you will start ranking better with those highly competitive keyword combinations, because of this relevance.

Writing titles this way also makes it easier for people to filter the search engine results and choose your page title to click on, as it gives more information about the topic of that page. In simple words, it becomes more clickable because of that extra information. In Joomla! you can also change the page title, without changing the URL of that page. This means that your current rankings are not affected by the change, as long as you use the **Alias** as a part of URL creation.

With the SEF patch in place, you can write the main title as you normally would and use the **HTML Title** field for the extended version. The previous screenshot shows the normal content title for the article.

In the following screenshot you can see the extended version with the **META tag description** and **META tag keywords** added. You will learn more about these options in the following pages.

Making sure you stay focused

One of the biggest mistakes you can make with your web site is to write about tons of different things that are not related to each other. If you write about garden design on one page and then about diet pills and exercises on another page of your site, it will not only confuse your readers, but also the search engines. They will be wondering, what your site is about, as they wouldn't see any relationship between the two topics.

If you build a web site that you want to rank well in the search engines it is very important to stay focused. Pick the main subject of your web site and stick to it. Don't make the mistake of taking a very broad topic unless you want to build a really big web site. It is much easier to look at the subject of your choice and see if there is a special topic within that subject on which you can focus in order to attract lots of visitors to the site.

For example, instead of trying to rank for "landscaping gardening", you can choose "Japanese Garden" design and start building your site on that topic first. Once you have visitors for that topic, you can expand your site to other topics such as "English Garden" design and build your site brick by brick. This approach will give you a solid base to work with and the possibility to get lots more traffic from both the gardening related topics, along with the flexibility to add other gardening related topics in the future.

Keyword density—what is it and why bother?

In writing your articles you will use the keywords related to the topic of the article many times in the content. You should use keywords in the most natural way so that the text is readable for normal visitors. The number of times you use your main keywords in relation to the total number of words in your article is called the **keyword density**.

Using the keywords too many times within your article will make it difficult to read and, from a search engine's point of view, it also looks like you are stuffing your keywords. Stuffing means you are trying too hard to rank for that word. The number of times you use the keyword in your article is related to the length of your article. If you have a short article, it is natural to use the keyword three to four times. Writing your keyword more than ten times in a short article will break the natural flow of your text. Most of your articles should not have this problem if you write them normally. If you are trying hard to get your keywords in place in the article, you will get the opposite result of what you wanted to achieve.

Look at your article after you finish writing it. If it looks like you have written your keywords too many times, try to change a number of them by using a synonym. This gives you an opportunity to rank for those words as well.

Using headlines in the best way

You have looked at your title and altered it to get better results, and also looked at the content to make sure you are not overdoing the placement of your keywords. Now it's time to look at the rest of your article. If you look at the web page, you have to keep in mind the following thing:

Web site visitors don't read, they scan!

This means that your page has to grab their attention right away as you only have a few seconds to keep them on your web page. You need to give them an overview of the subject of the page by leading them in and encouraging them to look over the content of that page.

Don't believe me? We will look at some statistics later on that will make it clear to you that this is really the case.

How to make your articles scanable

Filling your web page with large blocks of text will scare your visitors away. Here is an example, on how to improve a web page and make it more scanable. As you can see there is a lot of text and no real visual outstanding items that show what the page is about except for the page title.

Not using white space between paragraphs is also a great way of telling people not to read your article. It makes the content difficult to read as you don't see the end of one paragraph and the beginning of the next one. In normal books, it has its place if you need to explain a difficult subject that needs a lot of text to prove a point and show how things are done.

For web pages, however, it is the best way of losing your visitors. Such pages scare people away from your site, as they don't know if the page is worth the time they will spend reading the content.

As I said earlier, your visitors are scanners. They scan your page looking for resting points, headers, and structures. These page elements tell them that they have found the right page, to get the information they are looking for. In the previous example you see that white space was used to create text blocks that are not too lengthy to read. The use of introduction lines for each block is also well done for page scanning.

Getting keywords into headers and paragraphs

Using headers and paragraph layouts is one way to provide the specific information needed by scanners so that they start reading the article.

If you write a lengthy page about a certain topic, you can always split it into different paragraphs. If you do that, you will also have a clear idea of which paragraphs can be grouped together. Those paragraphs will have one keyword in common. Use that keyword to break the page.

A page on Japanese Garden design elements could be very long. You can easily break it into page sections. For instance, with headers such as "Garden design structures" and "Japanese Garden elements."

These headers should not be given a Heading level one tag, but one below that, such as Heading level two. If you don't want to use the HTML codes, or you don't know how to, just make them bold and use a bigger font to make them stand out.

If you have images on your page, place them near those breaks. If you still have a lengthy text section, place a smaller image in the middle of that text to break it into two pieces.

For a very long page, make a table of contents in the first paragraph and create placeholders for easy navigation. Placeholders are links to various sections on the same page so that you can jump to that location just by clicking on the placeholder link. To learn more about how to create such placeholders you can check the example on http://www.w3schools.com/HTML/tryit.asp?filename=tryhtml_link_locations.

The use of keyword-rich hyperlinks to the subjects placed in the table of content is also good for your Search Engine Optimization as you create extra keyword-rich links inside that page. Using bullet points, if useful, is also a good way to break your page and invite people to read on.

Using the metadata fields to your advantage

Some people, and yes some search engine optimizers also, will tell you that using metadata fields is a waste of time. That time could, in their opinion be better used for writing new pages on your site and creating better content. I think that is true, if you don't know how to write the descriptions, if it takes you too long to write them, and if you don't see the possible opportunities that the use of metadata will give you.

In Joomla! you will find the fields I am talking about under the **Metadata Information** tab. The fields shown in the following screenshot appear if you use the Joomlatwork SEF patch. If you don't have the patch installed you will not see the **HTML Title** field, the **Copy right** field, or the **Google settings** field, and the **Robots meta tag** field will not have a drop-down list.

Writing good meta tag descriptions

The **HTML Title** will be shown in the title bar of your browser and is used by the search engines. Make the best title you can and place it in the **HTML Title** field.

The **META tag description** is the place to write a small advertisement for your page. If done correctly it will show up under the title in the search engine results pages. The best way to write a description is to write it like an excerpt of the content of your article using the same keywords that you have used in your **HTML Title.**

The best time to write this is right after you have written the article. The article is fresh in your mind and you can write the description in less than five minutes. The best placement of your keywords in the description is at the beginning of your excerpt. Don't write long descriptions as they will be cut short by the search engines. Keep them short and sweet. You have only one second to get the click you want, make sure you get it! Writing good descriptions will help you get that click, even if you are not number one in Google.

How to use the Keywords field

The keyword field was used in the early days of the search engines to help get rankings. You just needed to stuff that field by repeating your keywords over and over again to get good rankings, even in Google. That was not the actual intention of that field, and search engines eventually started to give less importance to it.

Some search engines don't even use it now, and most give lesser importance to it. You can even get penalized for overuse of keywords in that field. Search engines don't like such keyword stuffing and will look at it as spamming. The best use of this field is to put in the most relevant keywords that are also used in the content of your page. Don't choose more than five to ten words to put in there. Whether you want them to be separated by a comma or not is your choice. I haven't found any difference between the two options.

The page we looked at earlier is now done, with some images added and the paragraph introduction headers displayed in bold. The overall view of the page is a lot more readable now, and with the proper use of images (see this in Chapter 8), we even have the possibility to rank better for the keywords in the page.

Crazy Beez Landscape Gardening
The California Landscaping Gardeners from Los Banos

Home   Garden Structure   **Plants**   Garden Design   Garden Center

Flowers   Trees and Shrubs   Herbs and Vegetables   Ground Covers and Lawns

Home ▸ Plants ▸ Flowers ▸ Showing First Class Flowers

Showing First Class Flowers

Showing your own First Class Flowers at Exhibits or Trade Fairs is a great way to get more knowledge about your own Flowers and Vegetables. You will come into contact with people who have the same passion as you have and you might even get som recognition for how you tread your garden. But there are some. basic rules for showing the fruits of your labor. You can read about that in the article below form Steven Karback.

Half the fun of growing first class flowers and vegetables is showing them. In showing follow the schedule to the letter, or should I say "number"? One too many or one too few will disqualify you. Also try to select flowers or vegetables of uniform size and if it is vegetables select those of uniform shape as well. It isn't the biggest tomato or the biggest eggplant that gets the prize but the best. Be sure to wash beets, carrots, or beans and avoid blemishes, broken roots, discolored or chewed foliage, cracked tomatoes, earworms in corn or disfiguration of any kind. Long stems on flowers are important.

Divide Peonies and Bleeding Hearts

Divide and split the peonies into sections with five or six eyes. In replanting there should be no more than one inch of soil over the crown. Bleeding heart is more difficult to handle because it breaks so readily into many seemingly useless pieces. Put together several pieces three or four inches long and plant them with two inches of soil over the crown.

Firm the soil around the roots with your foot. Since replanted perennials are not likely to be disturbed for several years, enrich the soil with manure and bonemeal before planting.

Plant Madonna lilies in August. Barely cover them and mark the spot so you won't disturb them when you cultivate. For a very beautiful picture plant the lilies beside blue delphiniums.

Sow winter rye in blank spots in the garden as they appear. Level the soil, sow the rye generously and rake it in. It is a grand soil conditioner and adds humus to the soil when dug under in late fall. Sown later, it is left all winter and dug under in the spring. Just as soon as a row or two of space is available sow the rye.

Greenhouse Task

Cuttings of tender perennials such as heliotrope, lantana, verbena, ageratum and fuschia plant care should be taken now. These cuttings will be the stock plants from which you will propagate in spring for your supply of bedding out plants. Some of the cuttings taken now could be grown into standards for next year's garden. Select a few of the strongest and pot them. Do not pinch. Instead, keep removing all the side shoots as they come along. Keep the main stem growing until the plant reaches the desired height and repot as they require it. Heliotropes and fuchsias make fine standards in one winter. Lantana takes two years to make a sizable head. Standards are fine material for adding height and interest to flower borders.

Bulbs to plant this month for winter flowering are freesias, ixias and lachenalias. Plant 12 to 14 bulbs per 6-inch pot with the tips of the bulbs exposed. Use 1 part sand, 1 part humus and 2 parts soil with 6-inch potful of fine bonemeal to each bushel of mixture. Place the pots in a coldframe and shade until growth takes place. Water sparingly until well started.

A compost pile for greenhouse and frame use is a must.

Ready to fix the confusion on the topic of fuschia plant care. We make the information simple, visit zone10.com.

Article Source: http://EzineArticles.com/?expert=Steven_Karback

The Garden Blog

Water Gardens
Fish Ponds
Koi Ponds

Garden Books

New Complete Home Landscaping
Ms. Catriona Tudor...

Buy from amazon.com

Privacy Information

Garden Information

Gardening Information

Landscaping

Projects
Garden Info Links

In the backend we also changed the **HTML Title**, added a **META tag description**, and some **META tag keywords**.

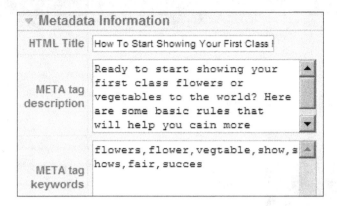

Putting it all together

Looking at this chapter it should be evident that you need more than just a better written, keyword-rich title to outrank your competitors.

If you want to enforce the great title you wrote, make sure you accompany it with:

- Good quality content with keywords in place
- Scanable page layout with keyword-rich headers
- A good/great **META tag description**
- A good set of keywords in the **META tag keywords** list

It is the force of these combined efforts that will give you better results in the search engines.

Another way of improving your page SEO is to use the "read more" option if you use introduction items, for example, in blog layout pages. In Joomla! there is a separate field where you can change the text of "read more" into a more keyword-rich link. This can be done by using the **Alternative Read more text** field in the **Parameters (Advanced)** section. Your template should support this, but not all of them do.

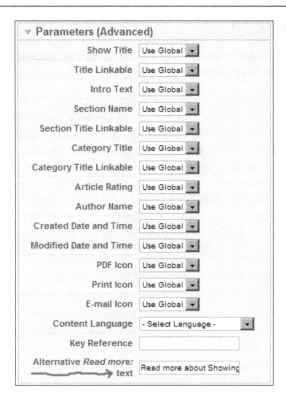

For example, you can change it to **Read more about Showing First Class Flowers** or even **Click to read more about Showing First Class Flowers.**

Using an article list layout when you create your menu link, instead of the blog layout gives you good keyword-rich links. I personally like this kind of layout especially for sites about technical topics, where there is little possibility to work with images. If you write about processes that need to be executed in a certain order, it makes sense to use a content table as you can simply order the pages into a certain sequence. If you create a web site such as the example site, people expect to see images, in that case a blog layout should be used and along with the "read more" option, to encourage users to click through from the introduction and to read the rest of the article.

Summary

In this chapter we looked at the options and the best practices for creating and laying out content that will do well in the search engines.

The topics we looked at are content ideas, keywords to target, and the importance of structure of your content. We also talked about keyword placement, how to enhance your titles, and the use of headers and paragraphs. Finally, in the content creation section, we learned about the meta tag description and keywords, along with the importance of proper use of those fields.

I also showed you a simple example of how to make your page more scanable and visually appealing for your visitors by using images and bold paragraph headers. Remember, good content is the most important factor in ranking well, but you need to have all the aspects of SEO aligned to outperform your competitors.

5
Joomla! Blogging and RSS Feeds

Blogging is a great way to get more traffic to your site and communicate with the community interested in the same topics as you.

Search engines such as Yahoo! and Google love blogs because of the fact that articles written in blogs are mostly up-to-date and they get the information about the update of a blog really fast using RSS Feeds and Pings. Articles posted on a blog with these two options in place can get into the search engine indexes within hours, sometimes even minutes.

So, let's see what we need for a site to be considered a blog, or to have a special blog section:

- Regular updates
- Chronologically ordered
- Commenting option
- RSS Feed and email update

We will work through these options to get you blogging with Joomla!.

I will give a short introduction to Joomla! blogging components at the end of this chapter just to show you an alternative. After that you can decide for yourself if you want to use them, and if they are worth the money spent. With a blog component, you still have to go through the basics of setting up a blog.

How is blogging good for SEO?

Using a blog has some advantages that fair really well if you want to have more visibility in the search engines. We will be looking at some of those advantages and how they can affect your search engine rankings. I am not saying blogging is easy, but it is very rewarding.

Creating fresh content

Creating short articles about your favorite topic and publishing them on a regular basis is the best way to get into the search engine results pages faster.

The number one thing about blogging is that you can write long articles or short articles. The combination of the two different formats won't break the flow of your site, unlike a normal web site, where you mostly write articles that are built with a certain length. You can also state an opinion about things that are going on in your community and write news items. All that in one web site without worrying too much about how to structure all the information.

I told you in an earlier chapter that you need a structure for SEO and that Joomla! will force you to use the structure you have chosen for your site. Using Joomla! as a blog will make it easier for you as you will be using the categories created in advance to hold that information for you.

Google and blog indexing

If you set up a blog and start using the sites and services we will be looking at, like FeedBurner and Technorati, you will notice that the major search engines also use these services to index blog sites and find new posts really fast. Now Google even owns FeedBurner! You will not only syndicate your articles using options such as RSS Feeds, but you will also push your articles through Technorati, the number one site to show your blog to bloggers.

Google has a special tool with some basic categorization in place for searching blogs; you can find it at `http://blogsearch.google.com`.

One good thing about this blog search tools is that it will show you how "old" a blog post is. For example, under the title you will see a statement such as **10 hours ago** just to prove how fast you can get an article indexed from a blog.

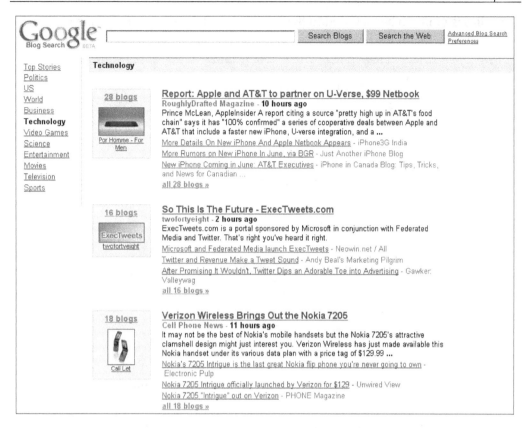

Setting up Joomla! as a blog

Joomla! was not built to be a blog in its basic form, unlike WordPress. However, Joomla! has a built-in layout function called **Blog layout** that can be used for sections and categories. RSS Feeds are also built in, but we need to put an extra component in place to get a commenting system.

First things first, let's set up the basic structure of your Joomla! based blog.

How to structure your blog section

The first thing you need to do is to come up with a section name for your blog.

You already have an extended keywords list, so it should not be difficult to set up a blog. In my example site I have set up a **Section** called **Garden Pools Blog** and the **Alias** I want to use is **garden-pools**.

This alias is going to be included in the SEF URL and contains some of the keywords I want to target with the blog.

Once that is ready, you need to create the main categories, which of course will be the main topics of your blog section.

Choosing your blog categories

Again you need to find the right keywords to put into your category names. The best thing you can do now is to focus on the topic you want to blog about. It is really essential that you think about these categories and name them the right way, or you will get into trouble later on. Once we get to the SEF URLs in the next chapter, you might find yourself in trouble if you have the same category names as in the main site.

In my category for this blog I have used the category name **Water Gardens**, depending on my choice of URL construction in the sh404SEF component. It is possible that I may not use the same category name for the main topics of my site.

If I were to use the same category name they both would get the URL
`http://www.cblandscapegardening/water-gardens/`, leaving one of the
categories not reachable. One workaround would be to change the alias of one of the
categories, but that would still leave a duplicate title on your site which you would
need to change. Google would show it as a possible duplicate title in its webmaster
content analysis. You can prevent this by choosing your categories wisely.

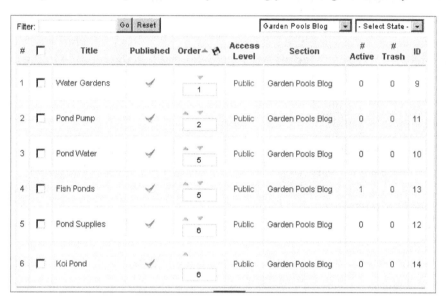

Therefore, it is important to think about these URL structures, when you start
naming and creating the blog categories.

Stay focused and limit yourself

If you start naming the categories make sure you stay on the same blog topic and
keep the terms as relevant as possible. Don't create too many categories as you are
going to create a separate menu for the blog. Too many categories will fill your menu
with a long list of topics, and the visitors will not be able to choose from this long list.
It is also not a pretty sight to have such a long list in your sidebar.

Limiting yourself to a smaller section of categories, which you want to connect your
articles to, will help you to stay more relevant to the topic of your choice.

Creating a blog menu

Once you have set up your categories, it's time to create your blog menu.

Start with creating a new menu and call it whatever you want to, give it a title like **The Garden Blog** as in my example site. To set this feature go to your administrator panel and choose **Menus | Main Menu** from the menu bar at the top. After that choose **New**.

Make it short and to the point so that it is really easy to find it on your site. Go to the **Extensions** menu, choose **Module Manager,** and **Publish** the module in the location you want it to show on your site.

The first thing you should do is create a link to the section in which you are going to put your blog posts, and change the **Parameters(Basic)** to match the layout you want:

- **#Leading** is set to **1,** which means one full length article to start with
- **#Intro** is set the **6,** so you have the introduction text (that is the text before the "read more" link) from six articles, getting a total of seven on the blog page
- **Columns** is set to **1** to get a complete overview of the articles in a listing that is not broken into two columns after the first **Intro** article
- **#Links** this is the number of links with the title of older articles that don't show on the blog page anymore

After setting the **Parameters(Basic)** you need to set the **Parameters(Advanced)** as well:

- Change the **Category Order** to **Order** and the **Primary Order** to **Most recent first**.

- Make sure you have the **Show a Feed Link** set to **Yes** — only for this menu item. This option is set so that we can get a full RSS Feed over all the blog categories

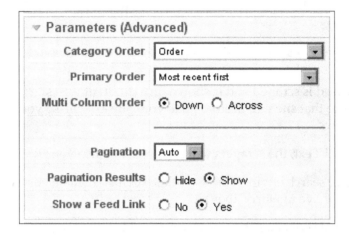

For a blog, you need to change some of the settings in the **Parameters(Component)**:

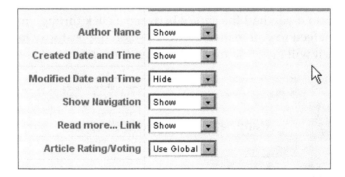

- For a blog you need to **Show** the **Author Name**, the **Created Date and Time**, the **Show Navigation**, and the **Read more... Link**

- The **Article Rating/Voting** depends on you, for me its set to off, as I don't like the dotted rating icons

The commenting system will give your visitors the ability to share their thoughts about your article, rather than just rate them, unlike the rating system. You will learn more about such a commenting system later in this chapter.

Why use a Full Text instead of Intro Text feed

For each feed item show is the last option you need to know in the **Parameters(Component)**. It is for you to set whether you want your RSS feed to include articles as Full Text or just the Intro Text. If you go for **Intro Text,** only the beginning of your article will be shown in the RSS Feed, with a link to the complete article. **Full Text** will show the complete article in your RSS Feed.

The choice between these two is a difficult one. With an **Intro Text** feed you will achieve two things:

- More page visits on your site, as people need to go to your article page to read the complete article
- If your feed is scraped and is shown on a different web site than yours, visitors to that site will need to go to your site as well, so you still get the page views

If you choose **Full Text,** the scrapers will love you, but also your RSS Feed readers!

Google and other search engines know that the scraped content comes from your site, so you don't have to worry about it.

However, your subscribers, subscribe to your feed because they want to read your articles in a simple and easy way. For most of them it means reading in their preferred feed reader, along with other RSS Feeds of their interest.

What would you do if you had the choice between a click through to the web site or reading the full feed in you reader? In my opinion the best way to go is to use a **Full Text** feed, as it will give you more readers in the long run.

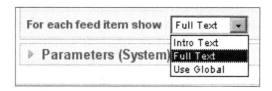

Separator and blog categories

To separate blog categories from the complete overview, place a separator just below the section link. Simply choose the option **Separator** in the new menu item and give it a title. I just named it "Blog categories". Now start adding the menu links to the different categories using the **Category Blog Layout** option.

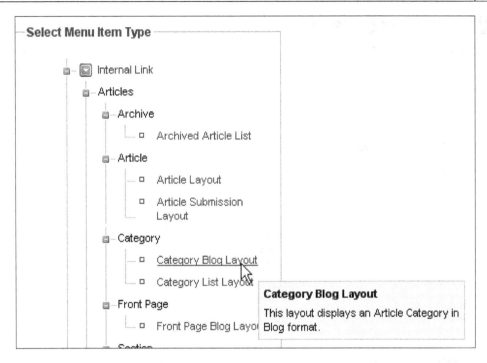

Make sure you change the menu parameters to match the ones you set previously in the section links. That way you will ensure a standard layout for every category in your blog section.

Commenting anyone?

One of the most important features of a blog is the commenting system, where visitors can respond to the articles posted on the blog. Comments can be a direct response to a post, questions, or additional information that can help others who read the article.

Joomla! at its core doesn't have a commenting system, with anti-spam features in place, so we need to look for third parties to provide this feature. You can choose from several components and plugins to get a commenting system in place. There are commercial ones such as JomComment and JXtended Comments, and free components such as !JoomlaComment, MXComment, and yvComment. Of the commercial ones the JomComment seems to be the most widely used, and of the free ones for Joomla 1.5 yvComment seems to be the most popular.

Why comments are important

From an SEO point of view, commenting is very good, as people will create extra content for your page with their comments. Those comments are mostly on the site's topic, so without writing the content yourself, your page content will grow. But it has another benefit, and that is the interaction with your visitors.

Interaction with your visitors

If you respond to the comments of your visitors in a respectful way and engage in the discussions, people are likely come back to your site to read your responses to questions.

They will eventually start asking questions and tell other people where to go to get answers to their questions. It will give you the possibility to get word of mouth advertisements that will increase the number of visitors to your site. They will share links on those articles and discussions, which leads to more incoming links to your site. As you can see, interacting with your visitors is really good for your Search Engine Optimization efforts.

However, there are people who will use your commenting system to spam your site with their own links and that is something we want to avoid. Therefore, a good anti-spam system and comment moderation facility needs to be in the system as well.

I am going to show you how to implement a third-party service that does all that and more. It is called Disqus and it's a free service.

Installation and configuration of the Disqus plugin

Disqus is not a component that you install on your Joomla! site, it is a free service provided by www.disqus.com.

To be able to use this service you have to get a free account on www.disqus.com.

Setting up your commenting service on Disqus

To get your configuration set up, log in to Disqus.

Once you are logged in look at the top right menu, there you will see small link that says **Add a Website**, and that is exactly what you want to do.

These steps are really simple—the first line is the URL of your site, the second is a description to identify the site in your administration and moderation panel.

You will need the **Short name** later on, make sure it is short and simple without spacing. You can even choose to remove any hyphens or underscores as well.

The next thing you need is to choose your platform.

Joomla! is not included in this short list, so move to the option **other platforms.** In the list that follows you see a link called **Joomla**, following this link will take you to the site www.joomlaworks.gr.

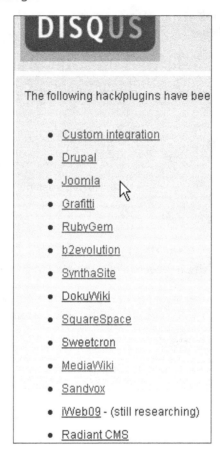

Find the plugin **DISQUS comment system for Joomla!**.

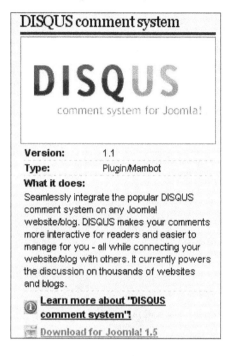

Download and install this plugin, it is also free. Install the plugin like any other plugin and we can get into the configuration of this plugin. The configuration of the plugin is really simple, but make sure you have the correct **Short name** for Disqus at hand.

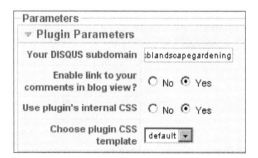

Change the content of the field **Your DISQUS subdomain** to the **Short name**. Your subdomain should be something like Short name.disqus.com.

After you enable the plugin you are ready to moderate the comments and trackbacks received through the Disqus web site. If you look at the pages on your site you will see that the comment feature is now in place and integrated into the site.

Disqus has the following advantages over comment components:

- Very good anti spam database that filters spam directly at the source
- Easy moderation panel

Can be used for different web sites and still have one moderation panel for all those sites

- It has a trackback system in place that most of the Joomla! comment components don't have

Limitations of Disqus

Are there any drawbacks of using this system? Yes, there are:

- You don't have control over the content of the comments like the real Joomla! comment components.
- The data is not stored in your database, but is with Disqus. If this service stops in the future, you could lose all your comments.

- You are also relying on servers that are not under your control, so if they have an outage it could hurt your site because of long loading time.

- You cannot limit commenting to one section of your site, so if you want to limit comments to the blog section only, you will notice that you cannot do that.

 This commenting system is for your whole site, so please be aware of that. This means, not only your blog has the possibility to receive comments, but all the other articles on your web site will receive comments as well!

Putting your RSS Feeds to work

Now that we have the blog and the commenting system in place, it is time to focus on your RSS Feed(s).

RSS stands for **Really Simple Syndication** and it simply means that the content of your site can be viewed easily using a RSS reader. More important is the fact that people can subscribe to your RSS Feed and get the new articles delivered to their reader or mailbox.

Search engines are looking at these feeds as well and they take them into their index really fast. You saw how fast you can get indexed in the blog search of Google. The only way it will happen that fast is, if you provide them with a sitemap and a RSS Feed. First you need to activate the RSS Feed option for the blog on your Joomla! site. To do that go to the **Module Manager** section in the **Extensions** menu and add a new module.

 Do not choose the Feed Display module, choose the Syndicate module!

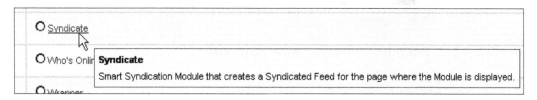

With a syndication module you are going to publish your content, with an RSS Feed module you are getting the feed from another site. Configure and publish the module to be active for the blog overview menu item only. For best results set **Format** on the right side to **Atom 1.0**.

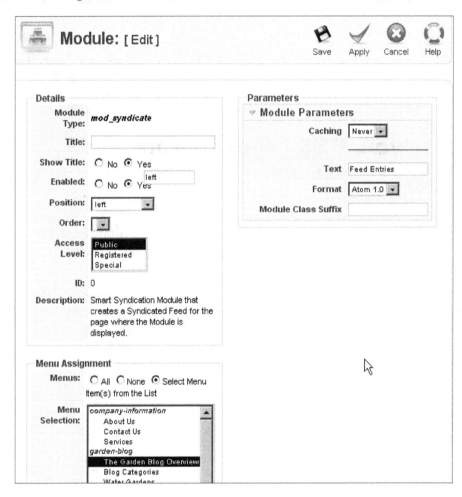

On the blog overview page you now see a small icon

Click on that **Feed Entries link** and copy the URL it goes to so that you can use it later when you are going to improve your RSS Feed to have the best possible effects for Search Engine Optimization.

Using Google's FeedBurner for SEO

The preferred choice for burning your feed was www.feedburner.com, and they were so good at it that Google bought FeedBurner. So now if you want to **Burn your Feed** you have to login to Google with your Gmail account. Once logged in, look for the service FeedBurner and click on it. You will find a small screen in the middle of the page that says:

> **Burn a feed right this instant.** Type your blog or feed address here:
>
> `ening.com/garden-pools-blog/feed/atom.html` ☐ I am a podcaster! **Next »**

Here you can paste the link that you got after clicking on **Feed Entries** on your Joomla! site. That is the public RSS Feed link that is shown by your syndication module. Once you click on the **Next** button you have a lot of options to improve your blog feed. The first thing you have to do is to make sure you have a nice feed URL.

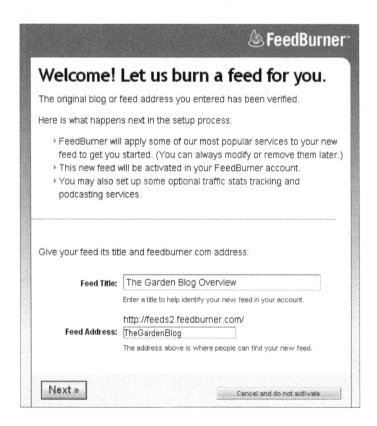

I wanted it to be **TheGardenBlog**, but it was already taken so I settled for **TheCrazyBeezGardenBlog**, which is also good. You can also adjust your **Feed Title**, if you think it will be better, this title will be shown in a RSS reader to identify your feed. Click on **Next** and there you are:

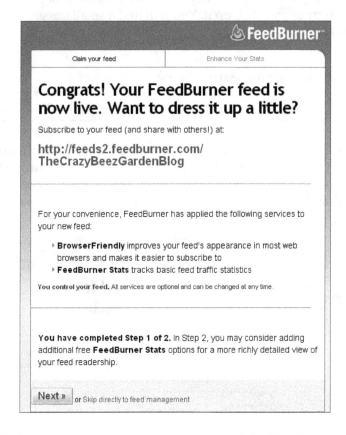

Are you done? No way, now we get to the best part of the FeedBurner by Google service.

Choosing your FeedBurner options for optimal results

The Google service has a lot of options in store that will improve our RSS visibility and provide us with some blogging features that Joomla! doesn't have. One of the most important services is the PingShot that we will be looking at later. Let's take small steps and see what we can configure to get the best of the best.

First we will go through the option tabs and check what you should really use:

- **Analyze**: This is where you will see how well you are doing looking at your feed reader's stats

- **Optimize**: Here are two services you need to activate, BrowserFriendly and SmartFeed

- **Publicize**: Most of your work will be done here with **Email Subscriptions, PingShot, FeedCount**, and **NoIndex**

- **Monetize**: Only if you want AdSense advertisements into your Feeds

- **Troubleshootize**: A great place to start if your feed doesn't work the way it should

From the tabs mentioned, we will be looking more closely at some of the settings in the **Optimize** and **Publicize** tabs.

Let's take a look at the **Optimize** tab settings:

- **BrowserFriendly: This** makes your RSS Feed that comes out of Joomla! a lot better, because it turns the not-so-nice looking feeds into human viewable HTML pages. For this, compare the following two screenshots.

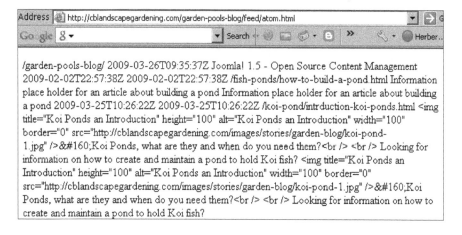

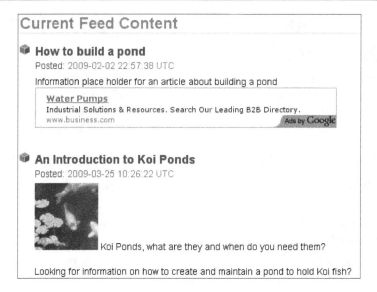

And all you have to do is activate the service!

- **SmartFeed** is all for your visitors, it will give them the choice of viewing your feed into their favorite feed reader. There are a lot of feed readers out there. If you activate this service you give your visitors an easy choice to import your feed with a single click. If they click on your **RSS Feed** button, they get a list of services to which, they can add your feed with just a click on the button.

Now, let's take a look at the **Publicize** tab settings:

- **Email Subscriptions** makes it really easy to offer an email subscription to your RSS Feed.

  After activation of this service, copy the code from the **Subscription Form Code** field, and paste it on your site in a HTML module. To create such a module, go to your administrator panel. Choose **Extensions** from the top menu, then choose **Module Manager**. Then click on **New** and choose **Custom HTML**, give it a **Title**, **Position**, and publish it after you paste the code. The subscription form and fields are now ready for use.

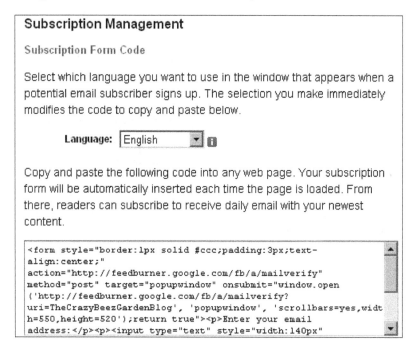

  You can also configure the time when you want those emails to be sent to your visitors using the **Delivery Options** setting.

- **PingShot**: **PingShot** does something that Joomla! cannot, but is essential for a blog.

  It sends a ping after you publish your post to several services such as Technorati, My Yahoo, and Bloglines.

  Make sure you activate the other two and add up to five extra options. For example, **Ping-o-matic** which will ping several other services for you, and **Newsgator**, which is another good service.

From the drop-down list you can add a few extra services of which **Google Blog Search Pinging Service** is one.

The other choice of services is dependent on the niche you work in, but for me the following ones work great:

- ◦ **icerocket**
- ◦ **Weblogs.Com**
- ◦ **FeedBlitz**
- ◦ **Syndic8**

- • **FeedCount**: This is a well-known counter. You can show it on your site to let people know how many subscribers are there on your feed. Don't show the feed count until you have over a minimum of 100 subscribers. There is a psychological effect behind this tip.

Nobody will subscribe to your feed if it shows that there are only 3 subscribers. The thought behind this is that it is probably not that interesting because there are few subscribers.

If you get over 100 subscribers, start showing the count! With over 100 subscribers there must be value in that feed! If you reach that limit and show it you will see that the number of subscribers will soon start to grow faster than before.

- **NoIndex:** This option makes sure that your own feed is not indexed and ranking higher than your pages. This means the feed from `burner.com` will not be indexed, because of that it is not possible to have it outrank your pages. If you don't use that option the feed itself has the possibility to outperform your pages (this is not likely, but I have seen it happen on some sites, although that was before Google bought FeedBurner).

Replacing your RSS Feed with the FeedBurner feed

If you are done with the configuration of your feed we are going to replace that nice Joomla! feed button and link.

To do so, go to your administration panel and create a new **Custom HTML** module. Open the FeedBurner configuration page in your browser, navigate to the **Publicize** tab and choose **Chicklet Chooser**. Use the standard feed icon and copy the code that is way down at the bottom of the screen and paste it into your new module. If you want the email subscription field as well, copy the code and paste it below the previous code. Publish the module to be shown on the site.

As this is HTML code you can change it to make it even better:

- Use the alt tag, which is now empty and write something like **Subscribe to The Crazy Beez Garden Blog**.

- Change the RSS Feed button to a larger one by uploading it to your site and change the src value with a link to your button. The src value is the HTML value for an image output. For example, `src="http://www.cblandscapegardening.com/images/stories/gardening-blog-rss-feed.png"`.

In the following screenshot you will see a subscribe module on top of the menu sidebar for my example:

How to claim your blog on Technorati

Technorati is the leading site when it comes to blogs and having your link on Technorati helps you to get more visitors to your blog. Technorati also has a blog search engine and it is used by a lot of people. The more people that subscribe and link to your blog the higher your Technorati ranking will be. To get a ranking you have to claim your blog. You need to get a free account and register with Technorati before you can start claiming your blog. Once logged in, go to **Blogs | My Blogs**.

At the right hand side of that screen you will see a link that says **Claim a new blog**, click on it to start the process. First, fill in your Blog's URL, and then click on **Start Claim**. Technorati will then check that it can find your URL, which should not be a problem. After the check you will get a link that you have to copy and paste into your site. If you follow the instructions on the screen you cannot go wrong.

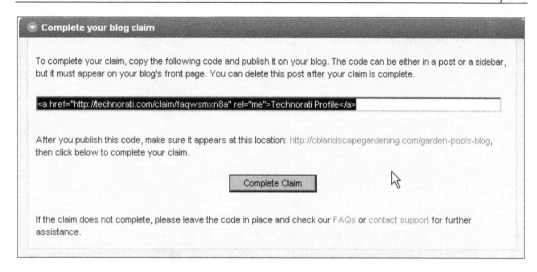

I have copied the link into the RSS Feed module, since that is already **Custom HTML**. If you look at your site now you will see a small line that says **Technorati profile**. Once you see that (you might need to clear your cache first) you can click on the **Complete Claim** button on the Technorati screen.

If the claim is successful, you can fill in the screen that follows and add some extra information about your blog. Also make sure that you add some of your keywords in the **Tags** listing. You can now remove the claim line from your site and put a Technorati favorite link into the RSS Feed module if you like. As this is the first time that Technorati is looking at your site, it might be a good idea to use the ping service that you will see if you go back to the **My Blogs** page.

After the initial ping you don't have to do that anymore as FeedBurner will ping it for you when you write a new post. If you missed something or did not get your description and tags in place, you can edit this later. Just go to your Technorati account and choose the **Claimed Blogs** tab. There you will find a listing of all your blogs and you can choose the **Edit Settings** option.

Once you click on that button a new screen will open. You can then correct, change, and add information and Tags.

Edit Blog Settings

Blog info for: Garden Pools Blog - Crazy Beez Landscape Gardening

URL http://cblandscapegardening.com/garden-pools-blog

Description Tell the world about your blog (250 characters max)   117/250²

> The Cary Beez Graden Blog is all about landscape gardens and fishing ponds, koi fish and garden design tips and trics

Tags Use tags to describe your blog (letters, numbers and spaces only)

gardening	flowers	garden design
landscaping	koi	ponds
landscape garden		

Using separate blog components

In this chapter you have seen that you can create a blog with a basic Joomla! site and some help from third-party services. So why use a blogging component such as MyBlog along with JomComment, or a combination of XBlog, IDoBlog, and a commenting component like yvComments? The answer is very simple. It will be good if you start a blog and have different authors for your blog.

However, there are also some downsides to the use of a blogging component. The drawbacks are:

- You have to learn how to use it the right way
- It can slow down your web site
- It adds a lot of bulk to your database since all the comments and posts are stored in extra tables
- With commercial components it will cost you money
- You have to update them separately from your Joomla! core updates
- If you want to use a blogging component look at what the **Big Boys** are using

By the Big Boys I mean the well-known Joomla! ambassadors such as *Steve Burge* from www.alledia.com and *Barry North* from www.compassdesigns.net. They blog with a basic Joomla! system, enhanced with commercial JomComment to handle the comments on their articles. And I must admit that I have rarely seen any spam comments on either of these sites. As for the Joomla! site, they use JXtended Comment from http://jxtended.com which is also a commercial commenting component.

MyBlog—a commercial blogging component

This chapter wouldn't be complete if there was no mention of the most widely used blog component MyBlog from www.azrul.com. Therefore, I bought and installed it on one of my sites, just to make sure that you can get an insight of what is incorporated into this component. First there is an admin panel for the component, where you can work through the component:

What you need to know after installation is, how to configure the general settings.

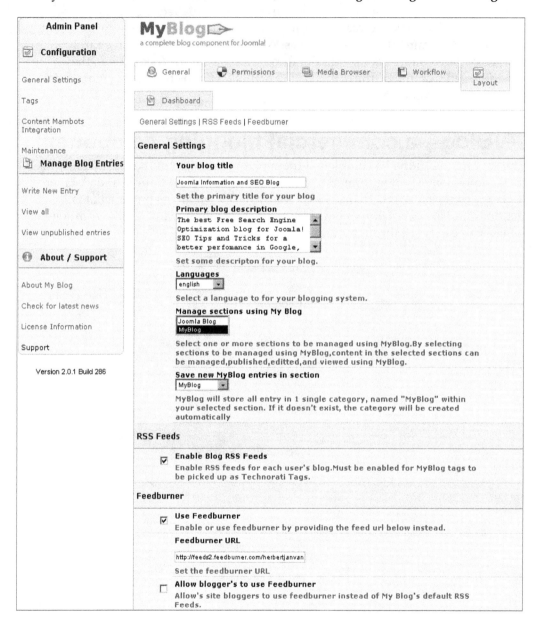

If you look at the settings, all the things you have read about will come back:

- The Blog Title
- The Blog section which MyBlog will use to handle to content
- Enabling the RSS Feeds
- Use of FeedBurner service with the feedburner URL

If you start writing an article it is done in the same way a normal article would be done, but you have extra options such as **Tags** and trackbacks in a place that you can use. You can write metadata into the article by using a small link to your options screen called **Meta Info**. You can choose your publishing date just like you can in Joomla! articles.

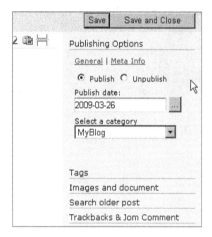

As for the use of SEF URLs for this component, there is a separate section in sh404SEF that creates nice URLs to each post.

I think the best additions that this component gives you for blogging are:

- The ability to use more than one section for your blog
- The Tags feature that is tightly integrated into the component
- Permission to handle more authors that can blog on your web site

Purchase and installation of this component is simple and it does the job well.

It is up to you to decide whether you want to pay for the extra functionality it brings. At the time of writing the standard version costs 35 USD, and the professional version without the backlink, and with more templates costs 45 USD.

Summary

In this chapter you have learned:

- Why blogging is good for your Search Engine Optimization strategy
- How to set up a blog section in Joomla! and how to build a blogging menu and RSS Feed
- Why the use of comments and interaction with your visitors is important, and how you can handle spam and comments by the integration of Disqus
- The use of RSS Feeds and how to improve your Joomla! RSS Feed, using the Google FeedBurner service
- How to claim your blog on Technorati, and a short introduction of the commercial blog component MyBlog from www.azrul.com

6
Create Search Engine Friendly URLs with sh404SEF

Using a component that creates better and more search engine friendly URLs is one of the best things you can do to improve your site to get better rankings in the search engines.

We will be looking at the following in this chapter:

- Why you need an SEF component
- What SEF components are available
- What makes sh404SEF a good choice
- How to install sh404SEF and its basic configuration
- Choosing the best URL options for your site
- Using the best options for metadata
- How to implement Search Engine Optimization on Non-SEF components
- Solving and preventing possible problems

Now this may seem like it is a lot to handle, and it really is, but this is one of the best and biggest improvements you can use for your Joomla! site.

What are the best SEF URLs?

First of all you need to be clear about what kind of URLs will provide you with the best results in the search engine rankings.

If you look at the **search engine results page (SERP)** you will find that the best performing URLs are the clean ones — the ones without a lot of parameters. If you look at a Joomla! URL that is created without any SEO options active on the site, you will see a URL similar to the following:

```
http://cblandscapegardening.com/index.php?option=com_
content&view=article&id=3:a-quick-guide-to-landscape-
gardening&catid=1:garden-design&Itemid=2.
```

But with all the default SEO options set, along with an SEF component, the URL will become similar to the following:

```
http://cblandscapegardening.com/garden-design/a-quick-guide-to-
landscape-gardening.html.
```

Not only is it a shorter URL, but is also in a better shape for people to remember. Another thing you should notice is also the category in which the article is placed is "keyword rich" now and is placed before the article title.

In the first example the Joomla! article ID, category ID, and item ID were in the URL. With both standard SEO options and an SEF component these numbers are gone. Now search for the keywords you are targeting in Google and look at the URLs of the top ranking web sites. In my case it would be the term **landscape gardening**.

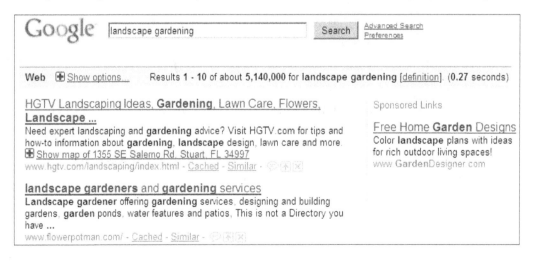

As you can see, all the top performers have clean URLs and their lengths range from short to very short! So, what we are aiming for is a short, keyword-rich, easy-to-remember URL. The best way to accomplish this for your Joomla! site is by using the standard SEO functions, enhanced with a SEF component that is able to deliver to you the best possible options.

Available choices for SEF components

Let's look at the options we have if we are looking for an SEF component? Well, luckily we have an array of options to choose from and we will look at the most well known ones.

- **Artio JoomSEF 3**: This is a semi-commercial SEF component, which means you can download and use it for free. But there is a little catch in the free version—in the metadata of all the generated pages there is an advertisement. This advertisement is probably not related to the content of your site and can harm your SEO efforts while you are linking to non-related sites. With the commercial option these links are taken out, it costs 24.99 Euro.

- **SEF Advance**: This is one of the oldest components. It is a commercial component that will cost you 40 Euro. It is indeed a very stable version and it is well supported. However, it needs **Ion Cube Loader (ICL)** to be installed on your site; this is clearly mentioned in the documentation. The Ion Cube Loader is a PHP based software that needs to be installed to decrypt the SEF Advance software to make it work. Not all hosting providers will allow such software to be installed as it eats up a lot of CPU power to decrypt software. Ion Cube is used by the developer to protect his/her software code. What I don't like about this component is that you need an extra license if you want to create a subdomain such as `blog.example.com`, or if you want to install WordPress on that subdomain.

- **sh404SEF**: This is a free SEF component that is well maintained and has some extra options such as built-in native support for Virtuemart. It has a lot of configuration options that we will be looking at in this chapter, as this is my and the Joomla! editors' choice for SEF URLs. The Joomla! editors are the webmasters who maintain the Extensions Directory and they keep track of third-party extensions and reviews placed in that directory. The Joomla! editors also have a short list of featured components, which are the current best components for a certain task. You can find this list at `http://extensions.joomla.org/extensions/featured`.

Why you should choose sh404SEF

As you have read before, there are several reasons why sh404SEF is the best choice of SEF components for Joomla!

Let's look at some of the reasons in detail:

- **Free**!: Yes, it won't cost you any money to use it, but since a recent change the download access will cost you about 35 USD a year to get the most recent version. Besides that it takes time to install and configure. One drawback can be that there is no paid support—you have to post in the forums or read the rest of this book to get more insight.

- **Advanced URL choices**: This is one good option, as you can choose for long, medium, or short URLs with or without the section or category in the URL. You can even choose to have only the article alias in the URL.

- **Creating your own URL**: With this option you can create your own URLs in combination with components that do not support the creation of automatically-generated SEF URLs.

- **Meta tags plugin**: Using meta tags such as keywords and descriptions is also a good practice, as you can set your description and keywords for Non-SEF component links, but that requires more work at your end.

- Rewrites for popular components such as **Virtuemart, Docman, Community Builder, MyBlog, Joomfish 2.0**, and lots more.

You can read more about reviews on the extension page about Joomla! at `http://extensions.joomla.org/extensions/site-management/sef/2380/details`.

How to get hold of sh404SEF

Getting sh404SEF was easy. You could download it from `http://joomlacode.org/gf/project/sh404sef/frs/`, but now it is on `http://dev.anything-digital.com/sh404SEF/` and you need a valid download subscription available for 35 USD a year to get the latest version for Joomla! 1.5. You still can use it for unlimited number of sites.

Don't be scared due to the fact that it is still in beta, I am using it on several web sites and have not had any problems.

Package Name ◇	Latest Release ▽	Maturity ▽	Files ▽
sh404SEF_for_Joomla1.5	sh404SEF-15_1.0.16	4 - Beta	com_sh404SEF-15_1.0.16_Beta_build_222.joomla1.5.zip
sh404SEF	sh404SEF1.3.9	5 - Production/Stable	com_sh404SEF_1.3.9_build_357.joomla1.0.x.zip
		5 - Production/Stable	com_sh404SEF_1.3.9_build_357.mambo.zip

Installation and basic configuration

Installation of the components is similar to any other component. Simply install it using the normal installer, but this time, read the screen after installation or even print it.

This screen has a lot of information on how to make sure the SEF URLs are as clean as you want them to be. If you closed the screen and missed the information, you can read it again in the documentation of the component, which can be reached from the component's control panel. Most important information is the .htaccess content. For now, you can go ahead and read the information is this chapter.

If you want a URL without /index.php/ in it, you need to run your web site on a Linux-or Unix-based hosting platform with the Apache mod_rewrite module active. If that is the case, check the information on how to construct your .htaccess file in the Appendix B of this book. You can find the information from your hosting platform in the Joomla! administration menu under **Help | System Info | PHP Information**. You will find some extra information and examples on .htaccess files in the Appendix B of this book.

The basic configuration of sh404SEF exists in two parts. One is the control panel, which we will be looking at in detail later.

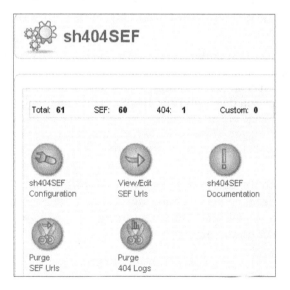

The second part is the sh404SEF Plugin that is enabled after the installation. Please check that as it sometimes fails to start. If it is not running you won't be able to use the metadata control option. You can activate the sh404SEF plugin using the plugin manager. A simple click of the button is enough to publish this component. There are no extra parameters in the plugin.

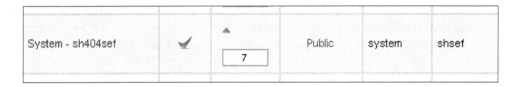

The plugin is needed to enable the component to place and change the meta tags description and keywords in the source code of your site pages.

Looking for the optimal basic configuration options

If you haven't used an SEF component before, don't worry. The standard Joomla! URLs and even the Joomla! core friendly URLs will be picked up by sh404SEF and will be redirected to the new and improved URL with a **301 redirect**.

If you have pages ranking very well in the search engines with SEF URLs, make sure you keep the URLs as they are or redirect them to the new URL. If you change any settings in sh404SEF, you are advised to clear the cache. This will delete all your previous URLs and build new ones. If you did not change old article titles, URLs, or moved them to new sections or categories, you should not have any problems. However, it's better to check them before than to fix afterwards.

I will take you through the basics of the standard configuration options that you need to change, or at least consider changing. Some of the possible changes are affected by what kind of web site you are building, so read carefully and consider the options that meet your site model.

We will be going through some basic stuff where you need to go to your **Components** menu and click on **sh404SEF** from the drop-down menu. The following screenshot shows the main settings, the basic configuration and the settings that you have to look at more closely:

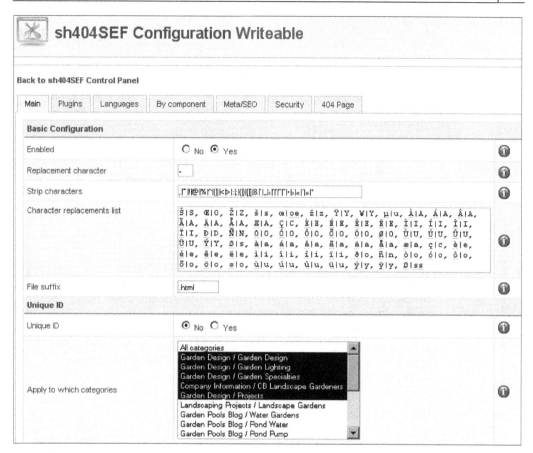

Now let's look at each setting:

- **Enabled**:

    This is pretty clear, whether you want to use the sh404SEF component or not. Of course you want to use it, you installed it—right? But sometimes we need to disable it to get the standard Joomla! URL, so sometimes this option needs to be set to **No** for a short while.

- **Replacement character**:

This character is used to replace the blank spaces from your title. Joomla! converts your **Title** to an **Alias** once you save the article you write. It is best if the blanks in your alias are filled with characters such as"–". Some hosting platforms change blanks to "%20%". As you saw before, that is not good for Search Engines Optimization.

Title	A Quick Guide To Landscape Gardeni
Alias	a-quick-guide-to-landscape-gardening

How to further improve your URLs

Once you have published the article, go and strip the stop words and small text from your **Alias**. You can also change the **Alias** by hand directly when writing the article. In the above example you can change the **Alias** from **a-quick-guide-to-landscape-gardening** to **quick-guide-landscape-gardening**.

You might want to do this with your old articles as well, but I strongly advise you not to! If those pages are indexed by Google or other search engines, it would lead to an Error 404 page. Therefore, think carefully before you change them.

- **Strip characters** and **Character replacements list**:

These are options that you don't need to change unless you have a special need for them — for example, if your site is written in certain foreign languages. For most web sites these settings are fine. Strip character strips out all characters that are not allowed or wanted in your URLs such as — ,~!@%^()< >: ;{}[ ]&`„‹" " " •›«'»°

Character replacement changes the special language characters that are not allowed in a URL and replaces them with the one that is allowed. For instance, if you have a German site, you can have a "ü" in your title which is then replaced by a "u". However, if you prefer to replace it with "ue", you can change the behavior in this field. From a German perspective it might be better to change "müller" to "mueller" instead of "muller". So, look at this option if you have a site that needs these replacements.

- **File suffix**:

  This is the extension you want to set at the end of your SEF URL. The best option for you is to use the suffix .html, but some people like to end the URL with .php or .htm. My advice is to use .html because I feel some people who look at the results in search engine results page see other extensions as a directory of articles instead of the page they are looking for. This can have a negative effect on the click-through rate of your site.

- **Unique ID**:

  This is a unique ID added to the URL, and is made up of date such as 02-09-2009 and the internal ID from the database for that article. The ID added will then be 2009090200000, which of course is not good for a standard web site.

  However, if you want to set up a news site that is also focusing on getting your articles included in news search engines such as Google News, this is the way to go. To get into Google News, your site has to have a minimum of three numbers in the URL. With this option set to active, you are ready to get into the news.

Setting up the plugin

The plugins tab in the default configuration gives you three options:

- **Use Title Alias**
- **Show section**
- **Show category**

Here are the settings I normally use on my web sites:

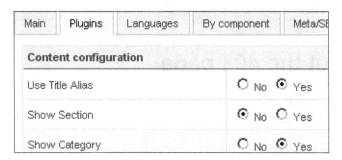

Use Title Alias is set to **Yes**. You have seen how to change the title **Alias** to create shorter URLs. Therefore, that one is definitely set to **Yes** to give you the possibility to work with the option shown in the previous screenshot about using the title alias.

If you set it to **No**, your title will be used as the URL. Here is an example for use of alias in articles:

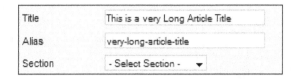

We will continue with the sh404SEF plugins configuration. **Show section** is set to **No** because I want short URLs. If you set it to **Yes**, the section of your article is also included in the URL. It is then built like `www.example.com/section-name/category-name/article-alias.html`, instead of `www.example.com/category-name/article-alias.html`.

Depending on your section name that can be a much longer URL. If you think your web site still needs it, go ahead and use it. However, make sure that your section name is short. For example, you might want to build a site about WordPress, Joomla!, or Drupal and create categories for each system with names such as installation, themes, and plugins. In that case you can have URLs such as `/wordpress/themes/introduction.html` and `/drupal/themes/introduction.html`. Think about that before you set up or change the structure of your site. My choice is to create category names such as `drupal-themes` and `wordpress-themes`, which gives me the advantage of having the keywords `wordpress` and `theme` in the URL instead of `wordpress/themes`.

This may sound like a minor issue to you, but it does make your site rank slightly higher and that is what we are aiming for. All the minor subtle changes that you read about here, add up to better performance of your site. Set **Show Category** to **Yes**, this should be obvious if you read the previous paragraph, as you want to have your keywords in the URL and using the right category names works great.

How about the 404 page

You don't have to set an option here, it is there and active already. You might have noticed that I skipped the META tags option, but that is because we will be looking at that once we get to the advanced section of sh404SEF.

But this 404 page. What do you want to do with it—just leave is as it is? After all it's just an error page that you get if something goes wrong. Is it? Or is it an opportunity to help your visitors and Search Engine Robots, and to draw them in to your site? Let's look at that later, as I have a special section about 404 pages for you.

What you need to know right now is that sh404SEF helps you find the errors and resolve them next time. If you look at the basic control panel, you only have the option to purge the 404 errors and not to look at them. Therefore, you need to switch to the panel overview, which is just one click away at the right side of your screen.

 Click here to switch to extended display (with all available parameters)

Using the icon **View/Edit 404 Logs**, you can select the option to view and edit the URLs that came into the 404 logs. This will give you the opportunity to set it right, but you need to know the Non-SEF URL to point the wrong URL to the right article. If you want to find that Non-SEF URL you have three options:

1. Deactivate **sh404SEF** and **SEF URLs** in the **Global Configuration**. Note that if you do this, your site will not be reachable using the SEF links in the search engines, so you need to have this re-enabled as soon as possible.

2. Look into the SEF URLs of sh404SEF and find the article you want to link to

3. Use the module from `http://www.joomlapraise.com/free-joomla-extensions/praiseurl-module.php`. We will look at this option in the last part of this chapter.

This means a lot of work which does not always pay off, but if you are changing your site or restructuring it, this is the best option to keep your rankings and still be able to change your URLs.

Keeping a close look on the 404 errors after your changes will give you the opportunity to redirect your old URLs to the new ones without having to put all kinds of 301 redirects in your `.htaccess` file. The sh404SEF sends a 301 redirect from the error URL to the new one, which is really nice as the search engines will drop the old URLs in favor of the new ones. In time you should see fewer 404 errors from search engine results page coming to your site. So, we are done with the basics and had a taste of the extended control panel. Now it's time to get even more advanced and dive deeper into those extended settings.

Looking at advanced configuration settings

Advanced means that we get into the real options that matter for optimizing your web site for the search engines. Most Joomla! webmasters will install sh404SEF and get it working by implementing an `.htaccess` file that works for their site. As you want all the best SEO options active and implemented on your Joomla! site, you have to go the extra mile and switch from basic to extended.

If you haven't done so in the previous paragraph, it's time to do it now. Just click on that blue banner on the right side of the sh404SEF control panel.

After the screen is updated you have several more options.

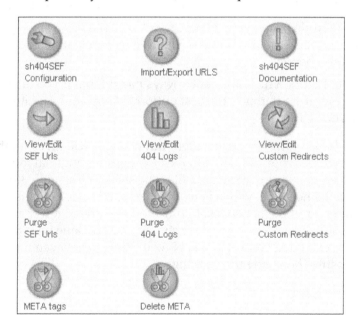

Here are some of the extras:

- **Import/Export URLs**
- **View/Edit 404 Logs**
- **View/Edit Custom Redirects**

- **Purge Custom Redirects**
- **META tags**
- **Delete META**

But that is not all... Just click on the **sh404SEF Configuration** button, where you first saw the default tabs such as the following:

Now, you will see the following tabs:

If that doesn't impress you, as there are only two extra tabs, have a look at the following main configuration page:

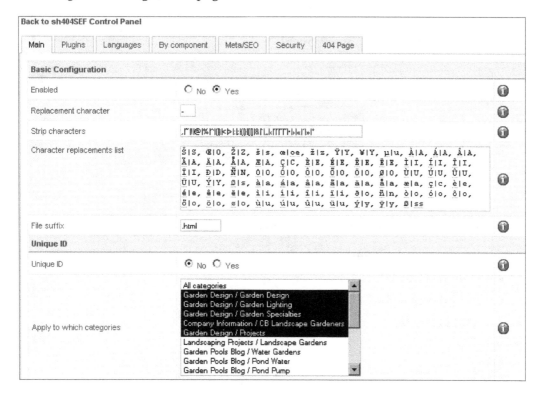

The above page changes to the following screen once you activate the extended view of sh404SEF, giving you some extra options that you want to activate and have to set it right:

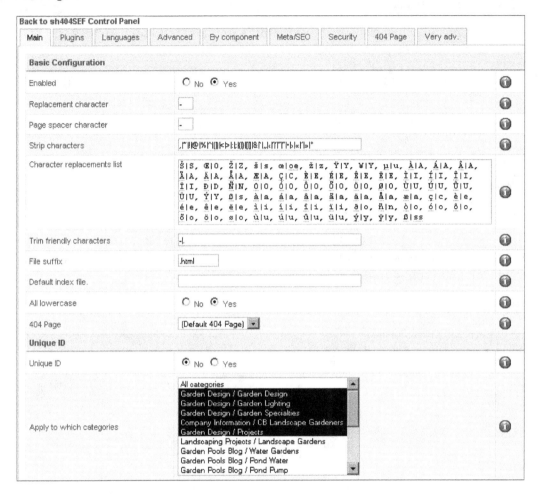

Now you see the following extra options to change:

- **Page spacer character**
- **Trim friendly characters**
- **Default index file**
- **All lowercase**

The same goes for **Plugins** section. Following is how the plugins section looks before the Sh404SEF patch is installed:

The screenshot now changes to the following once the patch is installed (I am showing you only the content part now):

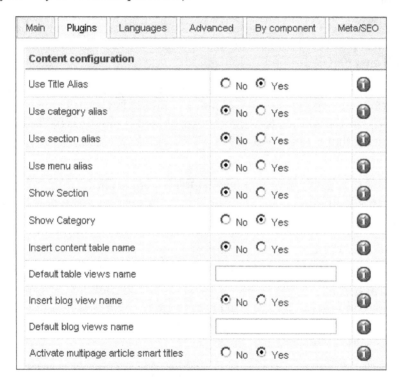

Overwhelmed? Don't be, I will show you what you need to change and you can look at all the other options once you need them, or at your leisure. You will quickly learn, to work with these options as most of them are self explanatory. Once you get an understanding of the basics of SEF URLs and improved SEO, you know what you want for your web site. So, I won't go into every detail of the extended configuration as that would take another book as this component is so large and advanced.

It is stunning that Yannick Gaultier has created this enormous component based on 404SEF and ported it into a Joomla! 1.5 native component. As I did not mention it before, a large Kudos to him! Also a big thank you for giving it to use for free!

Taking care of extended basics

Now, like I said we are not going to go through all the options, but only the ones you need to improve for your site.

Starting with the **Main** tab, there is just one extra field you are going to change. Set **All lowercase** to **Yes**. This is to make sure that you stay consistent once we get started with custom URLs.

On a Linux-or Unix-based server, which most of the hosting companies use, there is a difference between lowercase and uppercase letters. If you have a file called `welcome.html` on a windows server, it will also open if you type `Welcome.html`. On a Unix server that is not the case. For a Unix server `Welcome.html` is a different file to `welcome.html`.

Now you want to be consistent then let sh404SEF convert everything to lowercase. If you want to link to another page on your site, you don't have to worry if it is written with capitals, you know the link will work if you write in lowercase.

How to optimize your plugins

If a component has an `extended.sef` file, then that file contains the rewrite rules for that particular component. If such a file is present, the SEF component will use that information to create a clean URL. If there is no `extended.sef` file, sh404SEF will use its own plugins to create clean URLs.

Insert content table name	⦿ No ○ Yes	ⓘ
Default table views name		ⓘ
Insert blog view name	⦿ No ○ Yes	ⓘ
Default blog views name		ⓘ
Activate multipage article smart titles	○ No ⦿ Yes	ⓘ

In the default installation of sh404SEF, you will find that the **Default table views name** is **Table**. If you set this option to use, you will get the /table/ added to the URL of any table view that you use in your menu.

Default table views name	Table

If you want to create different views in the same category, which I advise you not to because of duplicate content issues, then you want this set to **Yes** and use table, overview, or something you like. The same goes for the blog view, you could insert / blogs/ or /blog-overview/. If you just set it to active with no name, sh404SEF will insert /blog/ for you.

The last option is to make sure that a multi-page article is getting the title URL you set for the extra page. Instead of article-page-2.html, you now get article-second-page-title.html. This gives you a better chance to get more keywords in your URL than just page-2.html.

Extra components, SEF, and other plugins

Looking at this massive page of plugins, you see that there are a lot of options for SEF URLs already built into sh404SEF. You will find options for:

- Virtuemart
- Community Builder
- Fireboard
- Docman
- Remository
- Letterman
- MyBlog
- Mosets Tree
- SMF Bridge
- iJoomla Magazine
- News Portal

Each of them have the basic options already set for you, check them to see if they are to your liking. Here are some special items that you might want to change.

For **Virtuemart** you should check the **Insert flypage name** and set it to **No** if you have only one flypage. That way your URL gets shorter and more focused on the products.

For **Community Builder** you might want to give users a possibility to have short URLs for their profile, but that can cause some issues. For instance, if a user called himself/herself Joomla! and on your site you have a category named Joomla!, sh404SEF doesn't know which is the right one, so be careful with this option.

MyBlog has an option **Insert post ID**, which adds the internal ID of that post, thus preventing a possible error if you use a post title twice. If you are sure that you will never use a blog title twice, you might want to set it to **No**. Leaving it to the default **Yes** has another advantage than prevention of duplicate URLs. After you post more than a 100 posts, which if you are a heavy blogger should not be a problem, you get three digits in your URL. With three digits, you could be included into **Google news**—an automated news aggregator provided by Google Inc. Google news requires you to have a minimum of three digits in your URL.

There is an option in iJoomla Magazine, **Insert magazine name in URL** based on the menu title with which you point to that magazine. If you have several magazines on different topics you might want to set this to **Yes**, so you get extra keywords in the URL. This prevents duplication of URLs if you write the same article titles in the magazines.

Language setting and SEF

This part is only relevant if you have a multilingual web site with a component such as Joomfish 2.0 or above.

If you have a single-language site, set both the options at the top to **No**. If you have a multi-language web site you will see that there are separate sections for each language installed. In that case change the **Page text** to fit your language and your likings. For example, if you want to use the Dutch language, you may not like "paginas" and prefer to change it to "bladzijde". If this option is not working as you expect, do remember that we have set the **Activate multipage article smart titles** to **Yes** in the plugins configuration screen.

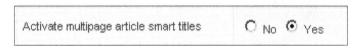

Only if you have set this last option in the main content to **No** you will see the **Page text**. If you want to use this option, make sure to deactivate it on the main plugin configuration page.

Getting advanced, are you?

The next configuration tab is of great importance as these options will provide you with more control over the URLs.

Cache management

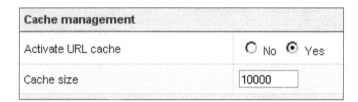

Using the URL cache means that the SEF URLs created by sh404SEF will be stored in a separate cache on your server. This is meant to decrease the loading time of your site, as it eliminates the need for sh404SEF to query your database for the right URL to a page, it will use the one from the cache.

Using the standard cache size of **10000** Kb means you are using approximately 1 MB of your server space. This means there can be around 5000 URLs in that space. If you have more than that, increase the size of the cache if you need to, count 1MB extra for every 5000 URLs. You can check the number of URLs created by sh404SEF on the control panel and if you want to know how many articles you have, check the last page of **Article Manager** and look at the last article number, that would give you some idea. Be aware that the installed components will create extra URLs. Although it is a great way to speed up your site, if you run into trouble with URLs not working right, make sure you set this option to **No** from the beginning.

Caching is great and we will be looking at that when we get to speed up your site, but they can also get corrupted. If that happens, clear the cache and start over. (Refer section *Solving and prevention of possible problems.*)

Advanced component configuration

This is the part that you were looking for, right?

First things first, this setting makes it possible to exclude /index.php/ from your URL. This option was not found in the basic default configuration, but with sh404SEF, the **Rewriting** mode is set; it is by default set to use without .htaccess. To change this use the drop-down selection and set it to **with .htaccess (mod_rewrite)**. However, before you do that, make sure your .htaccess file is working. It should be changed to work with third-party components (check the Appendix B for .htaccess examples).

Advanced Component Configuration		
Rewriting mode	with .htaccess (mod_rewrite)	
301 redirect from non-sef to sef URL	No ○ Yes ●	
301 redirect from JOOMLA SEF to sh404SEF	No ○ Yes ●	
301 redirect www/non-www	No ○ Yes ●	
Record duplicated URL	No ○ Yes ●	
Log 404 errors	No ○ Yes ●	
SSL secure URL		
Force non sef if HTTPS	No ● Yes ○	
Encode URL	No ● Yes ○	
Home page URL		
Log debug info to file	No ● Yes ○	

The standard setting will do just fine to start with, and to give you some peace of mind if you start using the sh404SEF component. Here is a short explanation of why you should keep the 301 redirects active at all times.

- **301 redirect from non-sef to sef URL**

  This is where the real power of a SEF component lies. Your old, already indexed URLs will be transformed and your visitors will get the page loaded under the new URL. At the same time if a Search Engine Robot comes along, it will also find a 301 (permanently moved) redirect to the new URL.

- **301 redirect from JOOMLA SEF to sh404SEF**

  If you had already set the basic SEO options in your Joomla! configuration and those URLs are in the search engine index they will get the same treatment as Non-SEF URLs. This means if you change over to sh404SEF you should not loose any rankings.

- **301 redirect www/non-www**

  With this option set, your main choice for www/non-www (usually the one set on the apache server) is used. This means that if your site is found without www, that is, example.com instead of www.example.com, all links will be set to **non-www**.

This prevents duplicate content issues by eliminating one of the two URL options to reach your articles. Make sure you set this option in the Google webmaster setting for your site also. You can find it by selecting your web site, then click on **Site configuration**, and choose setting. Now, you can set the preferred option for your domain:

Preferred domain	○ Don't set a preferred domain
	◉ Display URLs as **www.cblandscapegardening.com**
	○ Display URLs as **cblandscapegardening.com**

The two extra options that you can change over time or you might need right away are as follows:

- **Log 404 errors**

  Use this option if you have changed anything on the site. Initially set this option to **Yes** to discover any problems with redirections. This could cause problems with Non-sef components (we will look at solving some problems in the **Components** section) or some strange URLs that cannot be redirected at first.

  If the initial logging is done, you might want to shut it down for performance reasons as every error is written into the database.

- **Home page URL**

  This might sound a bit strange to you, so let me explain and show you a possible usage of this option. If you have created a special splash page for your web site and placed it in the root as `index.html`, then this page is shown, if you type in the URL of your web site. That could be a special flash embedded intro page or a selection page if you have separate sites on the same account.

  But if you build the menu for your Joomla! site and point the **Home** link to the top URL, your visitor will always get the same page. To prevent it you need this option.

| Default index file. | http://www.cblandscapegardening.com/index.php| |

As you know the main page for your Joomla! site is always the `index.php`, for that matter you place the full URL of your Joomla! site in the **Default index file** field. Be careful with your `.htaccess` file, not to give a redirect to the `index.php` file (see Appendix B). For example, you should write `http://www.example.com/index.php`, and you will find that your **Home** link now works as expected.

By component settings

The **By component** settings allow you to skip the process of creating the SEF URL for a specific component. This means if you have a component that breaks if you set the SEF URLs, you can take it out of the process. To do so, just change the options to **skip** and you are done, nothing else will happen if you set that option.

The next two options are for translation to other languages, usage of language code in the URL. The last option can be used if the `sef_ext` file from the component itself is better than the SEF option from sh404SEF.

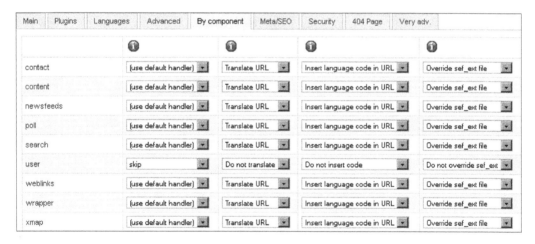

Using the best Meta/SEO option settings

The following are some of the most important Meta/SEO settings:

- **Activate Meta Management**

  For the best meta tags and options we need to make sure your **Activate Meta Management** is set to **Yes**. That way sh404SEF will take care of correctly using the options below this setting.

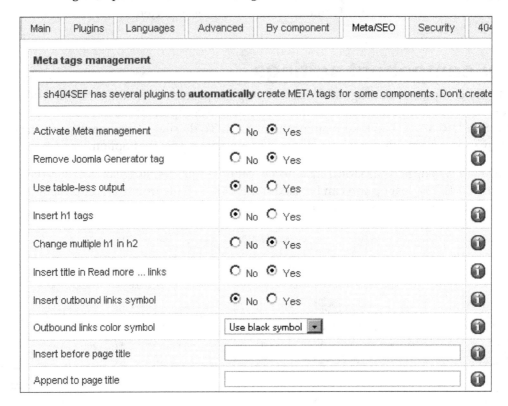

- **Remove Joomla Generator tag**

  You should set this to **Yes**, especially if you are concerned about security because Joomla! shows which version you are using. If a security hole is found in a certain version, it shows that your site could be vulnerable. If you have implemented the Joomla SEF patch, you don't need to set this options as the tag is already removed.

- **Use table-less output** and **Insert h1 tags**

    These are also good options, but check how your template holds up. You don't want to mess up your site. Also if your template is already in good shape, you don't need these options. For example, the standard Beez template was created to have all these practices built in.

- **Change multiple h1 in h2**

    This option is set to **Yes**. It makes the most important title text on your page stand out in h1. If you have several h1 tags, search engines can't easily tell what this page is really about. An h1 HTML tag should be used for the article title on the article page, and h2 tags can be used if you have a blog layout with several titles. In that case the category title should be the only title to have a h1 tag. This could happen to you if you use a blog layout with several "read more" lines to go deeper in your articles.

- **Insert Title in read more...links**

    Set this to **Yes**, we will be looking at templates later. Not all templates give you the choice to make changes manually, so this options works fine. Even if you forget to set your own text there, the best thing is that you create an internal link to the entire article with your title and keyword(s) in it.

- **Insert outbound links symbol**
    It is fine if you want your visitors to see that a particular link will take them to another web site. For me, it is a way to improve usability and nothing more than that.

- **Insert before page title** and **Append to page title**

    These are good options if you want to work on branding of your web site. I don't advise you to insert anything before the page title, because you want to keep your keywords that you are targeting for in the best place. The best place in the title is right at the start! For branding, use the last option. Appending your brand is a great way to get recognized as a brand in the search engines.

    If you want to use this option, make sure you have a blank space and then whatever you want, but keep it short. In the case study site I put in "Crazy Beez—Los Banos". This way I can promote the shop's name and get local traffic because of the city's name.

Security 404, and advanced

These options are better kept as they are, although you will read about optimizing your 404 Page in the next chapter. Security is also a part of your SEO efforts, as getting your site hacked will make it drop in the search engine results faster than you can build a new page. Use these options and check them on a regular basis and, if you want to give something in return, participate in the **Honey Pot project**. You get a complete overview of the control panel as shown in the following screenshot:

Security stats: Apr-2009 [Update] (2009-04-12 19:31:44)	
Attacks count	**0**
mosConfig var in URL	0
Base64 injection	0
Script injection	0
Illegal standard vars	0
remote file inclusion	0
IP address denied	0
User agent denied	0
Too many requests (flooding)	0
Rejected by Project Honey Pot	0
PHP, but user clicked	0

How to change your Home page Meta settings

With the Joomlatwork patch active, you could set the meta tags description and keywords within the **Home** link of your main menu. To move forward with the next item, save changes made in the **Plugins** option and go back to the main panel of sh404SEF. If you install sh404SEF, the meta tags description for your **Home** menu item doesn't work anymore as we let sh404SEF handle some of these items.

If you activate the meta handling option, you can set the options you want for your home page. Go to the **Meta tags** option and click on the link in the top right menu as shown in the following screenshot:

Just copy and paste the text you had inserted in your **Global Configuration | SEO** options.

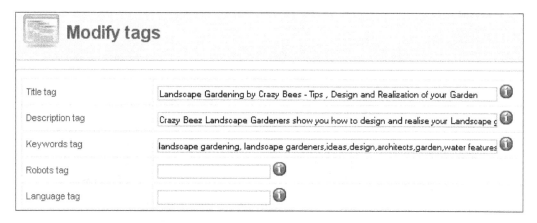

You don't need to use the **Robots tag** for the home page as you want it indexed and followed. You only want to use the language tag if you write in a language other than English. So if you don't need them, why are they there? Simply because a large part of the screen layout used by sh404SEF is same. For the next option we are going to look at—the **New Meta** option—the only difference is the URL part.

Putting meta tags on Non-SEF components

You will get, or may already have, some components on your web site, for which there is no possibility to put meta tag keywords in the output pages of that component. With the **New Meta** option you can get those **Description tag** and **Keywords tag** for every article or page produced by that component. Putting that data in is hard work and if you have lot of articles in that component it will take a lot of time to fix it!

If you use this option directly after the installation, you need to be aware that you have to create new metadata for every article.

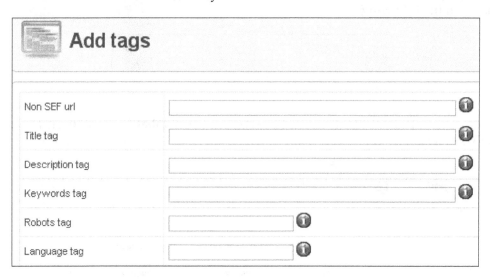

This screen is pretty easy to follow, but there is one snag to it that most people don't get. You really have to put the **Non SEF url**, which means a URL without the standard SEO and sh404SEF options active. Yes, that means a URL similar to:

```
http://cblandscapegardening.com/index.php?option=com_
content&view=article&id=3:a-quick-guide-to-landscape-
gardening&catid=1:garden-design&Itemid=2
```

You only use the part starting with `index.php/` without the domain name and without the "/" before `index.php`. This is the case for most SEF components, they use this basic **Non SEF url** for the rewrites.

Recently, a module available at `www.joomlapraise.com` shows the Non-SEF URL in a module position. You can find the **PRAISE URL** module at `http://www.joomlapraise.com/free-joomla-extensions/praiseurl-module.php`. Before using this module you needed to deactivate sh404SEF and the Joomla! SEO options as described earlier, and to do that you needed to make your `configuration.php` file writable, and so on.

You need to install and publish the module so that it can be seen by only special access level users, and deactivate it once you are done with filling the SEF URLs for your special meta titles, descriptions, and keywords.

PRAISE URL

$_SERVER["REQUEST_URI"]:
/index.php?option=com_content&
Itemid=6&catid=6&id=6&lang=en&
view=article
JRouter::getVars() and buildQuery:
/index.php?option=com_content&
Itemid=6&catid=6&id=6&lang=en&
view=article

This module will also come in handy with the next option of sh404SEF that will take your Non-SEF URLs and transform them into any URL you like.

Taking it one step further—special URLs

We looked at special metadata such as titles, description, and keyword in the last paragraph. You saw how this works for Non-SEF components and how to improve those pages. There is also an option in sh404SEF to create SEF URLs for those pages. Go to the control panel and click on **View/Edit Custom Redirects** and choose **New**. You will see the following screen:

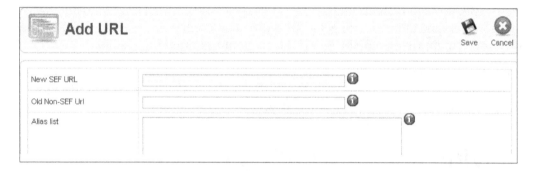

Again we start with the **New SEF URL** because this is the URL that Joomla! will always build from the database. Use the URL without the root of your Joomla! installation and without the `"/"` before `index.php/`. Put that in the **Old Non-SEF Url** field. In the field before that you write the URL that you want. Make sure you don't create duplicate URLs. I have a sample screen from a Joomla! 1.0 site to show you the usage of that field.

Edit Url	
New SEF URL	bentley-arnage-rl.html
Old Non-SEF Url	index.php?option=com_productbook&Itemid=39&func=detail&id=13&lang=en
Alias list	bentley-arnage-rl

You create a new URL that comes right from the root of your Joomla! installation. In this case it creates the URL such as `www.example.com/bentley-arnage-rt.html`. You could also create a URL that would say `www.example.com/catalog/luxery-cars/bentlry-arnage-rt.html`.

If you decide to do that later, you will see that sh404SEF will create an alias such as the **bentley-arnage-rt** (without the `.html`). The old URL, which might already be in the search engine indexes, will get a 301 redirect and will point to the new URL. That way you can improve your site without losing your old ranking results.

If you get used to reading from the Non-SEF URL of the component in question, you can duplicate an already created custom redirect and just change the item ID and some other ID values to create a new entry.

Solving and preventing possible problems

The sh404SEF component is a really powerful component, and certainly a must for every Joomla! site if you are aiming for better rankings. It is also a possible source of problems, because of the following:

- **Overcoming slow loading times:**

  If you have a very large web site you will find that sh404SEF slows down your web site's loading time as it needs to build the SEF URLs. One way to solve this to a certain extent is to increase the cache size for the URL cache so that more URLs can be stored in that cache.

- **Prevention of non-reachable URLs:**

  After you change some options in the configuration of sh404SEF it wants you to clear the old cache to generate new URLs. You have to be aware that it really creates new URLs for your articles. If you have changed the article title's alias, or moved the article to another section or category its URL will change.

  Be aware of this and create a custom redirect for that page using the old URL in the alias field. You can see an example of that in the previous paragraph about special URLs.

- **Recreate SEF URLs with one Click:**

  The SEF URLs are built upon the first request of that page. This means, after you clear the cache and a visitor from the search engine results page has clicked on a SEF URL, it will not find the page. To solve this you need to have a Sitemap component such as Xmap active. After you have cleaned the SEF Cache, directly visit the menu link you have created for the sitemap.

  The sitemap is now recreated and calls every page that is in the sitemap. Now all SEF URLs are again active and you don't lose any visitors. You can check this by going again to the sh404SEF control panel and you will see that there are again a lot of SEF URLs in the database.

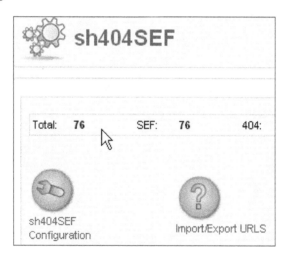

If you don't see the numbers showing up again, clear the Joomla! cache (In your Joomla! administration panel under **Tools | Clean Cache**), then visit the sitemap page and reload again, that should fix it. Check some of the links in the sitemap page to see if they work.

Summary

In this chapter you have learned about the sh404SEF component and why you need it. You also saw that there are a lot more improvements that sh404SEF makes than just creating short and better SEF URLs. Using each of the following options:

- Using the best options for metadata
- Creating and using special meta tags such as title, description, and keywords
- Creating special redirects for moved or Non-SEF URLs

This will give your site the power to do even better in the search engines. In the next chapter we will also look at a better 404 page that can be edited from within the sh404SEF component, and in the Appendix B you will find several .htaccess examples that can help you get this component working.

Using sh404SEF and setting the configuration right will give your site the something extra that it needs to outrank your competitors. However, it is not a miracle component that will boost your site without even working on your content. Writing good keyword rich articles and titles is up to you, but you will atleast have a place for them from where they can be picked up by the search engines.

7
The Importance of Good SEO Joomla! Templates

Templates in Joomla! are of course an easy way to change the look of your web site. A nice looking web site will keep visitors on your site for longer time than a web site with an old, worn-out layout, and color settings. But there is more to templates than what "meets the eye". There are some SEO factors to consider when you are looking for a new template for your web site.

A few things we are going to cover in this chapter are:

- Finding the right template for your site
- What to look for in a template
- Why validation of HTML, XHTML, and CSS matters
- Choosing between free and commercial templates
- What does usability have to do with SEO
- Going for fixed or fluid

Now that may seem like a lot to handle, and it really is, as this is one of the best and biggest improvements you can use for your Joomla! site.

Finding the right template for your site

Getting the right template for your site can be a long and cumbersome process. You want to check the best resources to find just the template that will show your visitor what your site is about. More importantly, you want to capture your visitors and draw them in to your web site to read more of your content and to have them do what you want them to do. This means you want to get the conversion goals you have set for your web site. These may include reading information, contacting you for service, signing up for your newsletter, and so on—you know what your goals are better than anyone else.

So, your template is really the first impression that people get and you should make it as clear and as compelling as possible. Keep not only your goals in the picture, but also the audience (your target group of visitors) in mind when choosing a template. The people working in business domains like to see more white space whereas gamers like to see more black or dark blue for some reason. Check the following sites as examples:

- www.nytimes.com
- www.mtv.com
- www.worldofwarcraft.com

Once you have an idea about your visitors and how you want to brand your site, it's time to check some of your competitors' web sites. If you have already set up a web site, then this would also be a good time to check what the top 10 sites in your niche look like. If you do that (and you should really look at how the layout of the site is set up), look for the following things:

- Where is the main menu
- What information or topic sections/categories are there
- How is the general look and feel of the site
- Look at the source code of several pages, and check if and how meta tag description and keywords are used

Back to the templates, let's see what is important for search engines and their robots, before you choose and possibly buy a template, or have it custom built.

What to look for in SEO templates

Although I say SEO templates, SEF templates would be a good term as well. W3C compliant templates are focused on XHTML (eXtensible Hyper Text Markup Language) and CSS Cascading Style Sheets, which means the markup of the site's template is split into generating the HTML code, and the real layout is done by a CSS file.

Templates you use for your web site should follow the W3C coding as closely as possible. Search Engine Robots are built to look for proper coding and get their impressions from that. This means you want your page titles enclosed in H1 tags (meaning this is the most important line on this page), subheadings in H2, and so on. Subheadings in H2 can be used on the site for multiple headings, but H1 tags should appear only once.

Some templates form the site title in a header like text and post it as H1, this is of course not the most optimal coding decision but it is very common in Joomla! templates. If you want to check the used elements of a template, you could read through the source code, or use the Web developer extension for Firefox which you can find at `https://addons.mozilla.org/en-US/firefox/addon/60`.

Once installed set the following options under **Outline**:

- **Outline Block Level Elements**
- **Show Element Names When Outlining**

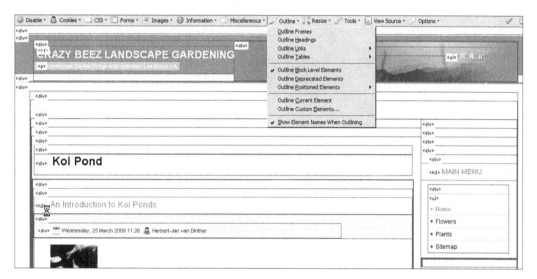

In the previous screenshot, you can see that the main title of the site is set as H1, the article titles are set as H2, and the menu titles are set as H3. Although not optimal, this is workable, but in this case you need to make sure that your main keywords are in the site title. So, does that mean you should not use templates that are not completely XHTML and CSS compliant? No, you can use templates that are not fully compliant but you should look for the ones that are built to get close.

Even if you have a completely valid template, you will break it. Once you implement some JavaScript counter coding such as Google Analytics or default StatCounter, your code is no longer a valid XHTML code. You do have an option to keep your compliance by using XHTML coding from StatCounter, but that will give you less information about your visitors. If you want to check whether a template is valid just head over to `http://validator.w3.org/`, and enter the URL of your web site. You will get an overview of how well you are doing:

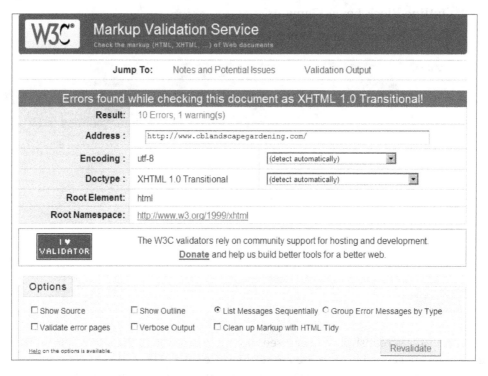

If you have any errors and warnings, it's time to check the cause of these errors. All the errors and warnings are pointed at the message section of that screen. If you don't have any experience with markup validation tools, you should check the **Verbose Output** option. This will give you more information on each of the errors and suggest changes that could fix them.

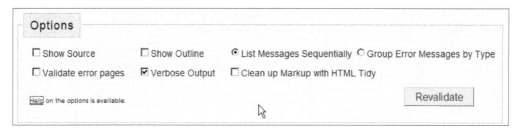

Most of the errors are caused by the StatCounter JavaScript in this case and there were no errors that could prevent a Search Engine Robot from searching the site. Search Engine Robots will not run any JavaScripts, so don't worry about that. You could have bigger problems if you find real errors that break parsing of the site such as never ending tables or unclosed H1 or H2 tags.

There are a few DOC types available in the W3C recommendations (`http://www.w3schools.com/tags/tag_DOCTYPE.asp`). For Joomla! templates you will find that the majority will be HTML 4 or XHTML 4 Transitional and very few XHTML Strict.

The biggest difference between the two is the fact that with the transitional DTD you are allowed to use all HTML elements and attributes, including presentational and deprecated elements. For XHTML, the template must be written in valid XML (`http://www.w3.org/XML/`).

Why validation matters

Apart from the reasons discussed in previous section, one more important reason to get a W3C-valid template is to get the best performance in terms of the loading time of your web site. W3C validation makes loading of pages faster in your visitor's browser, as that browser has to do fewer corrections to the markup. Spiders such as Googlebot and Inktomi slurp can read the code faster and can easily find the real content on your page. With the right validation, your page loads faster and this is also one of the aspects that Google takes into account. The better and faster your pages are loading, the better your position will be. So, try to find a template that has 80, or if possible 90 percent valid code after you have installed your extra code and components.

Why you should look at code positioning

What is code positioning anyway? In simple terms, it is the way in which the code for your HTML page is generated.

There are several ways in which you can generate your page using the template of your Joomla! web site:

- In sequential order, which means that the page is built following the guidelines from top to bottom—first the header, then the left side modules followed by the content, and then the right side modules and the footer

- In search engine optimized order, which means that first the content, then the header, followed by the left and right modules, and then the footer

A search engine optimized template will follow the latter, now why should you care? The page layout in both cases can be identical. There is no difference to the visitor of your web site, but there is a difference for the Search Engine Robots. They get the most important information first, before all the other code is shown to them. This is also the reason why I use the right menu option instead of the left one, as there are only a few well-optimized Joomla! templates.

Most template builders don't go that deep into Search Engine Optimization, currently I know of the following three:

- One site that has a few source coded SEO'd templates is `joomlashack.com`
- Second are the specially built Bolt and Breeze templates from `alledia.com`
- Third in line is Rocket theme with their free afterburner template `http://www.rockettheme.com/joomla-templates/afterburner`

There are a lot of great templates that are really well coded and could even outperform these special templates. If you feel that these special, highly optimized templates are suited for your site and, if your site's audiences like them, you should go for the best and fastest template you can get.

How to look for optimized code? Just open up a source code viewer and read through the generated HTML. If you find that the real content of your article is way down below all the other kinds of coding, you know it's not optimized with code positioning.

Leave your tables behind

Modern day templates should not use tables anymore to position their content, and neither should you. Stay away from templates that are built with tables to set the layout. Using tables in this manner provides you with a slow loading page as most of the positioning is done with tables in tables in tables, and so on.

Table-based templates are slow to generate in browsers compared to XHTML and CSS templates. Each table has to be completely built before the one inside it is built. You can see that if you have a large number of tables, it will take time to show the page to your visitor.

Even with the best template that is created with only XHTML and CSS, you will see tables in a Joomla! web site. Even with a Joomla! 1.5 site, Joomla! in its core system creates tables, rows, and cells to position the content. The work to get a table less Joomla! version is in process, but if that will make it into Joomla! 1.6 is not clear at this moment. However, you can still minimize the number of tables used by choosing a template that is not built around tables. To strip the tables from your output, `yootheme.com` offers a free template override (`http://www.yootheme.com/member-area/downloads/category/templates-15`). Make sure to carefully follow the instructions for implementation and check your layout and CSS afterwards. Not all templates will work with this override so make sure you make a backup of your template.

You can easily identify a table-based template by looking at the source code of the index file of the template. If you see all kinds of `<table>` `<tr>` and `<td>` coding, look further. If you see a lot of `<div>` and `<class>` tags in the source code, it is worth investigating if this template suits you.

Choosing between free and commercial templates

Let's talk about why you chose Joomla!. Was it because it's open source, or because it's free, or you were looking for one of the best content management systems? Why does it matter at this point? If you say because it's free, then you are more willing to look for free templates. If you say open source, your first bet will probably be a free template as well, along with the possibility to change it yourself as you have free access to the code. If you were looking for a very good content management system, then you are in the market for the best templates money can buy. Yet, it is possible that you could end up with a free template for your site.

Free is not the same as open source. There are some commercial templates that are open source. Open source means that you have access to the code, and hence the freedom to change it to suit your needs.

There are several good web sites that you can use to find great templates for free—for example, www.joomlaos.de which is the same as www.joomla24.com, but with a better gallery system for the templates. Don't worry about the language, you are looking for the most visual part of your site. Besides that, demo means demo and download means download.

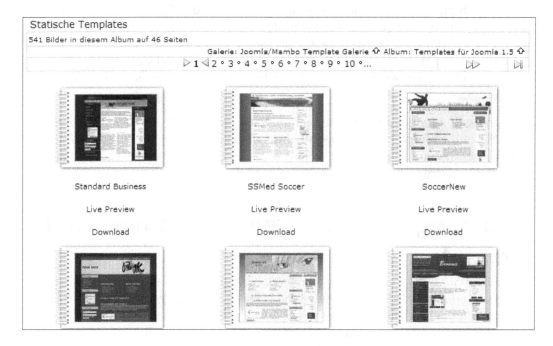

Let's look at the web sites where we can get templates. Most of these web sites offer free templates:

- www.joomlashack.com
- www.rockettheme.com
- www.pixelparadise.com
- www.joomlart.com
- www.youjoomla.com
- www.joomlabamboo.com
- www.joomladesigns.co.uk

Always look at the license that comes with such a template. It might not suit your site to keep a link to the web site builder. There is one problem with free templates—most of them state that you have to keep the link intact, and if you want to remove it you should pay for it. If you run a web site about Joomla!, you can easily keep the link because it points to another site that is also about Joomla!.

If you run a web site to sell gardening services, why would you link to a Joomla! site? That is not the best option for your Search Engine Optimization efforts.

Another problem with free templates

I use free templates. I always look at the source code of the pages generated after I install and activate them, and so should you.

The intention of the template builder is not always clear. It is possible that he/she built the template for a company that paid him to promote their site. Building a free template and sharing it with the Joomla! community is a great way to get lots of incoming links. You know that such a link is not always in your best interest, and the template builder will know that you will remove the link if it is too obvious—for instance, a link to an insurance company or a car sales dealer. If you know how to read the footer of the template file, or even the index.php file of the template, you know how to get rid of such a link.

So they changed their tactics, now you won't see the link on your page, because it is "hidden" using a CSS code such as .hidden. Therefore, you need to step up and check the .css file that is referenced in the template as well.

Another option that is now gaining momentum is to put in some extra JavaScript called PHP file, in which a hexadecimal code line is embedded. Now that is going an extra mile to hide your intentions. You have to decode the code and see what it's all about.

You could even end up with a link to a malicious software distribution site which will most certainly get you out of any search engine index. When you download a free template, make sure you check that it comes from a reputed source. It should deliver quality templates and check the templates they offer before they make it into the downloads section.

It's also good practice to check the web site of the template builder for two reasons:

- If there is an update for that template
- What the site is really about and if that doesn't look good, stay away from that template

Why go for commercial templates?

One of the reasons for choosing commercial templates is the fact that you get support if something goes wrong. Support should not be the only reason to go for commercial templates. Also consider the fact that there are a few other web sites that use the same template. This makes your site more unique than many free template-based sites. Search engines love unique templates.

Price is really not an issue anymore as most of the templates and template clubs will charge you between 20 to 50 USD per template for a three month membership with access to multiple templates. This is good value for what you get. If you want a truly unique template, then those template builders will offer you this possibility as well. However, you may have to dig deeper into your wallet.

The commercial templates are well formatted when it comes to standards such as XHTML and CSS. This makes it a good choice for your Search Engine Optimization efforts. Commercial templates use the most up-to-date settings for Joomla! and will use the possibility to incorporate parameters that make it easy for you to do some customization or add extra functionality.

Images used in commercial templates for the background, and other images used for the layout are also optimized to reduce loading time for the template. You will also see that commercial templates are making good use of getting CSS and JavaScript out of the main `index.php` file. Setting these files outside the template and including them using external files will get your main content loaded faster.

The main reason for choosing commercial templates is that they look really good and are specifically built for a certain purpose or niche. We will consider two examples of such templates. The first one is that of a blog-like template such as **Sketch** from `www.joomlabamboo.com`.

The second example is of a special **car magazine** template from `www.gavick.com`.

There are many others to choose from and you will find templates that will suit your needs without any major problems.

What does usability have to do with SEO

Working on the layout of your web site and making it better for visitors is also a key factor in Search Engine Optimization. It helps you to keep the visitor on your site and lead them through as many pages as possible. It will help you in the rankings because that visitor is not going to do his search again, after viewing only one page.

Google and other search engines track the behavior of searchers and how fast the searcher is coming back to search the same term again. If your visitor stays on your site for a long time, a message is sent to the search engine that says: "Hey, I found what I was looking for. This is a great site for that topic". This means you have won a small battle fought with the other sites on the same topic.

How to make your site sticky

One thing you need to do is to make the site appealing to your visitor. You can accomplish this by choosing a layout and colors that fit their interest. As I mentioned before, setting the right colors for your audience is one way to start, but you need to take an extra step to get it really right.

Use a featured content box/module to highlight the articles that you think are important. Add some movement using flash banners if that is what fits your site and your site's topics. You can also use leading images—for instance, your blog post intro field. Adding these images and moving elements is a way to tell your visitors that you care about their experience on your site. It is also a way to express the effort you are putting in to show them the pictures you selected or created for them.

Headlines and typography

Using typography is another way that could make your site stand out and is coded into the template of your choice. Templates use CSS to ensure things such as headlines, menu listing, and other typographic elements to stand out. Use of these elements in the content of your articles is also a great way to lead people through the content.

We talked about making your pages scanable, and you can enhance that scanability by using classes that are built into the stylesheet of your template. Most editors have the option to select a style such as H3 or H2 that you can use to highlight a certain portion of your page. If you want to get into those options, check how an item such as "quote" shows up on your page. Using quotes is a nice way to break a long paragraph and it will attract the attention of your visitor.

The following is an example on how you can mix up your normal template, set typography, and add some extra elements such as bolding, H2, a drop letter element used for complete call to action, and an image to complete the page.

Going for fixed or fluid?

For your web site you have to decide if you want a fixed width for the template or want to scale the template to fill the whole browser window no matter what resolution your visitor uses. In this case, you choose a fluid width template that spans about 95 to 98 percent of the screen leaving just a small space on both sides of the screen. If you use that option, check your site for different screen resolutions as it might break the layout of your carefully crafted page.

The following is a sample of a fixed 1024 pixel wide layout and the other of a 98 percent wide screen layout, both read on a screen resolution of 1920 x 1200 pixels.

You can see that the second option is not that much fun to read. How could you read that with more text? So choose wisely and think of your targeted visitors. What screen resolution are most of them using? Old computers or new ones, new flat screens with high resolution or old ones that can reach all the way up to 800 x 600 pixels?

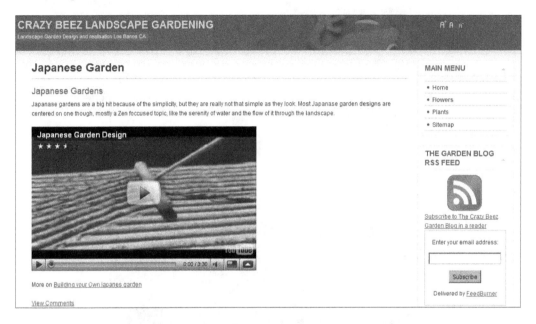

The difference between such a 1024 x 768 resolution and a new 1900 x 1200 widescreen can make your site look very "white" and it makes reading the content difficult.

Display font changes for bigger or smaller text

Looking at visibility, you should give your visitors a possibility to change the standard font size of your site. This option is really great if your target audience is somewhat older and they normally would have to use reading glasses. You will gain a lot of credit if they can increase the font size in your pages. There is a quick way to see if a template has that feature built-in. Just look for the larger and small A's in the header of the template.

With some templates you even get a choice to switch between colors, even black and white, just for usability purpose. In some countries, this option needs to be included by law, similar to other usability issues. Check if your web site template is taking the given guidelines into account.

If you think you have all basics covered, go and check your site in a text view browser such as **lynx** (`http://lynx.isc.org/`). That way you can see how your content holds up and is seen by a search engine spider.

Why use fast templates

One thing that is mentioned throughout this chapter is speed. In the next chapter we will be looking at options to speed up the loading time of your pages in general—it starts with the template of your web site.

Loading time matters a lot if you want to optimize your site for search engines. A great looking template might just be what you need for your web site and, if it fits your audience, you want to use it.

It might just be that this template is not fast because of errors in the HTML or CSS files, or because it uses a lot of images that are incorporated into the template. You need to check the files in the image directory of the template and see what elements are used the most. Using an image optimization tool could help reduce the overall loading time if you can reduce the size of the complete template by several KB(Kilobytes).

There is also a template I mentioned before and is fully optimized — **BOLT** from `alledia.com` — shown in the following screenshot.

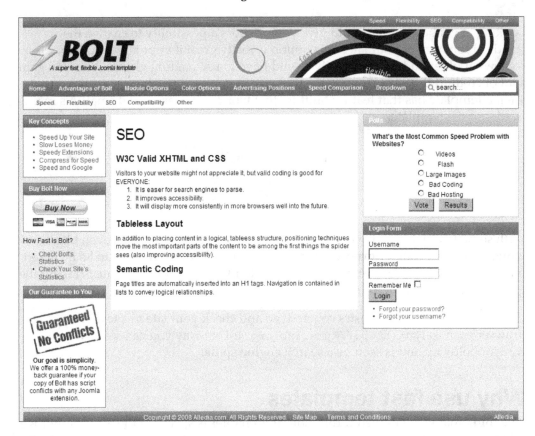

It might not look like a great template at first sight, but it has all the features we talked about in this chapter. And it has the power to change and fit your web site with its different color options and module positions. Buying one doesn't mean you have to mortgage your house, as it costs 25 USD for a personal license.

This is a straightforward template that can be used for a variety of web site topics. It is the opposite of templates that are created by great designers and web sites such as `www.joomlabamboo.com`, `www.gavick.com`, `www.joomlart.com`, `www.joomlajunkie.com`, and many others. These designers and template builders will give you a wide array of special niche templates. All of them are well built with lots of module positions.

All these features come at a price. It is not only the money you spend on them, but also the larger loading times that they come with. You need to make sure that if you use those templates your site is still loading faster than your competitors'.

Summary

Templates are of course the main reason why people choose Joomla! as their content management system. The possibility to change your web site with just a click of the mouse to select another template is really great, but it has to be used with caution.

Changing your template every month is not a good idea, you will frustrate the frequent visitors of your web site. They have to find their way through your site again, even if you keep the modules and menus at the same position. So, stick to your template for a longer time if the number of your visitors are rising and you see that there are a lot of returning visitors.

In a search engine optimized template, you should look for the following items that we talked about in this chapter:

- Valid W3C compliant XHTML and CSS coding
- Fast loading template images
- Free of hidden and non-relevant links
- Clean coding
- Source code optimized to improve the probability to easily find the content for Search Engine Robots
- Use of typography

It cannot be stressed enough that the template of your site needs to fit the visitor groups you are targeting. Having a large template is not that much of a problem for design nuts, as they tend to have fast Internet access. But for Search Engine Optimization you should rethink the strategy, as Search Engine Robots are not into design but into speed.

Why Speed is Important in SEO

8

The speed and performance of your Joomla! web site is one thing that can help you get better search engine ranking for your web site. Speed is not only important for your visitors, but is also a key factor for your Google rankings.

If you look at your Google webmaster warnings, there might be some warnings related to the speed of your web site. Google will tell you if your site was unreachable, gave a timeout, or a certain page had a very high loading time.

We will be looking at the following things that can help you improve the performance of your site:

- Finding your slowdowns
- Using the cache function of Joomla!
- Looking for errors in log files
- How to improve your images

Finding your slowdowns

Before you do anything to speed up your web site, the first thing you need to check is, how well it performs. If you don't do that, you won't have a baseline to see how the improvements you make are affecting the loading time of your site. With this baseline you can check if the change is really an improvement, or if it is slowing down your web site. So, let's start getting that baseline.

Using OctaGate for insight

Using the OctaGate service, you can perform the first check of your site (`http://www.octagate.com/service/SiteTimer/`). Once you get there, just fill in the link of your web site.

After you hit the **Start** button, you have to wait for a few seconds until the page is completely loaded. After the check is done, you get a full view of what is using up your download time.

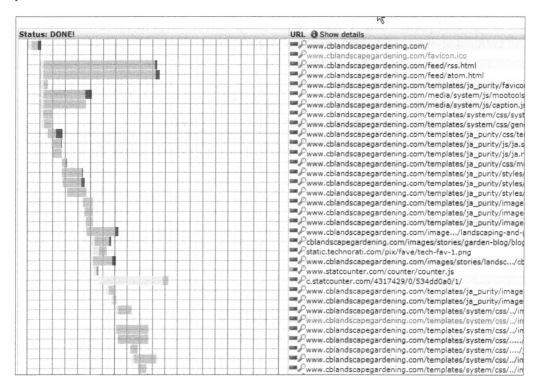

In the following screenshot we can see what each color code represents:

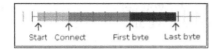

Let's look at the meaning of each color code:

- The first block shows when the element in that line is called
- The second block indicates the time between the first connection and the time when the first byte of that item is received
- The last block indicates the time elapsed before receiving the last byte of that item

To get a better understanding, if the second block is long, it takes more time for the server to respond to get the item. If your third block is long, it is probably a large image that takes time to be downloaded. As you can see in the previous figure, sometimes a third-party resource could slow down the loading of your site. In this case StatCounter takes some time to connect and get the scripts from their servers. But as it is not a significant slowdown and the service is great, I will leave it up there.

What you also see in the picture are two empty lines:

- There is no `favicon.ico` in the root of the site
- One of the images in the template images directory is missing

You might think that if there is no line, there is no problem. But there is a problem as both items are called either by a browser (`favicon.ico`) or by the template that is installed. So, once called, your browser stops for some time to wait for that item to arrive. For me, the total loading time of the template of this web site made me rethink whether I should use this specific template.

If you find that the loading time for your template is long, you should think about changing that template as well. In any case, you should fix the problems you find. We talked about templates in the previous chapter, and I will show you how to get a great `favicon.ico` file later in this chapter.

YSlow is what you need

One of the tools you really need if you get into Search Engine Optimization is Firefox. In Firefox you should have already installed the Web developer plugin from `https://addons.mozilla.org/en-US/firefox/addon/60`. Now, you need to install YSlow from `https://addons.mozilla.org/en-US/firefox/addon/5369`. The first plugin is for analyzing all the on page source elements and outlines. You will use the second one to analyze the page from a loading point of view. To get this plugin to work, you need to install the Firebug plugin from `http://getfirebug.com/`. Just install the plugin to Firefox and you will see a small icon on the status bar of your browser.

Now go to the page you want to analyze and hit that button. Here is the grade report of the previous page, which is the home page of my example web site:

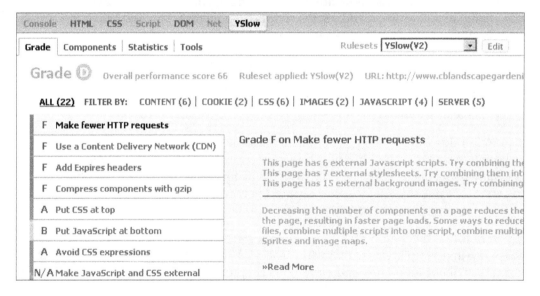

Yes, your web site gets a grade. In my case a D, which is of course not good enough. But this tool also shows which elements of the page are pulling you down by grading them with an F. For each of these F grade items you will get an advice to improve that factor. Some of them will take a few tweaks only, while others may take a significant amount of time to fix. In either case, you have to make a simple decision: *How much time will it take and what will the speed advantage be?*

If it is a simple fix, go ahead and make that change. If it takes more time and knowledge to fix it, get some insight into the problem and a possible fix. Don't spend too much time getting an A. You are not going to get it as you are using StatCounter or Google Analytics. I prefer using both, but they are both out of your control and you need their service to know what is going on with your web site.

To show you how simple some fixes are, I installed and activated an optimized Joomla! template. In the following screenshot you can see the new grade:

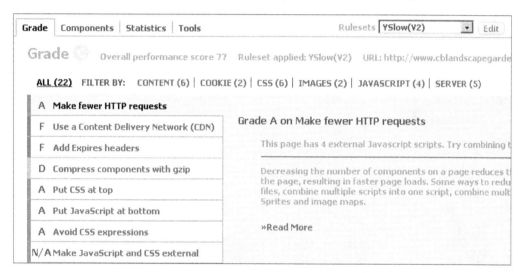

On the OctaGate service page, the total time was reduced from six to four seconds, which is a 33.3 percent improvement in loading time. Go through all the items, read the explanation, and see if you can fix it fast. If you can't, get someone to do it for you or decide if it's worth the effort.

Look at the tools provided with YSlow. One of them gives you the possibility to get a printed report that you can use to get a smart and fast overview. The following image shows just a part of such a report:

Components

The page has a total of **13** components and a total weight of **189.5K** bytes

TYPE	SIZE (KB)	GZIP (KB)	COOKIE RECEIVED (bytes)	COOKIE SENT (bytes)	URL	EXPIRES (Y/M/D)	RESPONSE TIME (ms)	ETAG
doc	10.7K	3.5K			http://www.cblandscapegardening.com/	2001/1/1	404	
js	74.4K				http://www.cblandscapegardening.com/media/system/js/mootools.js	no expires	134	"a818c7-122a4-4947f950"
js	1.7K				http://www.cblandscapegardening.com/media/system/js/caption.js	no expires	10	"a818c2-6b9-4947f948"
js	7.7K	2.6K			http://www.statcounter.com/counter/counter.js	2009/5/13	11	"268021-1e4a-49f049e3"
js	22.7K	9.1K			http://www.google-analytics.com/ga.js	2009/5/19	11	
css	15.0K				http://www.cblandscapegardening.com/templates/allediabolt/css/template.css	no expires	141	"aac64e-3ac3-4a09d546"
cssimage	0.1K				http://www.cblandscapegardening.com/templates/allediabolt/images/blue.png	no expires	137	"aac536-b1-4a09d546"
cssimage	0.4K				http://www.cblandscapegardening.com/images/logo.png (status: 404)	no expires	135	
cssimage	0.4K				http://www.cblandscapegardening.com/templates/allediabolt/images/icons.png (status: 404)	no expires	133	
image	38.5K				http://www.cblandscapegardening.com/images/stories/landscape/landscaping-and-gardening-services-2.jp[snip]	no expires	10	"a8825e-96a6-49f4aaee"
image	7.3K				http://cblandscapegardening.com/images/stories/garden-blog/blog-rss-feed.png	no expires	62	"a882d6-1c94-49cb57c7"
image	-1.2K				http://static.technorati.com/pix/fave/tech-fav-1.png	2009/5/12	72	"4c6-27dab80"
image	34.8K				http://www.cblandscapegardening.com/images/stories/landscape/cb-landscape-gardens.jpg	no expires	74	"a886b2-8805-49612d6a"

* type column indicates the component is loaded after window onload event
† denotes 1x1 pixels image that may be image beacon

Stats

The page has a total of **13** HTTP requests and a total weight of **189.5K** bytes with empty cache

WEIGHT GRAPHS

Empty Cache		
HTTP Requests - 13		
Total Weight - 189.5K		
■	1 HTML/Text	3.5K
▨	4 JavaScript File	87.9K
▩	1 Stylesheet File	15.0K
■	3 CSS Image	1.0K
▦	4 Image	81.9K

Primed Cache		
HTTP Requests - 12		
Total Weight - 19.6K		
▧	1 HTML/Text	3.5K
▨	3 JavaScript File	0.0K
▩	1 Stylesheet File	15.0K
■	3 CSS Image	1.0K
▦	4 Image	0.0K

Now as you know you have to improve some of the items that showed up in the reports. It is time to get into some of the basic stuff that you need to do in your configuration panel. Don't forget to reset the `configuration.php` file's security using your FTP program to read only (Mod 644) after the settings are activated and tested.

Using the cache function of Joomla!

Setting the cache function in Joomla! to **Yes** is just the first step towards getting a better performing web site. You have to open the **Global Configuration** panel and go to the **System** tab. On the left side of the screen you can change the settings for the **Cache Time**. **Cache Time** is the time taken for a cached page to be regenerated after somebody opens the page. The page is stored in a special directory to be shown to a new visitor who wants to look at the page. This reduces the number of queries to the database, which will improve the loading time.

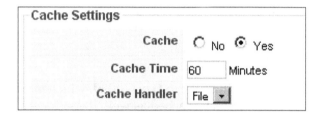

How you set the time for the cache depends on what kind of site you run. A news site needs to have a shorter cache time than a web site on which there are only a few updates per month. For the first case you can set it to around five minutes, and for the later you can easily go for several hours. You can clear the cache to show your content immediately after writing by using your Administrator panel (**Tools | Clean Cache**). You can do that only if you have minimal administrator rights at the backend.

Set the caching for your modules

If you have set the caching option, you still need to check the modules you use on your site. If you have a module that shows updates or changes according to the page that is visited, you should deactivate the function of module caching.

A standard **Caching** module will be set to **Use Global**, which means if the cache is on then the module content will be cached as well. If you have a module such as Related Articles, you need to change this and set it to **No Caching** as every page has different related items. Using cache on such a module will prevent the system from showing the real related pages.

Optimize your server settings

You can also optimize some server settings that can affect the loading time of your site. To change the settings, go to the **Server** tab in **Global Configuration**.

The first option is to set the **GZIP Page Compression** to **Yes**, in order to reduce the file size of the downloads. If you set this option, make sure to check your site for the next couple of days. In some cases the GZIP compression will effectively stop your site from showing its pages. You might even find that your hosting provider does not allow the use of GZIP because it uses more CPU time.

The standard cache function may prevent you from seeing the problems that may occur. Therefore, it is important to check the site until you are sure it is running fine. The second option to change is to set **Error Reporting** to **None**. This ensures that any errors that may occur are not written to the database, reducing the number of write actions to the database and also keeping it smaller in size.

Caching outside Joomla!

You can move your caching and do it outside your Joomla! installation. At `joomlatwork.com` they have a separate component that makes your Joomla! web site much faster.

The component takes the generated pages and puts them in a separate cache, so it's not the same cache as Joomla! uses. After the component has done its work, surfing your web site is like looking through static HTML files (to be honest, it's even faster).

This component is tested on a huge Dutch web site called `www.kika.nl`, which is about helping cancer-prone children. If you browse through this site, you will see how fast it performs. Although the site is built on Mambo, the page loading time is very short. The caching engine was completely rebuilt for Mambo 4.6 and Joomla 1.5. If you use it, it should bring the same benefits to your site. You can find more information at `http://www.joomlatwork.com/products/components/joomla-performance.html`.

There is also a downside to this component—it alters the `index.php` file from your Joomla! installation. If you use other components that do the same, you will run into trouble. You will need to check if everything still works after a Joomla! core version upgrade.

Optimizing CSS and Javascript

The Joomla Performance Booster component (I don't know if you should call it a component as it runs largely on top of your Joomla! installation) combines, compresses and compacts JavaScripts and CSS files into one file each. This means your CSS files will be put into one file for your browser to load.

There can be a lot of CSS and JavaScripts on your site, depending on the Joomla! template and the number of components you use. Sometimes a component comes with several extra CSS files to handle the layout items for that component. Just for fun you should look at your source code (shown in the following screenshot) to see how many CSS files you are loading at the moment.

```
<!DOCTYPE html PUBLIC "-//W3C//DTD XHTML 1.0 Transitional//EN" "http://www.w3.org/TR/xhtml1/DTD/xhtml1-transitional.dtd">

<html xmlns="http://www.w3.org/1999/xhtml" xml:lang="en-gb" lang="en-gb">

<head>
  <title>Landscape Gardening by Crazy Beez - Tips , Design and Realization of your Garden | Crazy Beez Los Banos</title>
  <base href="http://www.cblandscapegardening.com/" />
  <meta name="description" content="Crazy Beez Landscape Gardeners show you how to design and realise your Landscape garden, read more about
  <meta name="keywords" content="landscape gardening, landscape gardeners,ideas,design,architects,garden,water features" />
  <meta name="robots" content="index, follow" />

  <link href="/feed/rss.html" rel="alternate" type="application/rss+xml" title="RSS 2.0" />
  <link href="/feed/atom.html" rel="alternate" type="application/atom+xml" title="Atom 1.0" />
  <link href="/templates/ja_purity/favicon.ico" rel="shortcut icon" type="image/x-icon" />
  <script type="text/javascript" src="/media/system/js/mootools.js"></script>
  <script type="text/javascript" src="/media/system/js/caption.js"></script>

<link rel="stylesheet" href="http://www.cblandscapegardening.com/templates/system/css/system.css" type="text/css" />
<link rel="stylesheet" href="http://www.cblandscapegardening.com/templates/system/css/general.css" type="text/css" />
<link rel="stylesheet" href="http://www.cblandscapegardening.com/templates/ja_purity/css/template.css" type="text/css" />

<script language="javascript" type="text/javascript" src="http://www.cblandscapegardening.com/templates/ja_purity/js/ja.script.js"></script>

<script language="javascript" type="text/javascript">
var rightCollapseDefault='show';
var excludeModules='38';
</script>
<script language="javascript" type="text/javascript" src="http://www.cblandscapegardening.com/templates/ja_purity/js/ja.rightcol.js"></script

<link rel="stylesheet" href="http://www.cblandscapegardening.com/templates/ja_purity/css/menu.css" type="text/css" />

<link rel="stylesheet" href="http://www.cblandscapegardening.com/templates/ja_purity/styles/header/green/style.css" type="text/css" />
<link rel="stylesheet" href="http://www.cblandscapegardening.com/templates/ja_purity/styles/background/lighter/style.css" type="text/css" />
<link rel="stylesheet" href="http://www.cblandscapegardening.com/templates/ja_purity/styles/elements/green/style.css" type="text/css" />
<!--[if gte IE 7.0]>
<style type="text/css">
.clearfix {display: inline-block;}
</style>
<![endif]-->

<style type="text/css">
#ja-header,#ja-mainnav,#ja-container,#ja-botsl,#ja-footer {width: 1024px;margin: 0 auto;}
#ja-wrapper {min-width: 1025px;}
</style>
<meta http-equiv="Content-Language" content="en" /></head>
```

The following is a detailed image showing you the javascript and stylesheet calls.

JavaScripts are called using:

```
<script type="text/javascript" src="/media/system/js/mootools.js"></script>
```

Stylesheets are called using:

```
<link rel="stylesheet" href="/templates/template_name/css/template.css" type="text/css" />
```

```
44  <script type="text/javascript" src="/media/system/js/mootools.js"></script>
45  <script type="text/javascript" src="/media/system/js/caption.js"></script>
46  <script type="text/javascript" src="http://www.cblandscapegardening.com/plugins/content/slimbox/slimbox.js"></script>
47
48  <link rel="stylesheet" href="/templates/js_inspirion/css/reset.css" type="text/css" />
49  <link rel="stylesheet" href="/templates/js_inspirion/css/960.css" type="text/css" />
50  <link rel="stylesheet" href="/templates/js_inspirion/css/template_css.css" type="text/css" />
51  <link rel="stylesheet" href="/templates/js_inspirion/css/dropline.css" type="text/css" />
52  <link href="/templates/js_inspirion/css/style1.css" rel="stylesheet" type="text/css" media="screen" />
53  <link rel="stylesheet" href="/templates/js_inspirion/css/sanserif.css" type="text/css" />
54  <link rel="stylesheet" href="/templates/js_inspirion/css/j15.css" type="text/css" media="screen" />
55  <script type="text/javascript" src="/templates/js_inspirion/js/matching_columns.js"></script>
```

I counted seven .css files and four JavaScript files in the header of the template I used, at the start of the site. So, this component will reduce it with six .css and three JavaScript files, which in turn will lead to faster pages. I will later show you how to reduce the number of .css files manually, but Joomlatwork can do this for you.

Looking at drawbacks and warnings

There are a few things to be aware of before you consider this as a valid option for your web site:

- If you have a lot of modules that change on every reload or refresh of the page, then do some testing to find the right cache time to set (for example, weather modules)
- If you use dynamic image rotations, these will remain still until the cache expires
- If you use clocks, user counts, or other on-page counters, they will be frozen in time
- If you use RSS Feeds to update your site content, they will not refresh until the cache expires

All the above drawbacks come from the fact that the database is not called frequently for these items. The pages come from the cache, which serves them very fast. Another thing to be aware of is the fact that you could run into trouble if the CSS files that are optimized call a dynamic CSS file. It might break because of an incorrect path call, as the originally called file is no longer there in the cache.

So, as a final warning I would say "test, test, and test" until you get everything working as expected. If it does, you and your visitors will enjoy a super fast loading web site. The Search Engine Robots will like it as well.

Optimizing your CSS files

To start with, you can just optimize your CSS files. This option is a very simple one, and you can implement it online using CSS compressor—a great tool available at http://iceyboard.no-ip.org/projects/css_compressor. Before you start this process, make sure you have a copy of the original CSS file as backup.

The tools used to optimize a CSS file will do the following things to your file:

- Convert colors to short HEX codes
- Combine rules
- Strip whitespace

Especially, the last option will make your CSS file very difficult to read. Consider a CSS file as shown in the next screenshot:

```
/* COMMON STYLE */
------------------------------------------------

html, body, form, fieldset {
    margin: 0;
    padding: 0;
}

body {
    color: #000000;
    background: #FFFFFF;
    font-family: Arial, Helvetica, sans-serif;
    line-height: 150%;
}

body#bd {
    color: #333333;
    background: #F2F2F2;
}

body.contentpane {
    width: auto; /* Printable Page */
    margin: 1em 2em;
    line-height: 1.3em;
    margin: 0px 0px 0px 0px;
    font-size: 12px;
    color: #333;
}

body.fs1 {
    font-size: 10px;
}

body.fs2{
    font-size: 11px;
}

body.fs3{
    font-size: 12px;
}
```

The Strip whitespace option will make it look like the following:

CSS

- Link to this output.

```
body{color:#000;background:#FFF;font-family:Arial, Helvetica, sans-serif;line-height:150%}body#bd
{color:#333;background:#F2F2F2}body.contentpane{width:auto;line-height:1.3em;margin:0;font-
size:12px;color:#333}body.fs1{font-size:10px}body.fs2{font-size:11px}body.fs3{font-size:12px}body.fs4{font-
size:13px}body.fs5{font-size:14px}body.fs6{font-size:15px}a{color:#069;text-decoration:underline}
a:hover,a:active,a:focus{color:#333;text-decoration:underline}.contentheading,.componentheading,.blog_more
strong,h1,h2,h3,h4{font-family:"Segoe UI", Arial, Helvetica, sans-serif}
small,.small,.smalldark,.mosimage_caption,.createby,.createdate,.modifydate,a.readon,.img_caption
{color:#666;font-size:92%}h1{font-size:180%}h3{font-size:125%}h4{font-size:100%;text-transform:uppercase}
p,pre,blockquote,ul,ol,h1,h2,h3,h4,h5,h6{margin:1em 0;padding:0}ul li{padding-left:30px;background:url
(../images/bullet.gif) no-repeat 18px 8px;line-height:180%}ol li{margin-left:35px;line-height:180%}th
{padding:5px;font-weight:700;text-align:left}fieldset{border:none;padding:10px 5px;background:url
(../images/hdot2.gif) repeat-x top}hr{border-top:1px solid #CCC;border-right:0;border-left:0;border-
bottom:0;height:1px}td,div{font-size:100%}form label{cursor:pointer}input,select,textarea,.inputbox
{padding:3px 5px;font-family:Tahoma, Arial, Helvetica, sans-serif;font-size:100%}.button{padding:3px
5px;border:1px solid #333;background:url(../images/grad1.gif) repeat-x top #333;color:#CCC;font-
size:85%;text-transform:uppercase}.button:hover,.button:focus{border:1px solid
#999;background:#333;color:#FFF}*+html .button,* html .button{padding:2px 0 !important}.inputbox{border:1px
solid #CCC;background:#FFF}.inputbox:hover,.inputbox:focus{background:#FFC}pre,.code{padding:10px
15px;margin:5px 0 15px;border-left:5px solid #999;background:#FFF;font:1em/1.5 "Courier News", monospace}
blockquote{padding:1em 40px 1em 15px}blockquote span.open{padding:0 0 0 20px;background:url(../images/so-
q.gif) no-repeat left top}blockquote span.close{padding:0 20px 0 0;background:url(../images/sc-q.gif) no-
repeat bottom right}.quote-hilite{padding:10px 15px;margin:10px 0;border:1px solid
#CACACC;background:#FFF}.small-quote{margin:0;padding:0;background:none}.small-quote span.open-quote
{margin:0;padding-left:20px;background:url(../images/so-q.gif) no-repeat center left}.small-quote
span.close-quote{margin:0;padding-right:20px;background:url(../images/sc-q.gif) no-repeat center
right}.small-quote span.author{padding:2px 5px 2px 20px;border-top:1px solid #DCDDE0;margin:.5em 0
0;display:block;background:url(../images/author.gif) no-repeat 5px 4px #EAEBEE;font-size:90%;text-
```

As you can see, for us, the mere mortals, this is very difficult to read. But the net effect of this action is shown here:

Statistics

- Original size: 25.95 kB (26,572 B)
- Final size: 19.62 kB (20,089 B)
- Saved: 6.33 kB (6,483 B)
- Reduction: 24.4%

- Duration: 0.44271 seconds

- Rules: 246
- Selectors: 389
- Properties: 620

As you can see there is a reduction in the file size by **24.4** % or a total gain of **6.33 KB**. We talked about the speed of your template and the effects on SEO previously. If you have a template that you really like and want to keep, do this exercise with all the CSS files of your template. It will reduce the size so that you can still gain momentum. The total time to perform this exercise is counted in seconds. Go to the web site, copy the URL or the CSS content of your template if you want to run this code in the optimizer, and paste the optimized code back into your Joomla! template editor. It's done!

Combining CSS files

This might take some more work on your part and is not as easy as the previous option. There is a reason why the CSS files in a template are separated. This is done to give you more configuration options such as changing the color of the layout. You can have a green.css, blue.css, red.css, and even orange.css, all separate from the general.css file. Combing them into one is done through a simple copy and paste technique. The code from both the templates are combined into one and saved.

That was easy — wasn't it? Now, you have to check how these files are called in the index.php file of the template. This should be changed to the newly-created and uploaded file.

Here is an example code for such a call:

```
<link rel="stylesheet" href="<?php echo $tmpTools->baseurl();
?>templates/system/css/system.css" type="text/css" />
<link rel="stylesheet" href="<?php echo $tmpTools->baseurl();
?>templates/system/css/general.css" type="text/css" />
<link rel="stylesheet" href="<?php echo $tmpTools->templateurl(); ?>/
css/template.css" type="text/css" />
<script language="javascript" type="text/javascript" src="<?php echo
$tmpTools->templateurl(); ?>/js/ja.script.js"></script>
<?php if ($tmpTools->getParam('rightCollapsible')): ?>
<script language="javascript" type="text/javascript">
var rightCollapseDefault='<?php echo $tmpTools->getParam('rightCollaps
eDefault'); ?>';
var excludeModules='<?php echo $tmpTools->getParam('excludeModules');
?>';
</script>
<script language="javascript" type="text/javascript" src="<?php echo
$tmpTools->templateurl(); ?>/js/ja.rightcol.js"></script>
<?php endif; ?>
<?php  if($this->direction == 'rtl') : ?>
<link rel="stylesheet" href="<?php echo $tmpTools->templateurl(); ?>/
css/template_rtl.css" type="text/css" />
<?php else : ?>
<link rel="stylesheet" href="<?php echo $tmpTools->templateurl(); ?>/
css/menu.css" type="text/css" />
<?php endif; ?>
```

This again is not that easy to read.

The following line calls the template.css file, which is the one you can edit with the template editor of your Joomla! site.

```
<link rel="stylesheet" href="<?php echo $tmpTools->templateurl(); ?>/
```

```
css/template.css" type="text/css" />
```

They are defined by the site's parameters in the templates configuration, as shown next:

```
<link rel="stylesheet" href="<?php echo $tmpTools->templateurl(); ?>/
css/template_rtl.css" type="text/css" />
<?php else : ?>
<link rel="stylesheet" href="<?php echo $tmpTools->templateurl(); ?>/
css/menu.css" type="text/css" />
```

If you want to combine the three files, you should not only combine them but also replace the existing references to these files with the reference to the new combined file. If you want to use this option, you will see it is not that easy to change these options. However, it is an exercise that will give you a better understanding of CSS and the `index.php` file of your template.

Doing easy file path optimization

We looked at the difficulties in combining CSS files. For that you looked at the `index.php` file of your template. One thing you must have noticed is that all calls to the CSS and JavaScript files are done like this:

```
<link rel="stylesheet" href="<?php echo $tmpTools->baseurl();
?>templates/system/css/system.css" type="text/css" />
```

This means for every file there is a call to the database to determine the file location. See the following line of code:

```
echo $tmpTools->baseurl();
```

This call is done within the template so that the template can be used on any Joomla! based web site on any domain. But you know your domain and the path to your files. So, you can just copy that information form the source view of a generated page of your site. Backup the information of your template's `index.php` file before you start. Keep a copy of the original template's `index.php` file, in case something goes wrong. Now get the links for the `.js` and `.css` files and replace them accordingly. In the previous example it ends up like:

```
<link rel="stylesheet" href="http://www.cblandscapegardening.com/
templates/system/css/system.css" type="text/css" />
```

Doing this for all the files in the template's `index.php` file, in case of my web site, reduces the number of calls to the database by a minimum of ten. Look at your `index.php` template file and see for yourself how many `baseurl` requests can be replaced by changing it to the full path to the file. Reducing the number of calls to the database improves your loading time and your hosting provider will find it a good idea as well. The fewer the calls to the database, the less resources are called from the CPU of the server. So, you get a faster loading site and a more stable hosting platform.

Looking for errors in log files

Log files on your hosting system are a good indicator of what is going wrong if you have a problem with long loading times. Look at the `error.log` files to find out if there are any problems with your site; you might even notice some attempts to hack your web site. Therefore, it's a good idea to do these checks at least once in a month, or instantly if you encounter a problem.

Error log files are sometimes difficult to read. With practice you will come to know the biggest problems very quickly. Reading log files can show you that the path to your `favicon.ico` is not what you expected it to be. It might also show you that a certain image is missing in your template directory. Both problems can slow down your page's loading time, as the browser will try to find the missing file, thereby going through the process of error handling. Eliminating the problems by providing the expected files can make a large impact on your site's performance.

Improving your images

Images can be a better part of the web site and it improves the site for your visitors as nobody likes to read through large pieces of text. Images make your site more alive comparatively. Images can set your site apart from your competitors', if you use better images to make things clearer. Images also slow down your page loading process if they are used the wrong way.

The following are the ways in which you can improve images:

- Modifying images to the right size
- Naming your images the right way
- Using size parameters
- Using caption, alt, and titles

Resizing your images

Many people, including me (when I started), make the mistake of uploading a large image and reducing it on the page. For instance, uploading an image that is 2500 pixels wide and then reducing it using the HTML code width="125px". It looks good on the page but, although it may seem fine, it is not. The browser still needs to load the file and then resize it to the parameters you set. Therefore, make sure you reduce the file to the size you are going to use on the page.

If you want to use the image in different sizes on a single page or on different pages, don't cut corners, create the right sized files and name them so that you can tell them apart. A file named `example-image-250.jpg` is then likely to be 250 pixels wide.

I know that there are many people who have a hard time when it comes to reducing the size of an image. In several graphical programs, I have seen that the end result of such an action can be terrible. Some details are blurred and there is no way you will want it on your web site.

Using the right program for the job

You can see two examples of file resize action in the following images. It illustrates reduction to 250 pixels width image from a 1600 x 1200 pixels image. The first one is done using Jasc Paint Shop Pro 8.

The following one is done using the free-for-personal-use graphics program called IrfanView.

I know it is difficult to make out the difference once this is in print, try this yourself. IrfanView is superior when it comes to resizing and keeping images sharp, even the minute details. You can download the installation and plugin package from www. irfanview.com. Download and install that package as it offers some extra features that you might want to use. Resizing an image with IrfanView is very easy, just open the image in the program and choose resize from the menu option **Image | Resize/ Resample**...

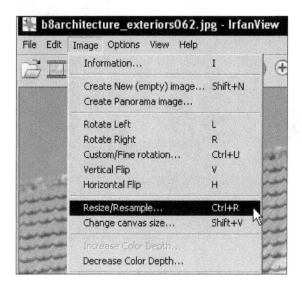

Then set the size you want using the set **newsize** option. With the option **Preserve aspect ratio** set, the height will be automatically calculated.

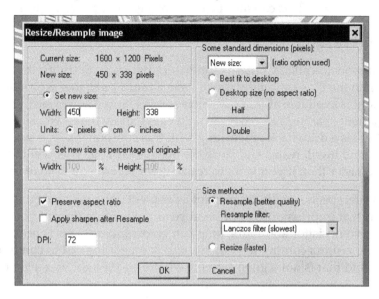

After you get it to the right size, save it as `.jpg` file. You can also use the option **Save for Web... (PlugIn).** It will give you some extra options to reduce the total size to an even lower value.

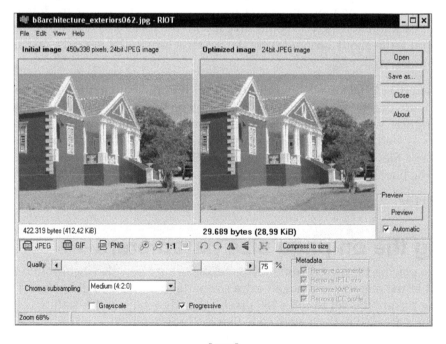

If you don't want to install IrfanView, or you are not on your own computer, you can use Smush.it — the image optimization tool available at `http://developer.yahoo.com/yslow/smushit/`. This can also be used through `http://smush.it`. This service lets you render a maximum of five images per session. With IrfanView you can work with batches of files.

There is a component called Content Optimizer, that you can try for image optimization on the fly — especially if you have a multi publisher web site. The component is available at `http://extensions.joomla.org/extensions/site-management/cache/6427/details`. Reviews show that it works fine. However, there is a drawback of working with this component. You can upload large images, and it will resize and store the images for you. This will use up your hosting space faster than if you were to resize them before you upload them.

For any web site, speed is really important as you get only one chance to create an impression. If that impression is poor because of the loading time of your pages, you lose! You lose your visitor and in the long run your ranking. This is because search engines see the visitors coming to your site and soon getting out to continue with their search. And that is not a good sign for what they thought was a good match...

Naming your files with keywords in mind

One thing I do with images for a web site is look at the text and subject of the article. I then choose an image that fits with the content, resize it, and save the file with a different name. The previous image is called `B1234xxx.jpg`. If you are doing an article on vacation houses, you could save it with the name `red-vacation-houses.jpg`. If you write about a triangle roof design structure, call it `example-triangle-roof-design.jpg`.

Do you get the global idea behind this exercise? It is all about getting an extra keyword into the source code of the page. If you have your image's path open to search engines, you are more likely to get traffic for those keywords from image searchers as well. If you use the Joomlatwork patch, this is already done in the `robots.txt` file, that is replaced by the patch. If you want to open the path yourself remove the line:

```
Disallow: /images/
```

Using the on page size parameters

If you are placing the file on your web page, make sure you also incorporate the file size, that is, the real size and not an extra size reduction like you did before. For the following picture it is set to 468 x 180 pixels. The advantage of this setting is that these values are also in the source code that the browser gets.

Having the size means that the browser can reserve that space for the image and go ahead with showing the text as it waits for the image to arrive. If you don't set those sizes, you have to wait until the image is downloaded before the browser will get on with the rest of the document.

People can start reading the content immediately instead of waiting for the image to display before they can read the rest of the article.

Using Caption, Alt, and Title

If you look at the screenshot in the previous section, you see that the field **Alternative Text** is also used to get keywords into the page.

 Don't go stuffing the **Alternative text** attribute with keywords. Search engines really don't like keyword stuffing and will reward it with lower rankings.

On some sites you may notice that they have only one word in the Alt attribute, or they have stuffed it with numerous keywords that they want to rank for. You should not use either of those options. Just write a fitting description, possibly with the same keywords that you used for the file name.

I also like to use the title tag, where I can just copy the **Alternative Text** into the **Advisory Title** field.

You can use the caption text, which is mostly displayed as text following the image to get keywords on the page. For this option the same things as mentioned earlier still apply — clear descriptions of the image and no keyword stuffing.

Summary

There are several options you can use to improve the speed performance of your Joomla! web site. From caching to image optimization, all options are aimed to make sure your real visitors and the Search Engine Robots like to come back to your site instead of visiting your competitors' sites.

9
Tracking and Tracing to Improve Your Web Site

Tracking and tracing—doesn't that sound a bit dull? Why would you even bother to spend your time in such a boring way? So the question is: *Why should you do it*?

One reason is because it is fun to see your site growing. You can see whether your SEO efforts are paying off and, increase your income if you use some form of advertising. Besides, you can learn more about how search engines look at your web site and what other web sites are referring back to you.

One of the most important tasks is to see how well your site is converting, along with what does/does not work from your SEO efforts.

In this chapter, we will be looking at some of the ways to get those statistics, and will later see how to interpret them. This chapter will talk about:

- Finding the options and tools for you
- Which service you want to use for your statistics
- How to look at your StatCounter stats
- How to analyze Google analytics
- What more can you learn from your statistics
- Putting to work the lessons you learned

Looking at your options

We are going to look at some of the statistics software you can use to monitor your web site from a traffic point of view. There are several options you can use such as:

- Hosting provider statistics
- Separate software installations on your hosting account
- External services such as StatCounter and Google Analytics
- Web Analytics software installed on a PC

You may not even know it, but your hosting provider also keeps a tab on your web site! Most hosting providers will give you the stats from **Webalizer** and you might even think that it shows how much traffic you got. Here is a screenshot for one of my web sites:

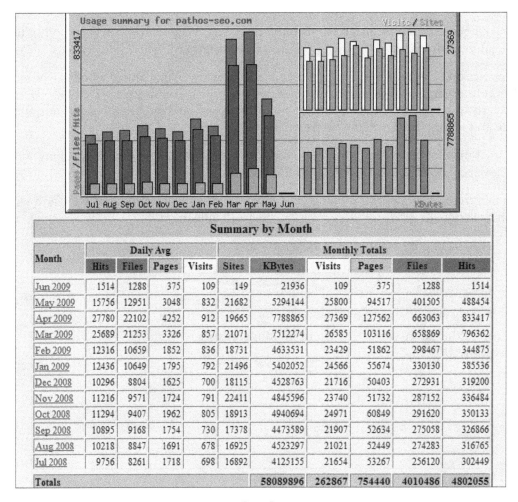

Summary by Month

Month	Daily Avg				Monthly Totals					
	Hits	Files	Pages	Visits	Sites	KBytes	Visits	Pages	Files	Hits
Jun 2009	1514	1288	375	109	149	21936	109	375	1288	1514
May 2009	15756	12951	3048	832	21682	5294144	25800	94517	401505	488454
Apr 2009	27780	22102	4252	912	19665	7788865	27369	127562	663063	833417
Mar 2009	25689	21253	3326	857	21071	7512274	26585	103116	658869	796362
Feb 2009	12316	10659	1852	836	18731	4633531	23429	51862	298467	344875
Jan 2009	12436	10649	1795	792	21496	5402052	24566	55674	330130	385536
Dec 2008	10296	8804	1625	700	18115	4528763	21716	50403	272931	319200
Nov 2008	11216	9571	1724	791	22411	4845596	23740	51732	287152	336484
Oct 2008	11294	9407	1962	805	18913	4940694	24971	60849	291620	350133
Sep 2008	10895	9168	1754	730	17378	4473589	21907	52634	275058	326866
Aug 2008	10218	8847	1691	678	16925	4523297	21021	52449	274283	316765
Jul 2008	9756	8261	1718	698	16892	4125155	21654	53267	256120	302449
Totals						58089896	262867	754440	4010486	4802055

But the problem with Webalizer is that *it does not exclude your own visits* to the web site, and it also counts the hits, files, and visits relating to your administration panel.

Therefore, if you have been working hard on your site, you will see a spike in the traffic it reports, which you can explain the day after, but will have forgotten about after a few months. If you have a subdomain that you want to track separately, that is not possible with a typical install of Webalizer — you get all the traffic from your entire domain.

However, there is some information that you can use. The following is a simple legend to explain some terms:

- **Hits**: The total number of requests made to the server
- **Files**: The number of files downloaded to your visitor's browser (not cached)
- **Pages**: The actual number of pageviews the site has served
- **Visits**: The number of sites that request a URL
- **KBytes**: The amount of data transferred from your web site — an indicator of your bandwidth usage

Clicking on the **Month** link from the first overview graph, you get a more detailed view of the traffic generated and the sources it came from.

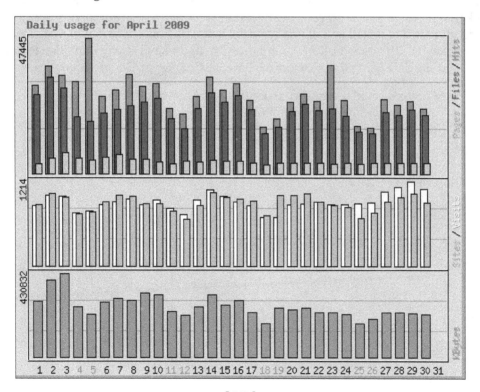

As shown here, the first image you get is a detailed graph of your daily stats over that month. It is followed by some tables and statistics that are not quite distinctive enough for you to get any information on it and use for further analysis.

The only table you want to look at, is the one at the bottom of the screen that says: **Top 20 of x Total Search Terms**. You will see a large number instead of x, but you get only 20 terms for which people have found your site in the search engines. Note these terms and write them down as they are most likely to fit into your keywords list. You can use these statistics and compare them with other options we are going to explore.

 If you have a provider such as hostgator.com, you will have a tool called **AWStats**, which we will be looking at next.

Using your own separate AWStats

As we looked at the Webalizer statistics, you can imagine that there are other similar packages you can use.

I have mentioned before, HostGator will give you AWStats, but as it is a free software package you can install it on your own hosting account if you want to. It is pretty straightforward to install and, if you have the space on you account, you might want to try it as well. This is an option you might want to consider if you don't like to track your web site data using free services such as StatCounter or Google Analytics.

The following is a small screenshot from the demo site of AWStats:

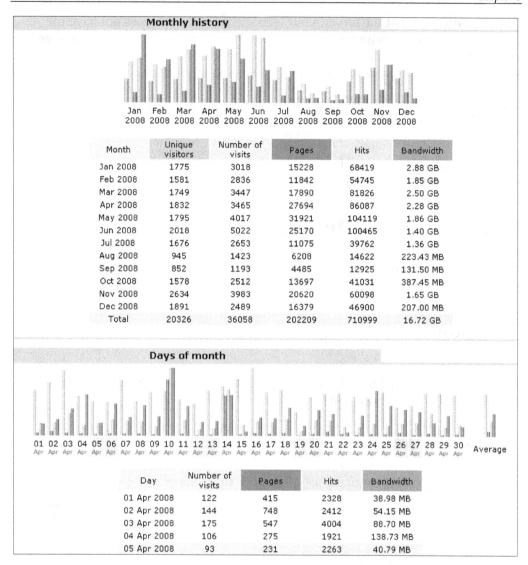

Month	Unique visitors	Number of visits	Pages	Hits	Bandwidth
Jan 2008	1775	3018	15228	68419	2.88 GB
Feb 2008	1581	2836	11842	54745	1.85 GB
Mar 2008	1749	3447	17890	81826	2.50 GB
Apr 2008	1832	3465	27694	86087	2.28 GB
May 2008	1795	4017	31921	104119	1.86 GB
Jun 2008	2018	5022	25170	100465	1.40 GB
Jul 2008	1676	2653	11075	39762	1.36 GB
Aug 2008	945	1423	6208	14622	223.43 MB
Sep 2008	852	1193	4485	12925	131.50 MB
Oct 2008	1578	2512	13697	41031	387.45 MB
Nov 2008	2634	3983	20620	60098	1.65 GB
Dec 2008	1891	2489	16379	46900	207.00 MB
Total	20326	36058	202209	710999	16.72 GB

Day	Number of visits	Pages	Hits	Bandwidth
01 Apr 2008	122	415	2328	38.98 MB
02 Apr 2008	144	748	2412	54.15 MB
03 Apr 2008	175	547	4004	88.70 MB
04 Apr 2008	106	275	1921	138.73 MB
05 Apr 2008	93	231	2263	40.79 MB

One big advantage of AWStats is that you can see the full list of search terms and keyword phrases that are used in order to get to your web site.

The major disadvantage for me is the fact that it is better to give it a separate MySQL database as you don't want to overload your Joomla! database with all this data. This means that you need to be able to get an extra database on your hosting account and use it for AWStats.

You may also find that the server, your web site is hosted on, does not have the capacity that you want and need in terms of CPU resources. In that case the speed of your web site, along with the rest of the sites hosted on that server, will suffer. So, if you want to do this, make sure you set all performance options correctly.

Again, you can use this software for free, but use it only if you are really concerned about your traffic data on other free resources. Most of these free resources are secure enough to protect the data you collect to analyze your traffic.

You may have a question: *Why did you mention it here?* Well, my answer is: To give you an alternative for the services you will be looking at next.

Getting your statistics for free

If you do a quick search on Google with the term "Website statistics", you will notice that the following three web sites in the top 10 on the list are the only ones that actually provide some kind of statistics service for web sites:

- alexa.com
- Google Analytics (www.google.com/analytics/)
- statcounter.com

The other results are large web sites that provide all kinds of statistics about Federal taxes and really old information dating back to 1998.

The Alexa web site information

When you open the link to alexa.com, you will see the section **Movers & Shakers** on the front page, along with the list of the web sites shown in the graph.

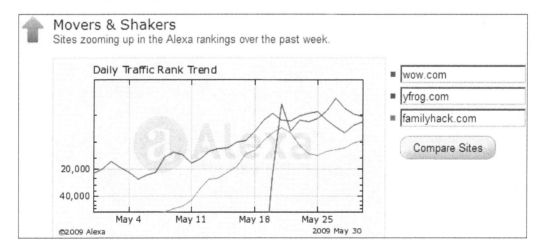

That graph is a nice tool that you can use to compare you web site to those of your competitors' sites. But if you want more data about your site (and that of your competitors' sites) click on the menu link on top that says **Site Info**. Now you get two option fields — **Keyword Search** (to enter the keyword you want to search) and **Site Lookup** (where you can put in a URL).

The first option is nice to work with if you need to find web sites related to your web site's topic. We will be coming back to this option once you start working on your incoming links. The second option is what we are looking for now — the data that `alexa.com` has about your web site. So, go ahead and put your URL in the right field and hit **Go**.

Ah, well… you might not be ranking in the first 100,000 ranking sites of Alexa and that is why you won't see a graphic for your traffic stats displayed. However, next to the graph your ranking is displayed, along with the progress (or regression) you made in the previous month and the previous quarter.

However, what you might be more interested in are the three tabs on the right — **Bounce**%, **Time on Site**, and **Search** % (the options shown in the preceding screenshot).

- **Bounce**%: This gives you an indication of the stickiness factor of your site
- **Time on site**: This gives you an indication if your content is read
- **Search**%: This offers you the percentage of traffic going to your web site through search engines

We will cover these topics in a detailed manner in the Google Analytics section where there is even more data to show, and more explanations on what you can do with this kind of data.

Two more tabs, namely **Related Links** and **Keywords** are also good to check to see if you are on track with your keyword list. More important is the fact that you can also get data about your competitors.

So the question that needs to be asked is: *Is Alexa.com a good tool to get your web site's statistics, and is it an depth analysis tool?* Well, it is not—it will give you only some insight into the traffic numbers of your competitors' sites. But it is a great tool, just like Webalizer if you want to get a global idea about the status of your web site when you look at traffic and search terms. You can do that in less than five minutes and for free as well.

But you want more. You want real data that you can use to improve your rankings. You want data that gives you the information you need to find the weak spots and the strong performers within your site! So, what you need is a detailed tracker that doesn't strain your hosting server, and wouldn't it be nice if it was available free of charge?

Getting free site analysis from StatCounter and Google Analytics

We have already seen in Chapter 1 how to put up these counters and how to implement them on your Joomla! web site. The best way to integrate them into your site is by using modules. This is because if you change your template the counters will still work, provided your template uses the module positions, else you just have to move the module to a position that is used. As we saw in Chapter 1, you can place it as the last module in the left or right menu position.

The main reason for giving you the information in Chapter 1 is to make sure that you started monitoring your traffic as soon as possible. If you have not yet implemented a counter such as StatCounter or Google Analytics, drop everything and get it into place! It will take you about five minutes only and the rewards are of a much greater value than you can imagine right now.

Looking at your StatCounter stats

A few years back you could get detailed information on the last 100 pageviews, which has now increased to 500 page views—thanks to the great service offered by statcounter.com, which has been running for many years.

If you want a large number of pageview details to analyze, you can upgrade and pay for a 1500 to 100,000 detailed page quota with a price that is stated on a per month/ per year basis. If you upgrade to 1500 pageviews, you get a total of 2000 because the 500 free pageviews are added to it. This is the one I implement on every site, along with Google Analytics, and is the one I look at every day!

Now, why is that? This is because I get an overview of all my web sites (project) on one page and with numbers that I can compare easily. I also have a separate account to monitor all my customers' web sites and I can even give each of them separate access to the statistics of their web sites only. Also, the statistics are easy to read, and the customers can look at their site's statistics without my help.

When you log in to StatCounter, you get a project page overview with the headers as shown in the following screenshot:

You also get the project details line, which has some icons displayed on it.

We will go into the details of some options and functions you get from StatCounter and learn how to use them.

- **Project Name**:

    This is the description of your site that makes it easy for you to identify it. In most cases you will have the URL of your site put in, but if you have more sites you might want to group them together on a certain topic or hosting package. In that case, you will be pleased to know that the page is sorted alphabetically and you can change the description by clicking on the wrench icon of the project at hand.

- **Type**:

    The project type will be **Standard** unless you upgrade. Once you upgrade, the name changes to the one you upgraded to.

- **Today**, **Yesterday**, **This Month**, and **Total**:

  These options will give the number of pageviews that your site generated. If you look at this every day, you will know instantly if something is wrong with your site. If the numbers you expect to see don't match with the actual numbers, it is time to investigate what happened — did your site get hacked, did its rankings drop, or was it a major holiday that impacted your numbers? All kinds of questions come up if the numbers are not as expected. Here is an example of a graph that indicated such an event:

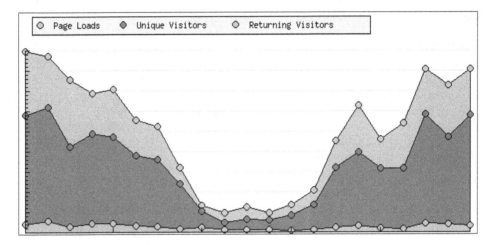

In this case a 301 redirect hack was placed in the `.htaccess` file, which led all visitors from Google, MSN, and Yahoo! to a different web site. In this case the effect was noticed within couple of days and corrected quickly. However, as there was no sign of a hack on the site, it took some investigation to determine what had happened.

Imagine if you did not have a tool like this, or you only looked at it once every three months or so. Your site could have been completely removed from the search engines and you would have to put in some major effort to get it back to the top position in the rankings. This example is just to show you why you need to look at those statistics at least once a week, and don't go crazy looking at them every hour! You can spend your time in a much better way by creating new content for your web site.

Don't count your own visits

One option you need to set within StatCounter is a blocking cookie and, if you have a static IP address from which you browse the Internet, it's good to block that too. If you don't know that static IP address (mostly used by broadband connections), visit your web site that has a StatCounter script running and click on a few pages, then look at the recent visitors activity and you will see your own visit and IP address shown so that you just have to copy it. To block that address you click on the wrench icon again and select **Settings**.

IP Blocking
You can specify your IP Address
86.83.117.90 or a range such as
212.14.23.* or even 212.*.*.* to be
blocked. This prevents you or someone
from your organisation inflating your count.
Put each IP address on a new line with no
spaces if you want it blocked. Or empty the
box if you want to count all visits.

Update IP Blocking in All Projects?
Tick this box if you would like your IP
blocking updated in all your projects.

In the lower part of the screen you will see a form where you can paste your own IP address. If you have multiple projects set up already, you can update this field across all projects at once. If you do this on the account where you have your customer's IP address blocked, the later options will overwrite all those values, so be careful in such a case.

Now go back to the wrench overview screen, go to the function **Create Blocking Cookie,** and click on the button that says **Stop logging my visits**. From this moment onwards, only the real visits from other computers are included in the statistics and your own visits are no longer counted.

If you want to change the display of your counter or if you need to retrieve the installation code again, you can get it from here as well. If you want to show off your visitor numbers and want the colors of that counter to match your site's layout, that can also be accomplished here.

Personally I don't like those counters anymore, they have these 90s look and feel and they don't provide any extra information to your visitors. In some cases I show a StatCounter button if it makes sense to show it, for example on site building web sites, otherwise I use the invisible option.

If you are worried about what search engines might think of such an outgoing link, keep in mind the statcounter.com is one of the very few web sites that have a PR of 8 and at one time even had a 10 (Google also has a PR of 8).

Looking at StatCounter information and graphs

Once you have logged in to StatCounter, you can select the project that you want to analyze. The first thing that will be shown is a graphic display of your web site's traffic. If you start with a project, it is shown as bar graph.

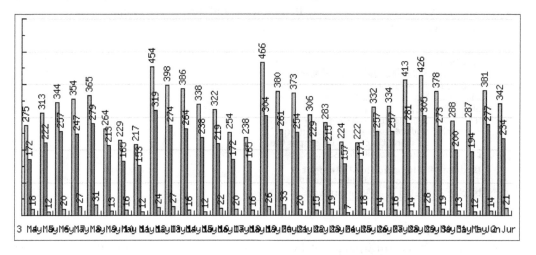

This is really horrible to read and it is advisable to immediately switch to the area graph, which is much easier to read. If you want this to be your standard view, select the little option **Save As Default** and push the **Submit** button.

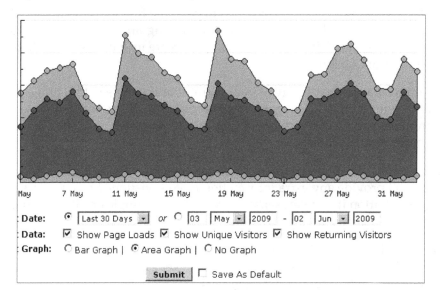

You can see several options to check your statistics over different time periods. Above the graph you have view options such as **Daily (default)**, **Weekly**, **Monthly**, **Quarterly**, and **Yearly**. If you use those options, you will also get an area graph with the data compressed for that time frame. On the yearly graph, you can see when you started with StatCounter, it shows data going back several years. This is useful for sites that have been established for a long time. Beside the graph you have a long list of menu options.

```
STATISTICS
Summary
Popular Pages
Entry Pages
Exit Pages
Came From
Keyword Analysis
Recent Keyword Activity
Recent Came From
Search Engine Wars
Visitor Paths
Visit Length
Returning Visits
Recent Pageload Activity
Recent Visitor Activity
Recent Visitor Map
Country/State/City/ISP
Browsers
System Stats
Lookup IP Address
Download Logs
```

You can go through all of these, but the things you should use are:

- **Came From**: To see where your visitors are coming from
- **Keyword Analysis**: To learn which search terms are performing well for you
- **Recent Visitor Activity**: Here you can see in great detail what your visitor is doing on your web site

Some items in the following screenshot have been altered for privacy reasons, but it should be is clear that you can get a lot of useful information. You can see the navigation path through your web site in a table following the text **Navigation Path**.

If it is a returning visitor, you can also see on which dates he/she visited your site.

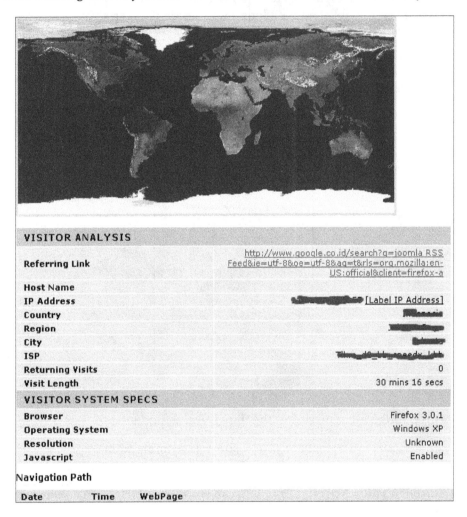

If you have an international site, you might be interested in the **Recent Visitors Map.**

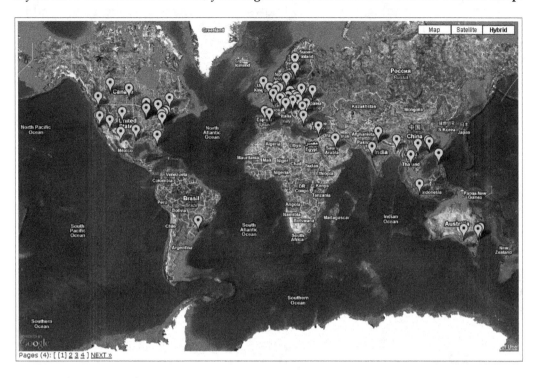

All these options and graphics tell you a lot about your web site. As I mentioned before, you not only see how your traffic is growing over time, but, for example, you can also analyze traffic spikes to see if somebody placed a link on Stumblr or even Digg. But it could also be because of a blog post you made, or perhaps somebody with a large number of followers posted a link to your web site. It doesn't matter who or what created that spike—it is important that you analyze and act upon it!

If somebody mentioned your site in a blog post, on a forum, or anywhere else on the Internet, you should at least check it out. In some cases it might be a great way to learn about somebody who writes about the same topic as you do, or you could help someone gain more insight into your writing.

If you are looking at building links to your web site, now is the right time to start as the person recommending you already knows what your site is about. You can add the results from the **Keyword Analysis** to your keyword list and see if they match with your initial research.

Analyzing your site's recent activity can give you a better understanding of the way your visitors navigate through your web site. It involves answering questions such as:

- Did you design the site for the visitors to follow a specific pattern, or the visitors can browse the site as they want
- Should you reflect those patterns in a new menu layout or design

We will see more information on the navigation issue in Google Analytics.

StatCounter is a great tool for getting insight into the main statistics of your web site really fast, and it presents it through nice visual graphics and elements. It is very user friendly and is easy to understand.

The biggest problem is the limited number of pageviews that you can analyze for free. You can upgrade to a paid account if you want to, but for such in depth analysis, I suggest we turn to Google Analytics instead.

How to analyze Google Analytics

As I mentioned before we will be looking at Google Analytics for several options that are not present in the other statistical service options or are very limited. We have already covered some parts of Google Analytics such as setting up the initial mail account and implementation of the code in a module. But now we need to set some extra options before start looking at a large amount of data.

First things first, when you log in and select the web site of your choice, you get a great dashboard that shows you the main statistics for that site.

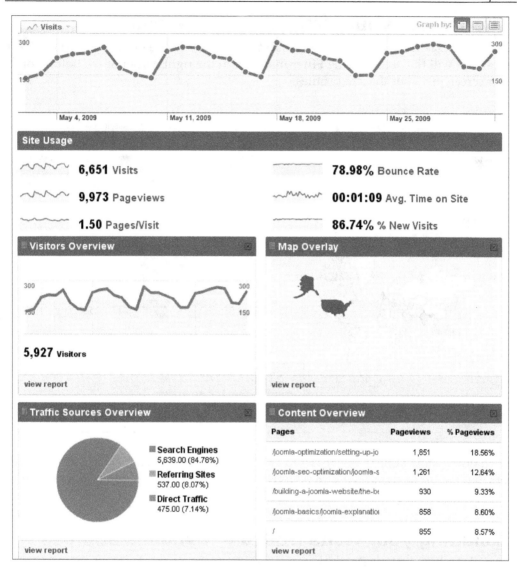

You can alter that dashboard later, if you want some different views. But one of the things that we really need to do right now is to filter our own visits. If you have a static IP address, you can set up a filter.

Filtering out your static IP address visits

Go to your **Dashboard** and click on **Analytics Settings** in the upper left corner of page. You will find a link to the **Filter manager** in the right corner at the bottom of your screen just after the site profiles.

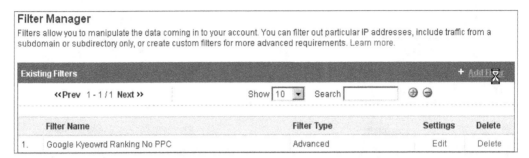

Now you can add the following filter:

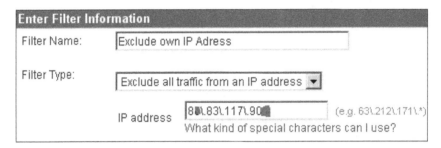

If you don't know your IP address you can look it up at www.whatsmyip.com. Please note that the input should be formed as 63\.212\., and so on, so don't forget to put the "\" in the right place.

Excluding your visits from a IP dynamic address

If you don't have a static IP address you need to create a page for your web site that contains a special string for a cookie to be set. The page should contain the following code:

```
<body onLoad="javascript:__utmSetVar('no_report')">
```

Create that page outside Joomla! as a standard HTML file that only you know about. The HTML page you create only needs to contain this string, so you don't need to create a new content page. After you placed the file online using FTP, you can browse to it using the URL you have chosen, and upon opening the page with your browser the cookie is set.

If you want to filter out other computers please go to that page using that computer. Now you are ready to create a new filter with the following settings:

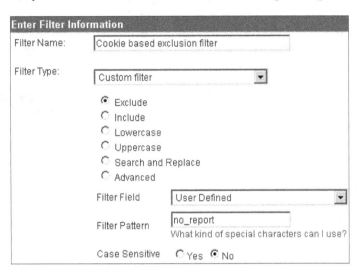

That should do the trick and clean your future visits. Looking at your Dashboard menu you have several options, the best to start with:

- Visitors — the overview
- Traffic Sources
    - Referring sites
    - Keywords
- Content
    - Top landing pages
    - Site overlay

Getting the big picture of traffic

Let's look into the specific areas of your Google Analytics and see what you can do with all that data.

Visitors overview

In the default screen of the visitor overview you get a graphical expression of your web site's state of growth over the last month. In this specific graph you can see the wave movement of weekend drops in traffic. You also get the numbers that give you an expression of how well your site is built to get people to read more than just one page.

In this case there is work to be done as **1.5 Average Pageviews** for the site in question is not good enough. If it was a blog, then it would not be a problem as blog post readers tend to read one article and then move on.

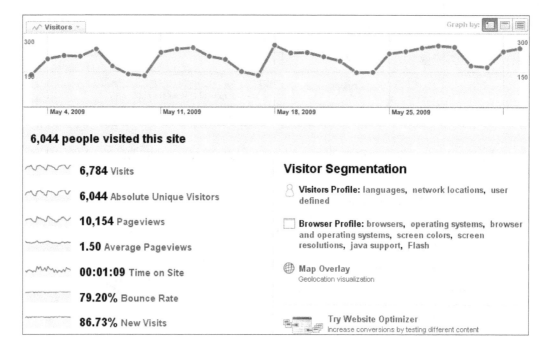

To compare the figures above, here is another screenshot of a different web site for the visitors overview:

As you can see, the numbers are very different. This site has many returning visitors and a very low bounce rate.

What to look for by numbers

Let's look at what information we should look for in the numbers shown in the preceding screenshot:

- **The visitors:**

  The numbers you saw in the two preceding screenshots tell you how often the site is visited. You can see how many visitors you get (in both cases for a month), along with the number of unique visitors. A unique visitor is tracked by a cookie that Google places on the computer of your visitor. These cookies have a long lifespan, some up to five years. This means if a visitor revisits your site in a month or two, he/she is seen as a returning visitor. If your visitor clears their cookies or has cookies disabled, his/her next visit is counted as a unique visit. The last option is an indication of whether your site attracts people who are coming back to your site to read more over and over again, or if they are just one day flies who move on and never return. If your site is an e-commerce site, then you really want more returning visitors because they are more willing to buy after a few visits to your shop.

- **The pageviews**:

  While the number of pageviews is a traffic indicator, the number of pageviews per visit is a quality indicator. A page in this respect is not a reload of the article your visitor is reading, but it is the page displayed if the visitor moves to read a new article on your site. The more pageviews per visit, the better the site is at retaining visitors and encouraging them click through to other pages on the same site.

- **Time on site**:

  The time that a visitor spends on your site is also a good quality indicator, but it can also have a different meaning. If your site is very fast loading (which it should) and mostly picture based, you can go through relevant pages very fast. If you have a long loading time, few pages, and short content per page, you need to check your loading time. It is very likely you will see fewer returning visitors as well.

- **Bounce rate**:

  A high bounce rate means that people will come to your site, read a page, and will move on to the next site. This can also be seen as a quality score. In most cases a low bounce rate means people have a higher interest in your web site and find the information good enough to browse around. A high bounce rate can also be an indication of good quality—it depends on what kind of site you have built. A site that wants to capture the visitors and keep them on the site has bounce rates and time spend on the site different as compared to a site made for AdSense or an affiliate site. The last two (AdSense and an affiliate site) want their visitors to click on an advertisement or move to a vendor's site. So, if they do that well, visitors won't stay long! If you have a site that presents people with solutions for their problems, then a high bounce rate could also mean that they have found the information they wanted right away and they are off to implement it.

In all the previous four cases, you need to take the actual purpose of the web site into consideration. An e-commerce web site has to have a different visitors' overview than an affiliate web site. The first one needs returning visitors to do well, the second one needs to get their visitors to act and buy the product from another web site.

If you find very large discrepancies for your site, you know that the layout of your site and the articles need more work to capture your visitors. A very good indicator is the **Benchmarking** function, which you can find a link to, in the visitor menu. To get those benchmarks you need to share your data (anonymously) with Google.

The question is: *Is it worth it?* Well, the answer is yes. Just look at the following picture and you will have some good indicators, which will show whether your site is doing above or below average.

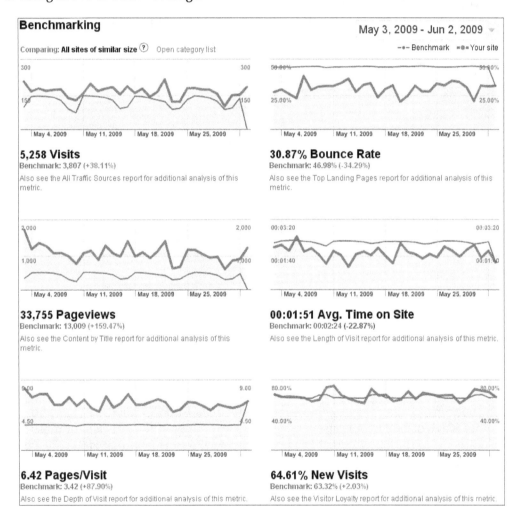

Learning more of you traffic sources

The traffic sources screen is clearly divided into several sections to give you a direct view of the different sources that bring traffic to your web site. Having a large percentage of visitors through search engines means you have done your SEO work well. But the higher it is, the larger the drop will be if your ranking in the results starts to fall.

What you are looking for is direct visitors who know your web site address already and more referring sites. We will be looking at ways to get those links to your site in the next chapter.

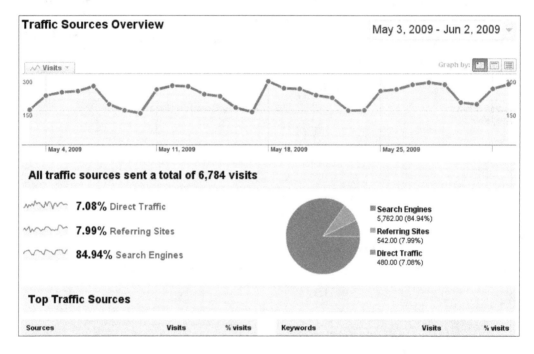

At the bottom of the screenshot there are two sections — one is called **Sources** and the other **Keywords**. There is also a table that shows the top five for each of those fields directly, and following that is a link called **Full report**, and that is the one you want for the keywords.

For the traffic sources, you need to look at the following two options in the traffic sources menu.

- **Referring Sites**:

    This is a great source overview to see what sites are linking to your pages and are sending you traffic. You can use this list to find possible partner web sites to start communicating, sharing, and exchanging links with. You can also identify possible scraper sites that use your RSS feed or articles to their benefit. It is up to you if you want to take action on those sites. It is possible that they are sending you more traffic than you might have expected.

- **Search Engines**:

    This gives you a table with the search engines that send you traffic. In most cases this will be Google, followed by Yahoo!, and then the smaller search engines. If you click on the search engine's name in that table you will get the keywords in that engine that have sent you the most traffic. It is very much possible that your Yahoo! keyword terms are different to those from Google.

Reading more about your Keywords

The **Keywords** section of Analytics will give you, just as the other statistics providers have done, the keywords that rank at top in the search engines at this time. Google does not stop after 500 pages. It will give you all the keywords for that month or any other time period you select. In the example we used it means there are 2.456 keywords that have directed traffic to your web site.

Looking through such a list will give you all kinds of variations for the same keyword combinations. You need to look at the top 25 or 50 and see if there is a pattern that matches your keywords list. If there is, you are on the right track.

Don't see a keyword pattern

If there is no pattern visible, you have to work harder as the visitors you are attracting are not the ones you want to come to your site. Most of them will be incidental visitors that were misdirected. As we have seen before, this might also be supported by a high bounce rate.

A large number of totally unrelated keywords means not only your visitors are lost but also the search engines. Go back to your keyword list and start working to get them a place in your articles and make sure that the menus and categories of your site match in a topical structure.

Structure and content analysis

The last, but certainly not the least important section is all about content, which is the cornerstone of your web site.

Take your time to go through all the different menu items to look at the pages in your site from different angles. One thing you might notice is the fact that your top landing pages are also your top exit pages. This is also largely dependent on the topic of your site and your site's "stickiness".

Again it is totally different for e-commerce sites and affiliate sites. If the top exit page for your e-commerce site is the page just before the checkout payment page, you need to analyze the process and see how to improve that final page. Just improving that single page may result in a lot more transactions being completed.

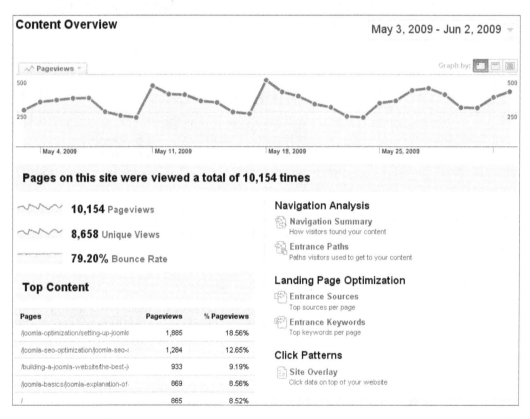

Another way to see how your pages are helping you to keep more visitors is by using the **Navigation Summary**. This will show you which pages your visitor visited next and tells you the exit click and next page click percentages. The entrance paths will show you in a clear manner the pages to which people are moving next.

Site Overlay

The **Site Overlay** is one of my favorite tools. It opens in a new window and puts an overlay over your web site as a kind of transparent sheet. On that sheet Google shows you the number of clicks that have been done on a specific item. You can click through and navigate your web site right through that overlay and see the click information in numbers and percentages for each item. Now, you can see where people click on your site and which items are not as popular as you might have thought. In one case I noticed that a certain image was clicked on a lot, but there was no action attached to that image. By connecting a link to a relevant page that fits the image I realized a higher click through rate, more pageviews and, even more important, a better experience for my visitors as they clearly expected the image to be clickable.

How to select a different time span

In the standard view, Google Analytics shows data for just a month. You can select another time span by clicking on the start date and an end date for the **Date Range** in the agenda and then hitting **Apply**.

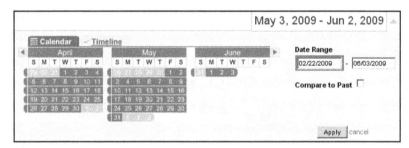

You can also select the **Timeline** and change it by moving and/or extending the sliders. This might give you a better view if you are looking for a special spike or drop in your site's traffic.

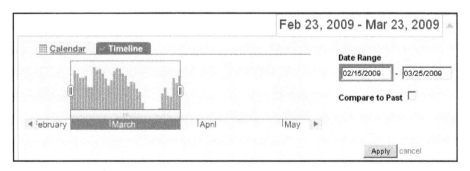

If you select a large time range, you may need to try and use the other views such as week-or month-based graph.

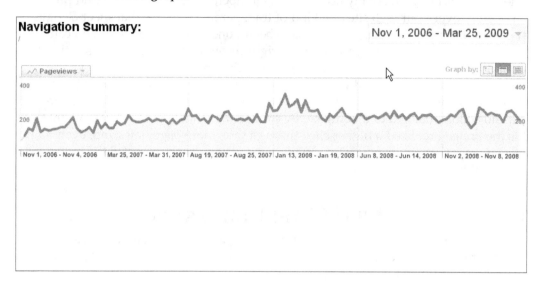

You can even compare two different date ranges to see how your traffic has changed.

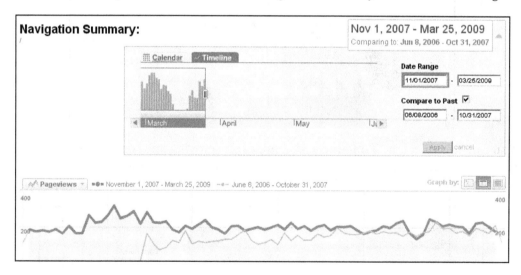

Joomla! statistics

If you are done with this chapter, you might be wondering why I have not mentioned the Joomla! statistics components and the statistics that Joomla! gathers. They will only show you the number of hits your articles have had and that can be cleared by clicking on the **Reset** button.

Article ID:	7
State	Published
Hits	4 Reset
Revised	1 Times
Created	Tuesday, 01 September 2009 15:00
Modified	Not Modified

The reason I haven't included any Joomla! statistics components is due to the fact that they slow your site down over time as the data in your database grows. Most of the components are also focused on visitor numbers and not on how they got to your web site. Having a nice module with a number of visitors to your site may sound appealing, but it offers no insight to the behavior of those visitors.

I have run Joomla! statistics components on several of my sites, but now, they are all replaced by StatCounter combined with Google Analytics. These services give you more information that you can use to further optimize your site than any Joomla! component I have seen.

Summary

The first lesson of traffic analysis is that you can never have enough data! You just need time to go through the different options and services. Using those data sources, you will come to know whether your Search Engine Optimization efforts have paid off.

If you follow the things explained in this book, you should see an increase in traffic coming from search engines as well as referring sites. You can also check if your site layout and visitor expectations match your web site building ideas. If they are better fitted together, you should see a lower bounce rate and a larger number of page views per visit. The time spent by the visitor on your site would then increase.

The nice thing about analytics tools such as StatCounter and Google Analytics is the fact that they store a large amount of data for you. They also operate on fast, special servers for data collection and, as their code should be somewhere towards the end of the HTML code of your site, there should be little to no impact on the site's performance.

As you start working further towards optimizing your web site, you can see which actions have a positive impact and which don't work for your web site.

Keeping tabs on your site with your statistics and analytics tools working on them, is an ongoing effort that you need to do at least once a month. That will give you a better understanding of the tools, a better insight into your web site and its visitors, and give you the joy of seeing your hard work pay off.

10
How to get Incoming Links

Incoming links are still considered one of the better ways of improving your rankings in the search engine result pages. But is every incoming link an improvement? Or, can there be incoming links that will bring your site down?

We will be looking at the different ways to get incoming links and how to avoid the wrong links coming in to and going out of your site.

There are a few ways to get links to your web site, which we will learn about in this chapter, including:

- Using paid options
- Using forums to get incoming links
- Commenting on other web sites to get links
- Building your own incoming links
- Using your best content for link building
- Writing articles for links
- Don't be afraid to ask

Do you want to use paid incoming links?

Paying for incoming links can be a tricky business if you do it the wrong way. Google doesn't like web sites that use this link building technique and their representative master anti-spam spokesman, Matt Cutts is very clear on this subject.

Buy links and get penalized… sell links and get penalized as well

The major penalty is a very likely drop in Page Rank. Although Page Rank is becoming less important as compared to your rankings on the search engine result pages, people still see it as a quality making if you do have a high Page Rank. Of course using AdWords to do a "Pay Per Click" campaign is also a form of paid links.

If you want to use the sponsored link options to get your site started, that is fine, but the ultimate goal of this book is to get higher rankings in the organic results of the search engines. Studies support the idea of using sponsored links to bring in more traffic from the organic searchers even after the campaign has stopped. It depends on how hard you need the traffic to your site for business, or if you want to go for organic results.

Helping people helps you with link building

If you have a topic that you are passionate about and you build a web site about it, then this option is one for you. Find a forum that matches the topic of your web site and start helping other people with your knowledge. On most forums there is a possibility to have your own "Signature", where you can have one or more lines of text with a link that people can click on.

For instance, the site `http://forums.digitalpoint.com` has a lot of requests for information on Joomla! where you can help people to solve their problems. After a number of replies to questions, you can put in your own signature such as:

Preview

Just Ask, or you never get an answer..
Joomla Search Engine Optimization
Joomla SEO Blog | WordPress and Joomla SEF and SEO Information and Tutorials

The links you put in there will not only bring traffic from your posts, but they also count as incoming links for Google. Not all forums have the same rules—for example, some of them have a rule that you can put a link to your site, but it should be the URL only without your main keywords in the link.

So, be sure to go to the best forums you can find on your topic and start helping others with your knowledge. In the meantime, work on your incoming links as well.

Commenting done the right way

Another option you have is to look for blogs about your web site's topic. You will already probably know the most useful ones in your field of expertise. Go to those blogs and read some of the posts they have published. If you are lucky, there will be some kind of widget that shows you how many readers they have on that blog for their RSS Feed or email system.

Large numbers are a good sign as that means a lot of people will read the blog and it probably has a good ranking in Google. Read the posts that are relevant to your topic and if you can, write a comment which shows that you know more about the topic. Also, if possible, make a new suggestion or correct an error in the article.

Don't write comments such as "I really liked this post", "Thank you for this information", or even "I really like your blog". If you write comments such as those you won't get any interaction with the blogger in question and you don't add value to the discussion. Such comments will get deleted or labeled as spam. When I get comment links such as these, I remove them as they add null to zero information for other visitors and they are clearly there just for link building. It won't work that way, and if you are outsourcing or want to outsource this kind of link building, here is a warning, make sure you state in your contract with these people that blog and comment spamming is not allowed!

If you don't add that clause, they may start commenting in your name, linking to your site (well, you paid them to do that...) with the same remarks over and over again. What happens next is that bloggers will ban you from commenting on their blogs, and in the worst case scenario you will loose a lot of credibility in your community. People are sometimes better informed than you think and a mistake like the one mentioned above will cost you more than money alone.

So, if you start commenting, ask yourself:

- Do I have something of value to add to the conversation?
- Will people read that comment?
- How effective will this blog be in sending me traffic?

Keep those in mind, with more emphasis on the first point, and you will do fine.

Finding places to comment

As I said before, commenting is a great way to create your own incoming links. But how do you find more relevant blogs to read and comment on? First of all, do a search for blogs about your web site's topic. You can use `http://blogsearch.google.com/` to find the most recent blog posts and see if the blogs it finds fit your web site's topic.

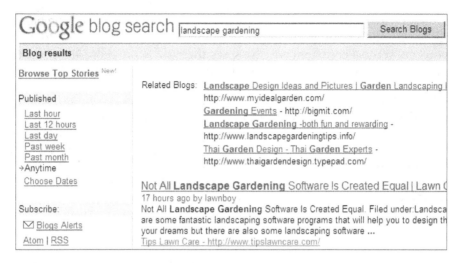

Technorati is of course the best place to look for blogs.

Go ahead and use the option **search the blogosphere...**. From the results of this initial search, you can filter based on several options. In the first selection list you will find options such as **Search Posts**, **Search Blogs**, **Search Photos**, and **Seach Videos**. The second selection list allows you to filter based on **entire post** or just **tags**. The third option is the one you really need to set and there you can choose to filter **on a lot of authority**.

This option means a lot of people are linking to that web site/blog and it will probably get lots of traffic and do well in the search engines. Those blogs are the ones you want your voice to be heard on and remember if you are going to comment, make sure it is a useful one.

What you need to do after finding the blog, is to really check out the site. In some cases there might just be one post about your web site's topic on that blog. And you really want it to be on topic all the way!

Two other blog search services you can use are:

- http://www.icerocket.com

- http://www.blogpulse.com

Both are set up to bring to you the most recent results like Google does but they have something extra. You can learn about trends as Icerocket has a trend tool and Blogpulse has its trend search option.

Using those trend tools will give you more insight on which terms are "hot" at the moment and growing. If you combine that with the blogs you just found, for your keywords, you could have a winning team.

Looking back at Alexa

We looked at alexa.com in the chapter about analytics and I told you we would be back later. Alexa is also a good tool to find web sites related to your own topic and check their influence in the blogsphere. Now is the time to head back to the blogs and web sites you have recently found and want to comment on. Check their ranking in Alexa and, most importantly, check the incoming links.

Use the tool that Alexa gives you to find a few web sites that you can really relate to. In my case I wanted a site about "landscape gardening" and I found www.thegardenhelper.com.

Now, The Garden Helper does pretty well in Alexa and is a very ancient web site, dating all the way back to 1998.

The site is not my kind of design and you cannot comment on the site itself, but they have a forum on which you can help and leave some traces. But what we are really interested in, from Alexa, are two items from this info page:

- **Sites Linking In:** It is on the top line with the traffic rank numbers and will show you other web sites that are linking to this site. You should check some of them to see if they have blogs where you can participate in the conversation. You can also ask them to link to your site if the topic is related and you think it would be of benefit to their visitors.

- **Related Links:** This tab will show you other web sites that are also on the topic of site you found. Sites such as `gardenweb.com`, have several subdomains including `voices.gardenweb.com`—a blog where you can leave comments.

As you can see finding relevant sites that give you the opportunity to comment, can be a cumbersome task. However it is worth the effort, especially in your initial link building. You might find that searching for blogs about the topic of your web site is a lot easier than it was for this gardening site. It maybe difficult also. It depends on the keywords you are going to target and the popularity of the topic of your site.

Commenting on a blog takes time and effort to do it the right way. Another way to comment is to link back to articles on a relevant web site and hope that they will show the trackback to your web site. If they don't show the trackback, you have at least provided your visitor with a valid link and you can hope that the webmaster of that site may link back to your site over time.

Creating your own linking empire

Besides blog comments and forum posts you can build your own little linking empire. To do that you can use several free blogging and page building services that are free of charge. We will be looking at services such as:

- Google Sites
- Blogger (`blogspot.com` domains)
- Squidoo
- HubPages
- WordPress

WordPress is the big one when it comes to creating highly relevant incoming links that will perform well in the search engines. We will be looking into WordPress in depth rather than the other services.

Remember, we are building links that themselves need to score well in the search engine results to get the most benefit from our work. So, how much work does it take and how difficult is it to work with those services to create good ranking results that will benefit your site in the long run?

Google Sites

If you have a Google account, go to your account page and look for **Sites.** Click on the **Create site** button and start building your pages. A sitemap is created directly and if you want to edit your page, use the **Edit page** button on the top righthand corner of your screen. In my case I got a nice URL, `http://sites.google.com/site/landscapegardening/`, to work with. Next to the edit page button is a drop-down menu named **More actions**, where you can select **Manage site** to change your theme and other settings later.

On this mini site you need to write some good quality content, that is also on topic, for your main site. Using these pages and the sidebar you can create links with your targeted keywords to link back to your main web site.

Blogger

Blogger is also a free service from Google. It will give you a URL that ends in `.blogspot.com` unless you host on a subdomain of your main site. However, in this case you are building links outside your domain, so the links will end with `blogspot.com`.

Again, if you are logged in to your Google account you will see the service **Blogger** on your account page. If you haven't used it before, click on the line that says **try something new** and choose it from there. If you click on it you go to `blogger.com` where you need to sign in with your Google mail (Gmail) account.

Once you are logged in, there is a three step track to get you blogging:

- Sign up with Blogger: Accept the terms and set your screen name.

- Name your blog: Give it a title and check if the URL you want is available. You might need to be somewhat creative here, as there are already a lot of blogspot sites around.

- Choose a Theme: You can change it later if you don't like the colors or layout.

Try using "-" between the keywords you want to use, if the name you want for your blog is taken.

Start blogging!

On a blog, you don't build a web site like you do with Joomla! it is just publishing posts that will show up in a top to bottom list starting with the most recent post. With Blogger you can also create trackbacks and links to your web site, again with the main keywords or a variation as the link text.

Depending on how much competition you are facing in the search engine results pages you may need to create several posts to be noticed. If you want to spend some money to use a better domain name than `yoursitename.blogspot.com`, then I suggest you pay for the option to switch to a custom domain. You could also choose to refer it to the subdomain of your site. For better value to building incoming links it is recommended to use a separate domain. This option will change the URL's to a `.com` or other domain name, but you still use Blogger to write and post your articles.

The custom domain will costs you approximately 10 USD per year (at the time of writing) and will give you more credibility than a `.blogspot.com` site.

Squidoo

On `squidoo.com` you don't blog or create pages, you build a **Lens**. A Squidoo lens is one big page where you can put in all your knowledge about the topic of your interest. For example, you can write text, embed videos, and embed RSS Feeds from your Blogspot or WordPress blog, so you only have to write things once and the lens will be updated automatically. Your Squidoo lens is built using modules that contain the content you want to publish. Creating a lens is not that difficult. Just follow the steps mentioned next:

1. Log in to Squidoo and click the button **Create a Lens!**.

2. Once you have done that, write the topic of your lens (What is your lens about).
3. What is the goal of your lens, here you can choose from four options. I suggest to start with the standard easy one.
4. Set the URL of your lens and the category.
5. Tag your lens with the most important keywords and fill in the security word.

Now you are done! Start working on the lens, and don't forget to include the link to your web site.

HubPages

A hubpage works the same way as a Squidoo lens. You create an account and start your first Hub. If you have set the basic title for your article the URL is taken from that title. In the next step you will get a warning about what you should not do on HubPages and a single line about **What Works**.

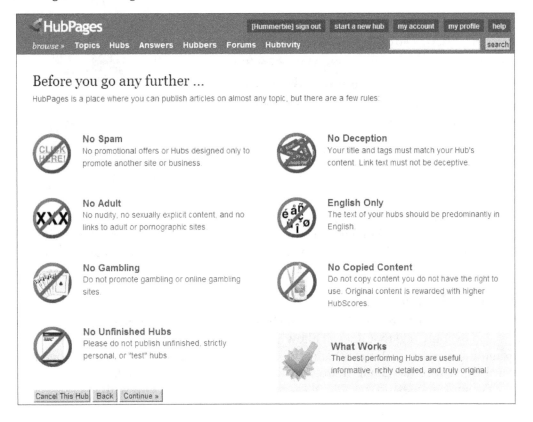

The next screen before you get your first Hub is a security screen to prevent automatic creation of Hubs. Now start building that Hub page and take your time to do it, write quality content about your topic, and make use of elements such as images to break the page.

 Create valid Hubs, otherwise they will not be given the power that you want them to have. HubPages has a system in place that will flag your Hub as over promotional or/and substandard.

Hubs are built with building blocks called capsules. On the righthand side you see an overview of all the different kind of capsules you can use, as shown in the following screenshot:

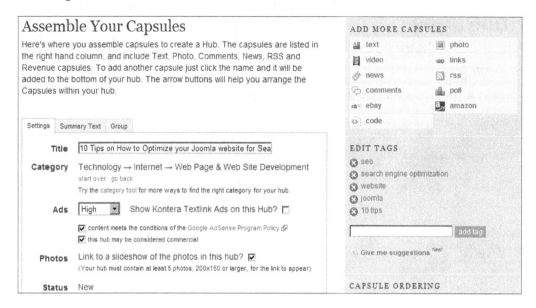

Naturally, you want to keep these capsules in mind as again there is a possibility to embed an RSS Feed. You should add the RSS Feed from your Joomla! web site to your Hub, in order to ensure fresh content every time you update your web pages.

WordPress

As I mentioned before, WordPress is the biggest scoring free service that you can use. It is also the only one that doesn't allow you to spam their system and use it just for promotional actions. All the other services mentioned earlier allow you to monetize your blog or web site. Some share a portion of their revenue as well. So, if you want to make some money on the side, these services will provide you with the possibility to do so.

WordPress doesn't allow you to build blogs just for Search Engine Optimization and I quote:

> *We have a very low tolerance for blogs created purely for Search Engine Optimization or commercial purposes, machine-generated blogs, and will continue to nuke them. So if that's what you're interested in, WordPress is not for you. A self-hosted solution would be much more appropriate for you; suitable hosts can be found at* `http://www.wordpress.org/hosting`.

Also see the following text taken from `http://support.wordpress.com/advertising`:

> *This might be just one of the reasons that Google loves WORDPRESS.COM blogs. So how is it possible to use WORDPRESS.COM to promote your website? Actually, you don't. On this service you are not going the promote your site in a way that you can do on the other services. On WORDPRESS.COM you truly build a blog or site containing pages with true value to the visitors of that blog. You can create an About page where you put a link to your main website and in that way show the readers where to get more information. You can also put a link to your website in the link section (Blogroll) together with a few other relevant links that contain valid information.*

Blogging on WordPress and your ranking

If you cannot promote your web site in a big way then what is the point of creating a blog on WORDPRESS.COM? A blog on WordPress can rank highly for the topic that you are blogging about and will give you some SEO love through those rankings. What is more important is the fact that you can take a special topic from your main web site's topic and create a blog around that.

If you write your blog posts well and start to rank on that topic you will be seen as an authority on that topic and people will want to know more about you. That is the main reason to invest time to blog on WORDPRESS.COM to be recognized as an authority in your field of expertise. As you took only one topic out of all the topics that your site is about, you can do it again for another topic as well.

You could also see these blogs as a collection of topic silos that create an array of highly related web sites that point to yours. This kind of link building takes time, and a lot of it! Is it worth it? Yes most certainly, and in more ways than one.

With blogging you can achieve the following:

- An authority status if you do it right
- More traffic to your web site
- Better rankings in the search engines
- More insight into what the visitors of your web site are looking for
- To interact with other people having interest in the same topic as you
- Fun in writing and that will reflect on your site as you want to create more content on that site as well

There is also a downside that you have to consider — it takes time away from building content on your main site and you have to cover more locations to maintain in the beginning. If you use that blog to write some timeless quality content on a niche part of your main site you will find out that you can stop maintaining those blogs after a short period of time. Remember, these are valid blogs to build incoming links to your main site!

Digging deeper into WORDPRESS.COM blogs

Creating a blog on WordPress is also very simple, go to WORDPRESS.COM and get a blog. Wait! Don't go yet! You need a few guidelines to start.

1. Your initial user account name is going to be the first part of your URL, so name it right and remember, you cannot use a "-" in your username. My first account was `seo4joomla` so what I got was `seo4joomla.wordpress.com`. When you are logged in to WORDPRESS.COM and you type in the URL with a new keyword that you want (if it is not taken); you will get the option to add that blog to your account so that you can manage all of your WordPress.COM blogs from one place.

2. Think about the title of your blog, if you want to change it later you can do that in the settings panel.

3. Once you have your new blog, start cleaning.
   - Delete the sample post and the comment along with it.
   - Delete all the links in the blogroll (unless you are going to write about WordPress).
   - Change the base post category from **Uncategorized** to a relevant topic name.
   - Change the name of the links category from **Blogroll** to your most relevant keyword.
   - Delete the **About** page and create a new one with the keywords of your blog in the title. That way your URL (page slug in WordPress) is containing the same keywords.

4. Choose a nice theme layout that fits your topic, and if possible use a customized header. Using a customized header will give your site a slightly different look from the other WORDPRESS.COM web sites.

5. Change the tagline in the general settings and start writing the way you do on your web site!

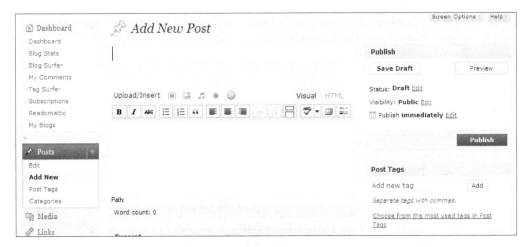

Using free blogging services

As you saw, there are several blogging platforms and free web site building platforms that you can use to promote your web site. There are a lot more out there on the Internet, but you need to look for the ones that rank well in the search engines before you put your valued time into building a linking "empire".

These services are free of charge and sometimes live on the revenue that comes from the blog content they host. If you don't want to be on such a platform where there are advertisements around your writing, don't use them. If you are afraid that you can lose your blog on such sites look for a way to make backups (for example, on WORDPRESS.COM you can use the Export function).

How to minimize your blog writing time

Keeping content fresh and up-to-date on all the blogs that you build is not that difficult. If you focus on blogging on your own web site, you should try to integrate the RSS Feed from your web site into those blog pages. RSS Feeds are the best possible automatic way of updating one-to-many, so use it to your advantage.

Using your best content for link building

Use the best articles from your web site to get into the picture of social bookmarking web sites. Find the most visited pages and the pages with the greatest number of comments, if you have a blog on your Joomla! site. Go to bookmarking sites and bookmark your pages using your own account.

There are a lot of bookmarking web sites that you can use, just make sure you send your bookmarks to at least the following:

- Delicous
- Digg
- Reddit
- Newsvine
- Bloglines
- StumbleUpon

These are some of the most influential ones that count towards your search engine ranking and are a great way to get traffic. Traffic from this kind of web site will come in bursts and mostly will not span a longer time period than a few days.

The real power lies in the long term effect.

Writing articles for links

If you like writing about your passion, you can consider writing articles and submitting them to article publishing services. People are always looking for information and, if you can provide that to them in a smart way, it will help you to gain recognition as a field expert.

You don't have to write long articles, but they must be informative and should give the reader an answer to a question they might have. Write those articles and submit them to services such as:

- www.thewhir.com
- www.ideamarketers.com
- www.goarticles.com
- www.ezinearticles.com

Each of those services have their own "Terms of Service" that you should read before submitting your articles. They have their quality guidelines as well. The length of the article might need to be of a certain minimum or maximum number of characters.

You might not be permitted to link deeper into your web site than the top level. Get that information before you choose a service to work with. Depending on the number of webmasters that will use your articles to republish, you could get a lot more incoming links from just a few well-written articles.

What you should NOT do is take an old article from your site and send it as an article to be republished. That could backfire, as the services mentioned have a clause in their "Terms of Service" stating that the article is original and not published before.

You should really not republish an already submitted article on your own web site, it could give your site a duplicate content penalty as that article will be published all over the Internet (with your link in it). An alternative could be that you publish some of your articles combined and rewritten into an e-book in PDF format that you give away for free from your web site.

Learning how to ask for a link

Sending an email to webmasters asking for a link to your web site is also an option to gain more incoming links. But sending an email with text such as the following will not get you a link from my site.

> *Hello,*
>
> *I have found your web site really informative and I think that my web site http://www.example.com could also be of benefit to your visitors.*
>
> *Please consider placing a link on your web site and send me the page with that link and I will link back to you.*
>
> *With kind regards,*
>
> *Webmaster of http://www.example.com*

So, what is wrong with such a request. You don't use the name of the webmaster or company involved. You don't show that you really visited the site and read some articles. You don't talk about the topics and benefits that visitors might find on your site. You request a link back before you consider placing the site link on your site (a dead give away of non-relevance, otherwise you would have linked to the site already).

You ask for a confirmation of the placed link, which tells me that you don't check the site and you don't have your analytics in order. You don't give out real contact information. Emails such as this look like they may have been sent out by a "link building company" that will spam all webmasters of sites that might be remotely considered "on topic" to your site.

So, don't buy into those services unless you are sure that they know how to do it right. Also include a so called "anti-spam" option in your contract with them to make sure they don't spam, otherwise your carefully built reputation may be shattered to bits.

A better request could have been, for example:

> *Dear Mr Boulden,*
>
> *I really liked reading your web site and particularly your page on xeriscaping. We have a web site on which we write about the elements used in xeriscaping that might be of value to your readers.*
>
> *It contains information about structure and placement of those elements and some reviews of pro and cons of the materials used. You can read it at* `http://www.cblandscapegardening.com/garden-design/xeriscaping.html`*.*
>
> *I hope you would consider linking to it from your page* `http://www.the-landscape-design-site.com/xeriscaping.html` *or from your link page.*
>
> *Maybe you could use this description and code:*
> * *Xeriscape garden elements*
> * *Materials and elements to use an xeriscape garden*
>
> *I hope you find the information on our site of value and would consider a link from your site as a privilege.*
>
> *Please contact me if you have any questions.*
>
> *With kind regards,*
>
> *Herbert-Jan van Dinther*
>
> *Director of Crazy Beez Landscape Gardeners*
>
> `http://www.cblandscapegardening.com`
> Email: `info@cblandscapegardening.com`

Knowing what to include in your link request

As you learned in our mail example, there are some things that you can do to get a conversation going with another webmaster within your niche to get a link.

- **Use the real name or company name:**

  It is much better if you use a real name or company name in your email, it shows that your are really interested in the content of his/her web site and you took the time to get the information.

  In most of the web sites you can look for a contact page and see if it's stated there. Otherwise, check if you can find the information on `http://www.whois.net/`, where you fill in the domain name and voila and you get the information. (In some cases you don't get it because of privacy settings from the hosting/domain provider.)

- **Show that you really visited the site:**

  This is key to your success and you have to read some of the articles. There must be some articles that you like, otherwise you wouldn't even contact the webmaster to get a link on that site. In your mail you can quote some of those articles, link to them, and give some good quality comment on those articles (short please! You don't want to over do it).

- **Tell the site owner about the topics of your articles and benefits to their the visitors:**

  Showing that there are real articles on your site, related to the topic of the site you want the link from, will create curiosity from the other party to check out your web site. Your web site content needs to be "link worthy" for them to host the link on their pages.

  At this point you should include the URL of your web site and you should do this by sending a link such as "Target Keyword and Domain" so that they can easily copy the link into their site and you have some control over the keywords used in the link to your site. This means, you have to provide them with a predefined HTML code that is ready to copy and paste, to make it easy for them to create the link to your site. For example, the HTML code would look like:

  ```
  <a href=" http://www.cblandscapegardening.com/">Landscape
  Gardeners Los Banos </a>
  ```

  If you don't, you will probably end up with `http://www.example.com`, which is not as good as a link with the keywords in it.

- **Put up a link first:**

  When you send a request to get a link to your web site, make sure you have a link to the other site on your web site. Also, make sure you clicked on that link to go to their site.

  It will show up in their statistics and they might even have checked out your site before you send the request.

- **Close your mail by giving out real contact information:**

  Putting the real contact information in the request mail gives you credibility and shows that you are really looking for a conversation with the other party.

  If they have a question for you, they can easily contact you.

- **Getting the link:**

  You send out the mails to the webmasters and you are awaiting a stream of relevant incoming links.

Don't be disappointed if it doesn't work right away. If it is a popular web site, emails for link requests will be coming in all the time, so it might take some time for the webmaster to get to your request. Some people are very picky when it comes to linking out to other web sites (I am), because they really want them to fit into the interest of the targeted audience of their web site.

If you don't get any response, try again in a couple of months and after that next year. Don't start spamming to get your link, it's a sure way of not getting it. The success rate of such link requests are really dependent on the kind of niche you are working in. If it is a high competition niche, you have to work harder and still you cannot expect a high success rate.

Summary

We looked at several options to get incoming links to your web site, including the following::

- Paid links
- Forum signatures
- Commenting on other web sites
- How to start building your own incoming links
- Getting your best content on social marketing sites
- How to publish articles on republishing services
- Asking other webmasters for a link

They all need you to invest time to do it right, and you have to check the results using your analytics options. If you see the traffic coming in, make sure you make the next effort of link building to be easier and more effective. You will know from your statistics what works and what doesn't in your niche.

It takes time to learn and execute the optons and ideas in this chapter, and you don't need to do them all and not even in the order it is written. What you should do is **start!** Start using those free services that can provide you with more incoming links and more direct traffic. It will take time and it will take effort to achieve your goals.

A
A Joomla! Case Study in SEO

In this appendix we will be looking into the complete process of building a demo web site through a case study. In this case study I will show you the steps I took to get a web site up and running with all the SEO options in place.

Is it a real live web site? Well, the answer is *yes*. But it is not for a real company, which limits to local search options using Google maps. Does it rank? Yes, but it needs to grow in content (once I finish writing this book!).

So, here are the steps we need to take, listed in chronological order:

- Pick the niche to build the site in
  - ° Brainstorm for ideas and choose a domain name
  - ° Buy the domain and arrange some hosting
- Set up the Joomla! 1.5 base installation
  - ° Install the SEF patch and sh404SEF component
  - ° Install a good Joomla! SEO template
- Name the sections and categories
- Build the menus
- Install and configure the sitemap
- Write the content
- Use Google webmaster tools
  - ° Analyze your results, rinse, and repeat

Choosing the niche

This involves finding a good niche to place and optimize the web site. This is not always easy to do.

Ideas such as digital photography and credit cards are just too saturated to even think about getting a new web site to rank well, especially in the time plan I wanted to use; you can try to rank for those words, but you will have to work long and hard to get there.

So, I came up with "landscape gardening" in the "Los Banos" CA area. I took a trip to Los Banos in 2001 to visit a family. I also needed a company name to go with the site and there the Beez theme came in and the idea was complete — "The Crazy Beez Landscape Gardening Company" was born.

Picking a domain name

With the niche, name, and location chosen, it was time to find a fitting URL in which it would be nice to have the main keywords. You can imagine that these names were already taken:

- www.landscapegardening.com
- www.landscape-gardening.com
- www.gardenlandscapers.com

Then I included the name of the company into the ideas, but that was getting too long.

- www.crazybeezlandscapegardening.com
- www.crazybeezlandscapegardeners.com

Also, there was some concern about people typing "crazybees" instead of "crazybeez". So, at the end, the domain www.cblandscapegardening.com was registered and put in place as a second domain on a hosting package that I already owned.

In retrospect I think it would have been better to host it with a USA-based hosting provider instead of a Dutch web hosting company. For the target audience this would have been a better choice as it would get an IP address in the USA and with that it would rank better based on Google's geotargeted search results.

Setting up the Joomla! 1.5 base installation

Installing the latest version of Joomla! is probably something that you have done a few times before you got your hands on this book. Basically, you just follow the steps presented by the installer and then delete the installation directory on the server. You can now log in to your web site's administration and configuration panel.

 Create a new "Super Administrator" user or at least rename the standard installation user to something other than "Admin". Use your imagination to make sure it is not simple to hack your site.

Log in with the new username and delete the standard one, which is there by default. Change the name of that user (not the login name) to something different to the username. Check if you can set all the SEO options in the **Global Configuration** and rename your htaccess.txt to .htaccess, so it works in the standard mode.

Installing the SEF patch and sh404SEF component

The JoomlAtWork.com's SEF patch is very easy to install. The free version (make sure you get the right version) is installed by uploading the files using FTP and overwriting the standard Joomla! files. If you buy the full version, it installs like a component, but you will need to change some permissions on a few files.

The component will show you which files need higher permissions to install the full component. The sh404SEF component is installed like a standard Joomla! component. You will need to tweak the .htaccess file a little, to enable support for a third-party component.

Set the configuration to reflect the choices that you made in Chapter 6. Also make sure you have the advanced options active.

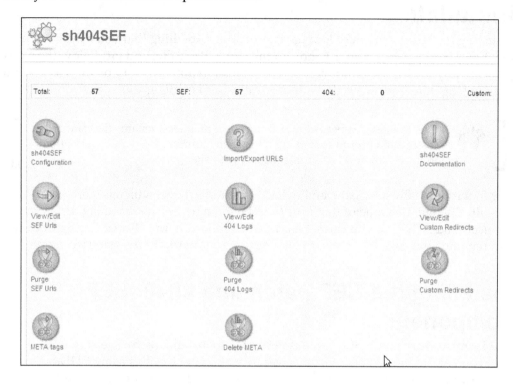

Installing a good Joomla! SEO template

During the process of setting up and creating a base for the landscape gardening site I had gone through three different templates. I started with the default Beez template, as shown in the following screenshot:

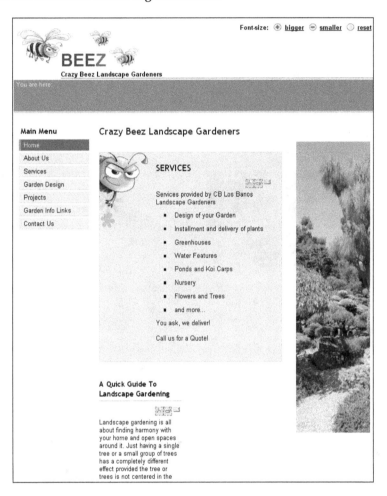

Then I switched to JA Purity, and I also tried Bolt from Alledia.

None of them offered the appearance I wanted for this web site. Fortunately, I discovered a new template called Inspirion, that was recently released by Joomlashack. This template was optimized for SEO, had the color schemes I wanted, and was affordable. So I bought it, installed, and started setting up all the modules to reflect the layout I was looking for. I ran into some issues, but the forum helped out there. The main problem I found was that the active menu tabs in the main menu did not follow once you clicked on one. After I set the module's **Caching** option under **Advanced Parameters** to **No Caching**, it worked correctly, setting all the layout options on the fly.

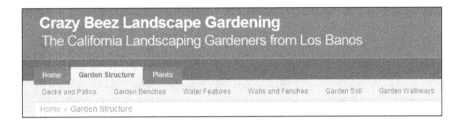

Naming the sections and categories

Once the template was in place, I could focus on improving the names of the sections and categories. Getting this right is critical for the success of the site as it will help the site to gain good rankings. Here the keyword list we built in Chapter 1 comes into play. It will be used to help us to filter and select the main structure and keywords of the site.

The right structure should reflect the "theme" of the site. So, from a long keyword list and with some help from Amazon (look inside the books on the topic of our site, it will give you some hints to create a good structure), the base of the sections is built as follows:

- Plants
- Structure
- Garden design
- Garden plans
- Garden center
- Company information (general information)
- Landscaping projects (used for references and ideas)
- Garden pools blog (the water blog about ponds)

As you can see, this is a large topic to build a site on and these are only the sections. Now, it's time to pick a section and make the category listing that is put into that section.

Here is an example for the Structure section:

- Decks and patios
- Garden benches
- Water features
- Walls and fences
- Garden soil
- Garden walkways

The rest of the categories will reflect a lot of the keywords that can help to attract traffic to this site. As you can see there is a lot of interaction between the categories, which is required to give the search engines an idea on what this site is about.

Even if you have a small site, make sure that the sections and categories are named according to your keyword strategy. It makes it a lot easier for you to structure the content within your site and, if you use other publishers, they will be able to place their articles in the right spot as well.

The way these categories and sections are shown on the site and reflected in the sitemap (that will be installed later) is determined by the menus. In the menu, the site's structure becomes clearer. Keep in mind that this part of building your site is not just for the search engines, it is also for your visitors as it will improve the usability of your site. Your visitors need to be able to find their way through your site as quickly and easily as possible. If you can achieve this, you have a clear structure for search engines in place as well.

Building the menus

The menus in Joomla! are one of the main things that make this content management system so great for some and so difficult for others. In the menu's modules and links, there are so many options to choose from. The following list shows the choices available to link to the articles.

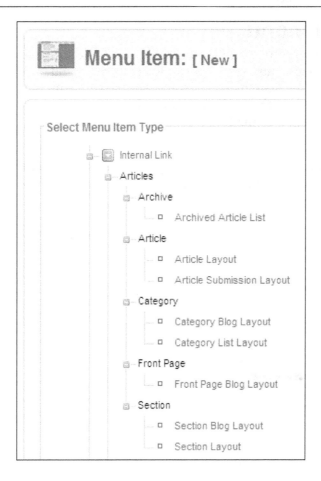

You need to decide the kind of layout you will be using for the site and stick to it. This is the only way to create an easy-to-use, consistent layout of your site. The only time you should divert from your chosen layout option is when a part of your site is really going to benefit from using a different layout. For instance, you could have a lot of table based layouts that hold all the articles to give your readers a quick overview of the content of the site, and use a blog layout for the blog section of your site.

That being said, let's start working on those menus.

The main menu

The main menu is of course the placeholder for the basic structure of the site and should reflect that structure as well. I wanted to have a standard site, so I used the first item from the main menu as **Home**. For the submenu items I placed the standard article links in the **Contact Us** and **About** page, along with the **Sitemap** link page. These pages are made as subpages for the **Home** link.

For the contact page you can use either the standard Joomla! contact component that is built-in or you can create a standard page and give it the layout you want. Here you can see the true power of the SEF patch, as you cannot do this with the standard Joomla! menu item.

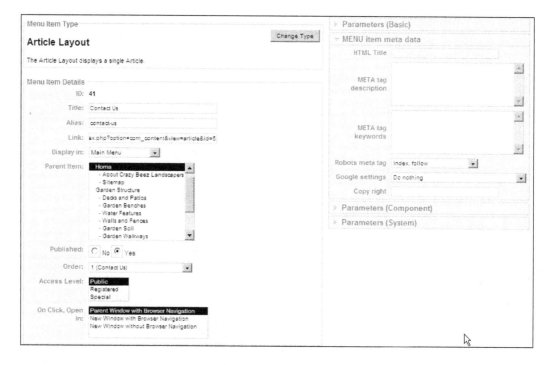

From the SEF patch you get an extra record and fields for the menu items. Consider you wanted to write a better title for the **Contact Us** page. If you used the standard Joomla! system parameter for the title you would see this:

However the HTML title that is seen by Google and other search engines is still "Contact Us" and you should do a Google search on that. With the SEF patch I can now create the HTML title "How to contact CB Landscaper in Los Banos".

If the changes you make are not immediately reflected, make sure to clean the cache of the site and check again. Even more important than the menu's HTML titles are the content HTML titles, which we will be looking at later.

Back to the menu, I have set up more menu items and linked them to the sections with a blog layout. As subpages, each category in that section gets a link to the blog layout for articles. Why choose a blog layout instead of an article list, which seems to do well also? The main reason is the topic of the site.

Landscaping and gardening are visual-orientated topics, and you can do great things with images to make things clear to the visitors of the site. If you have a web site that is really geared toward technical visitors who like, and are used to scanning through article listings, then make sure you use that option.

Using images in blog layout

In this section we will see an example of a page that has images in the category listing. The images are linked to the main category page and all of the images have Alt and Title tags in place. That way your visitor has two options—click on the category title or click on the image to go to that category.

At the end all blog layout pages with categories will show up in the same manner.

Installing and configuring a sitemap

The next thing we need to do is install the sitemap. Here I used Xmap, which is Joomla! 1.5 native. You can install Xmap in the same way you would install other components in Joomla!. Once the installation is complete, the first thing is to set the configuration options. One of the things we need is the path to our XML sitemap. That link is needed to show Google's webmaster tools, where to find the sitemap.

You also have the option to **Show Menu Titles** and **Include link to author** for the Xmap component. I have opted for both, but you might decide otherwise. The best way to decide is to see how the sitemap page looks and if you like it that way.

If you have separate menus for pages such as your disclaimer and privacy statement that you don't want to include in the sitemap, you can exclude their Item IDs. Last but not the least, use the sitemap link in your `robots.txt` file to promote your sitemap to all Search Engine Robots that come along.

```
sitemap: http://www.cblandscapegardening.com/component/option,com_
xmap/lang,en/no_html,1/sitemap,1/view,xml/
```

Make sure the statement is all on one line when you place it in your file.

Writing the content

It's time to start working on the content, and this should be fun as you will see your site grow with every article that you publish. The first page I want to edit is the 404 page. The 404 error does not say a lot to your visitors; it only indicates that they did not reach the page they expected.

The 404 page is great for guiding people back into your web site. So, change it to something more than just a "404 Page not found" item. Here is what I made of it.

Using 404 to guide visitors

I created a line with a link to the home page and a link to the **Sitemap** page. I pointed to the menus on top and the side, and used a **Search** box from Google that will allow visitors to search the site for the information they are interested in. Remember, I said that a topic should always be image rich, and so here you can see an image on the 404 page.

The image is linked to the sitemap. If you use images, be aware of the fact that your visitors will be clicking on those images irrespective of whether they are linked. You can use this to your advantage by linking your images it to a relevant article or category on your site whenever possible.

Whether you use the SEF patch or not, please set the **Robots meta tag** option to **noindex, follow**.

By using **noindex** you make sure the 404 page doesn't show up in the search engine indexes, but your links still count and you don't want Google to think that you don't trust your own site, so set the **follow** tag.

Using the HTML title and meta tags

When you start writing the site's content, use the fields introduced by the SEF patch to your advantage. If you don't, why did you install it? So, let's see how I have used it on a page with the title **Japanese Gardens**.

It is a very generic title and also very short. The title looks fine on the page, but it is too short to get good rankings. So, using the extra **HTML Title** field you can give the page a better title that will show in Google's search result pages.

For this page I chose **How to Design your Japanese Garden,** which should attract some more hits and also give extra keywords such as "Design" and "How to". On the page add a short description for the meta tag by the same name and use some keywords that are also in the content of the page.

As you can see in one of the previous screenshots, there is a You Tube video embedded with a green border. You can find the color options, under the embed function for the video on www.youtube.com.

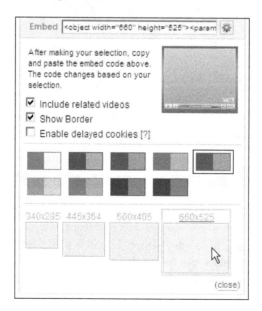

Fast and furious, or slow going

Writing and creating content can be done very quickly and, depending on the time you want to spend on your web site, your site can grow very fast. If you don't have that much time, make sure the number of pages grows to at least 10 or more. If you can rank with just five pages, you are in a niche without much competition.

Growing quickly gives you the possibility to rank with more pages in a short period of time, but it can be seen as a spam indicator also. You could get sandboxed by Google and it will take longer for your site to get the rankings it deserves.

Growing steadily means taking time to build the site piece by piece, by adding two or three pages per week, which will show very good results in the end. If you are looking for growth, you need to keep in mind that there should be enough content to encourage your visitors to come back to your site.

Using Google Webmaster tools

Once there is some content on your site and the menu structure is in place, you will see that your sitemap contains a decent number of links for Google to crawl. So, now it's time to give the search engines some food to eat by submitting the sitemap to Google Webmaster Central and placing a special spot in the `robots.txt` file.

Once you have submitted your site, log in to Google Webmaster Central and see if everything works without problems.

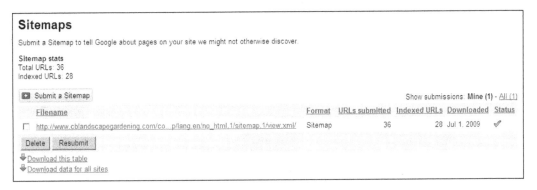

You can also get a nice overview on some of the terms you are ranking for at that moment. The ranking should grow in time as there will be more content to index, thus giving you more possibilities to rank.

Set your preferred URL

Using Google webmaster tools you can set the preferred URL that Google should use for indexing your web site.

Preferred domain	○ Don't set a preferred domain
	⦿ Display URLs as www.cblandscapegardening.com
	○ Display URLs as cblandscapegardening.com

This should reflect your own preference and your guess to what your visitors would use. In my case I opted for the **www.** version, as I think that the expected visitors to the site will use that option as well.

If you want to go full out in SEO terms, go for the non-www. version. It gives you four (4!) extra characters in your URL, as shown in the search engine results.

Google's help on meta tag errors

One other page for analysis of your site that you really need to check, but is mostly forgotten by a lot of webmasters, is the one under the Diagnostics section called **HTML Suggestions.**

HTML suggestions

When Googlebot crawled your site, it found some issues with your content. These issues won't prevent your site from appearing in Google search results, but addressing them may help your site's user experience and performance.

Meta description	Pages
Duplicate meta descriptions	4
Long meta descriptions	0
Short meta descriptions	2

Title tag	Pages
We didn't detect any issues with the title tags on your site.	

Non-indexable content	Pages
We didn't detect any issues with non-indexable content on your site.	

⬇ Download this table   Last updated Jul 1, 2009

If you click on those results, you will get a link to each page that has a problem so that you can easily fix the problems mentioned. Getting this page to show no problems at all will help you do better in your SEO efforts. The part of the webmaster tools that you will probably visit the most is **Your site on the web**.

This section shows you the ranking results you have achieved. There is also a page called **Keywords** that you need to check out. If the main keywords you want to target are not on that page, you need to improve your content so that they show up.

The results shown are from Google's Webmaster tool, but we also use Google Analytics and StatCounter to learn more about other keyword rankings you achieved. I found that these result pages give only an indication, but a check on the links and keywords that come in from the other stat programs will reveal a lot more.

Analyze results, rinse, and repeat.

With the first results from Google and StatCounter, it's now time to analyze the results so far. In StatCounter you can look at the keyword analysis to see if the most important keywords are indeed bringing you the traffic. If not, then again look at the content and the structure of the site.

		Num	Perc.	Search Term
Exit Pages				
Came From				
Keyword Analysis	▼	3	6.00%	landscape +bees
Recent Keyword Activity	▼	3	6.00%	site:www.cblandscapegardening.com
Recent Came From	▼	2	4.00%	guide to landscape gardening
Search Engine Wars	▼	2	4.00%	design a crazy garden
Exit Links	▼	2	4.00%	crazy design program
Exit Link Activity	▼	2	4.00%	los banos plants
Downloads	▼	2	4.00%	los banos landscaping
Download Activity	▼	2	4.00%	crazy garden designs
Visitor Paths	▼	1	2.00%	introduction to ponds
Visit Length	▼	1	2.00%	landdscape gardening
Returning Visits	▼	1	2.00%	cb landscape.com
Recent Pageload Activity	▼	1	2.00%	landscape design and realization
Recent Visitor Activity	▼	1	2.00%	how to build a great pond
Recent Visitor Map	▼	1	2.00%	los banos landscapers
Country/State/City/ISP	▼	1	2.00%	garden design realisation
Browsers	▼	1	2.00%	landscape gardening
System Stats	▼	1	2.00%	Landscape Gardening Tip
Lookup IP Address				

Also in Analytics, you can see the keywords used by your visitors to come to your site:

Dimension: Keyword ⌄	Visits ↓	Pages/Visit
1. cb landscape gardenging	2	12.00
2. landscapers los banos	2	12.00
3. cb landscape	1	1.00
4. cb landscape.com	1	1.00
5. cb landscaper	1	1.00
6. crazy garden blog	1	1.00
7. crazy gardens	1	1.00
8. crazy water feture	1	1.00
9. landscape garden blogs	1	1.00
10. los banos gardners	1	1.00
11. los banos landscapers	1	1.00
12. los banos plants	1	6.00
13. los baños c.b.	1	1.00

For me this list means that I need to check the site for spelling mistakes, especially the first and the eighth term. On the other hand, it was really nice to see the result shown in the following screenshot, the ninth position out of 4.85 million hits!

It's a promising start, but there is still a lot of work to do on the site.

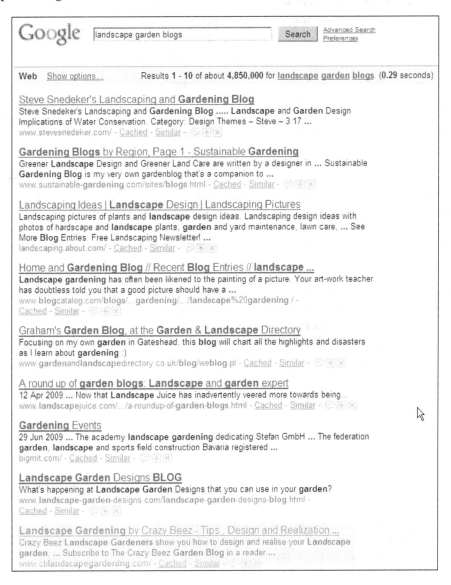

As you know, localization of the site title also helps. For example, if an individual staying in Los Banos searches for terms such as "landscapers Los Banos", then the site may appear in the top 10. If this were a real business site, it would definitely be very helpful to get it into Google maps.

Rounding it all up

In this appendix we looked at the complete process in a case study form. We looked at the way you can pick a niche to build the site on, in order to gain momentum for the most popular keywords that you ultimately want to reach for.

We did some brainstorming to get ideas for a domain name and we got the domain and the hosting to start building the site. The most essential part of the process of building your site is to set up the Joomla! 1.5 base installation. Once you have completed the installation, install the SEF patch and sh404SEF component and configure it.

We chose, purchased, and installed a great Joomla! SEO-ready template. We created a structure for the site and reflected it in the naming of the sections and categories. The best way to show your visitors the structure and lead them through your web site is to show the way you build the menus. After installing and configuring the sitemap, we gave the link to Google and placed the right command in the `robots.txt` file.

Writing the content and optimizing the content with text, images, titles, and meta tag descriptions and keywords is the most fun part. It is also the most time consuming part of the site building process. We looked at the use of Google webmaster tools to find possible problems with the site and learned how to analyze results to further improve the rankings.

As a final thought, make sure your site is secured to prevent hacking. The minimal effort you should take is to make sure the following files are set to read only:

- `configuration.php`
- `.htaccess`
- `index.php`
- `robots.txt`

If possible, get your administrator directory secured with a separate `.htaccess` username and password. You should also remove the default "admin" username and create a more secured login name and password for yourself as a "Super Administrator".

Now put down this book and start working on your Joomla! Search Engine Optimized web site and have fun in the process.

B
Joomla! robots.txt and .htaccess

The `robots.txt` and `.htaccess` files are important to help you gain more traffic from search engines. The `robots.txt` file opens up or restricts access to files on your server for Search Engine Robots. The `.htaccess` file takes care of creating great looking, search engine friendly, and easy to remember URLs for your web site.

However, they can also create havoc and dismay if used the wrong way, leaving Search Engine Robots locked outside your web site. It can also result in displaying those nice looking 404 pages under every link you touch on your web site. So, how do you know if the files are okay? Testing is the keyword here!

Making sense of robots.txt

The Googlebot and other Search Engine Robots will crawl your web site based on the rules you provide in your `robots.txt` file. This file needs to be in the root of your domain or Joomla! installation directory.

Setting your rules for robots

There are just a few rules that robots will take into account if they visit your web site. Some of the rules are in the `robots.txt` file and you can add another set of rules, either on a page-by-page basis or on a link in your web site.

In the `robots.txt` file you will see commands such as:

```
Allow: /folder1/myfile.html
Disallow: /folder1/
```

You can also have a link to the sitemap of your web site:

```
Sitemap: http://www.gstatic.com/s2/sitemaps/profiles-sitemap.xml
```

This will give the link to your XML or `.html` sitemap to the robots if you don't have an XML file. Small difference, large effect!

The following rule looks like it does the same thing, but it doesn't:

```
User-agent: *
Disallow: /
```

The "/" in the second line tells the robots not to visit your site's pages. In the following example, the robots are allowed to visit all pages.

```
User-agent: *
Disallow:
```

The previous example is to show that you really need to make sure to use the right syntax in your `robots.txt` file.

Standard Joomla! robots.txt

Joomla! comes with a standard `robots.txt` file:

```
User-agent: *
Disallow: /administrator/
Disallow: /cache/
Disallow: /components/
Disallow: /images/
Disallow: /includes/
Disallow: /installation/
Disallow: /language/
Disallow: /libraries/
Disallow: /media/
Disallow: /modules/
Disallow: /plugins/
Disallow: /templates/
Disallow: /tmp/
Disallow: /xmlrpc/
```

As you can see, most special directories are blocked from the Search Engine Robots. There is no need to let them visit and index these special pages that hold the core of the system.

Improving the standard for image searchers

In the standard Joomla! `robots.txt` file, the directory `images` is blocked by the following line:

```
Disallow: /images/
```

However, this is one line that you need to remove. In the `images` directory you have all the images that you so carefully named, to be included in the image search pages of the major search engines.

Make sure that the robots get access to this directory by removing that line from your robots.txt file. This will open up a new flood of visitors. If you installed the SEF patch from JoomlAtWork.com site, this is already done for you.

A complete example

The following is the complete `robots.txt` file of the site www.cblandscapegardenign.com—notice the long line for `sitemap:`, it must be on one line in your `robots.txt` file.

```
User-agent: *
Disallow: /administrator/
Disallow: /cache/
Disallow: /components/
Disallow: /includes/
Disallow: /installation/
Disallow: /language/
Disallow: /libraries/
Disallow: /media/
Disallow: /modules/
Disallow: /plugins/
Disallow: /templates/
Disallow: /tmp/
Disallow: /xmlrpc/

sitemap: http://www.cblandscapegardening.com/component/option,com_
xmap/lang,en/no_html,1/sitemap,1/view,xml/
```

Full access is now granted to include the `images` and stories directories, and a sitemap link is provided for all Search Engine Robots. The way in which pages and links are handled by the robots is a part of your content creation and that explanation is covered in Chapter 4, *How to write keyword-rich articles*.

Learn to love your .htaccess file

The .htaccess file is the most important file for having great, clean, and keyword-rich URLs. It is also a beast that can mess up your web site, making it totally inaccessible for every visitor who wants to move through your site clicking on a link from the front page and every link ends up telling them, "404 page not found".

The best part is that you might need to change it for every installation you do, even sometimes with the same hosting provider. Unfortunately, there are also some hosting providers that don't allow you to have your own .htaccess file because of its potential security risk.

If you have a hosting package that uses **IIS (Internet Information Services)** or even Apache on Windows, you will see that you will not be able to use the .htaccess file and you should use another option such as sh404SEF, which is discussed in Chapter 6.

The basics

There are some basic rules in the .htaccess file for Joomla! that should always be in place:

```
########## Begin - Joomla! core SEF Section
#
RewriteCond %{REQUEST_FILENAME} !-f
RewriteCond %{REQUEST_FILENAME} !-d
RewriteCond %{REQUEST_URI} !^/index.php
RewriteCond %{REQUEST_URI} (/|\.php|\.html|\.htm|\.feed|\.pdf|\.raw|/
[^.]*)$  [NC]
RewriteRule (.*) index.php
RewriteRule .* - [E=HTTP_AUTHORIZATION:%{HTTP:Authorization},L]
#
########## End - Joomla! core SEF Section
```

These lines make sure that your URL rewrite function is working if you renamed the file from htaccess.txt to .htaccess. Next, the **SEO Settings** in your Joomla! should be set to active.

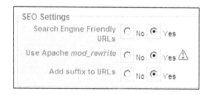

Test these settings first and get them to work before you install and configure any SEF component.

The good and the bad

As easy as it sounds to get the basic **SEO Settings** to work, it can be a challenge to get everything working the way you want it to. Every hosting provider has its own security settings that will affect the way the .htaccess file should be configured. You could even find that with the same provider, each new server needs different .htaccess file content.

The good thing is that once you've got the configuration right, you don't have to look at it again (unless your hosting provider changes some settings). One thing to remember is that you need to set the permissions for that file to 644 as it is a real threat to your site to leave the file world writable.

Some providers will not permit you to use your own .htaccess file because of this possible threat. In that case you can switch providers or just try to work with sh404SEF to overcome this limitation.

In the Joomla! .htaccess file there are some lines to prevent certain possible hacker attacks. Leave those lines in place as they are active by default.

Solving the most common problems

Looking at .htaccess configurations, there are usually a number of settings that can possibly hold you back in getting the URL rewrites to work. These setting are commented in the basic Joomla! htaccess.txt file, but somehow people don't really see what they need to do to get it right.

The first problem is the fact that the server is not set to use FollowSymLinks — one of the best options for fast file linking on a *Nix server.

Some common problems

This is the first option to comment, if you get 500 or 404 errors. Locate the following line in your .htaccess file:

```
Options +FollowSymLinks
```

And change it to the following:

```
# Options +FollowSymLinks
```

Save the file, upload it, and try again. The other option is the base for the rewrite action:

```
# RewriteBase /
```

If you have your Joomla! installation done in a subdirectory, you need to activate and change this setting to the following:

```
RewriteBase /subdirname
```

Your `.htaccess` file should always be in the root of your domain. If you don't have your site in a subdirectory, you might still need to activate this setting and change it to the following:

```
RewriteBase /
```

As I stated before, you need to do some testing to find the settings that work for your site. The above mentioned problems combined will give you several possible settings to figure out and test. These settings will be the cause of 80 to 90 percent of all problems in getting your `.htaccess` file to work.

.htaccess extras

Here are some extras that you might want to try once your basic `.htaccess` is working. First up, you can remove the `/index.php` and `/home.html`, by adding the following code at the end of your `.htaccess` file.

The last lines are there to make sure that your site is redirected from `http://example.com` to `www.example.com`.

If you want to use this, change the highlighted `www.example.com` references to reflect your own domain name.

```
# index.php redirect
RewriteCond %{THE_REQUEST} ^[A-Z]{3,9}\ /index\.php\ HTTP/
RewriteRule ^index\.php$ http://www.example.com/ [R=301,L]
# Homepage redirect
Redirect 301 /home.html http://www.example.com
# Redirect non-www to www version
RewriteCond %{HTTP_HOST} ^example\.com$ [NC]
RewriteRule ^(.*)$ http://www.example.com/$1 [R=301,L]
```

Final thoughts on 301 redirects

If you change your old URLs, you might encounter some problems with them and you need to redirect the old URLs that are still in the search engines to your new URLs. A code 301 will tell the Search Engine Robots that this URL is permanently changed and is now located at the new URL.

If you use an SEF component and change from Non-SEF URLs to SEF URLs, the SEF component will do this 301 redirect stuff for you. Otherwise you need to set some 301 redirect rules in your `.htaccess` file.

A basic 301 redirect rule will look like this:

```
Redirect 301 /blog/example-article.html http://www.example.com/
example-article.html
```

Make sure to accommodate the above rule in one line in your `.htaccess` file. The build up is as follows:

- First you set the 301 redirect—the command needed to tell the robots what is moved.

- The `/blog/example-article.html` needs to be a part of the URL after the main domain name, so in this case, `http://www.example.com/blog/example-article.html`.

- The last part is the "full URL" where the article has moved to. You cannot use a relative link for this part, you need to state the full URL.

Redirection to a new domain

In this example, I have changed the location of the previous blog placed in the `/blog/` directory to a completely new domain.

```
Redirect 301 /blog/ http://blog.hummerbie.com
```

This way you can redirect a complete subdirectory or subdomain to a completely new domain.

Working examples for your site

In the following pages you will find some examples of real .htaccess files, so that you can see how they were built for specific situations.

Standard Joomla! .htaccess

First, here is the standard Joomla! htaccess.txt for reference:

```
##
# @version $Id: htaccess.txt 10492 2008-07-02 06:38:28Z ircmaxell $
# @package Joomla
# @copyright Copyright (C) 2005 - 2008 Open Source Matters. All rights
reserved.
# @license http://www.gnu.org/copyleft/gpl.html GNU/GPL
# Joomla! is Free Software
##


#####################################################
#  READ THIS COMPLETELY IF YOU CHOOSE TO USE THIS FILE
#
# The line just below this section: 'Options +FollowSymLinks' may
cause problems
# with some server configurations.  It is required for use of mod_
rewrite, but may already
# be set by your server administrator in a way that dissallows
changing it in
# your .htaccess file.  If using it causes your server to error out,
comment it out (add # to
# beginning of line), reload your site in your browser and test your
sef url's.  If they work,
# it has been set by your server administrator and you do not need it
set here.
#
#####################################################

##  Can be commented out if causes errors, see notes above.
Options +FollowSymLinks

#
#  mod_rewrite in use

RewriteEngine On
```

```
########## Begin - Rewrite rules to block out some common exploits
## If you experience problems on your site block out the operations
listed below
## This attempts to block the most common type of exploit `attempts`
to Joomla!
#
# Block out any script trying to set a mosConfig value through the URL
RewriteCond %{QUERY_STRING} mosConfig_[a-zA-Z_]{1,21}(=|\%3D) [OR]
# Block out any script trying to base64_encode crap to send via URL
RewriteCond %{QUERY_STRING} base64_encode.*\(.*\) [OR]
# Block out any script that includes a <script> tag in URL
RewriteCond %{QUERY_STRING} (\<|%3C).*script.*(\>|%3E) [NC,OR]
# Block out any script trying to set a PHP GLOBALS variable via URL
RewriteCond %{QUERY_STRING} GLOBALS(=|\[|\%[0-9A-Z]{0,2}) [OR]
# Block out any script trying to modify a _REQUEST variable via URL
RewriteCond %{QUERY_STRING} _REQUEST(=|\[|\%[0-9A-Z]{0,2})
# Send all blocked request to homepage with 403 Forbidden error!
RewriteRule ^(.*)$ index.php [F,L]
#
########## End - Rewrite rules to block out some common exploits

#   Uncomment following line if your webserver's URL
#   is not directly related to physical file paths.
#   Update Your Joomla! Directory (just / for root)

# RewriteBase /


########## Begin - Joomla! core SEF Section
#
RewriteCond %{REQUEST_FILENAME} !-f
RewriteCond %{REQUEST_FILENAME} !-d
RewriteCond %{REQUEST_URI} !^/index.php
RewriteCond %{REQUEST_URI} (/|\.php|\.html|\.htm|\.feed|\.pdf|\.raw|/
[^.]*)$  [NC]
RewriteRule (.*) index.php
RewriteRule .* - [E=HTTP_AUTHORIZATION:%{HTTP:Authorization},L]
#
########## End - Joomla! core SEF Section
```

FollowSymLinks set Off

The following example has `FollowSymLinks` set to `Off` and most comments removed:

```
##
# @version $Id: htaccess.txt 10492 2008-07-02 06:38:28Z ircmaxell $
# @package Joomla
# @copyright Copyright (C) 2005 - 2008 Open Source Matters. All rights
reserved.
# @license http://www.gnu.org/copyleft/gpl.html GNU/GPL
# Joomla! is Free Software
##


##  Can be commented out if causes errors, see notes above.
# Options +FollowSymLinks


#
#  mod_rewrite in use

RewriteEngine On

########## Begin - Rewrite rules to block out some common exploits
# Block out any script trying to set a mosConfig value through the URL
RewriteCond %{QUERY_STRING} mosConfig_[a-zA-Z_]{1,21}(=|\%3D) [OR]
# Block out any script trying to base64_encode crap to send via URL
RewriteCond %{QUERY_STRING} base64_encode.*\(.*\) [OR]
# Block out any script that includes a <script> tag in URL
RewriteCond %{QUERY_STRING} (\<|\%3C).*script.*(\>|\%3E) [NC,OR]
# Block out any script trying to set a PHP GLOBALS variable via URL
RewriteCond %{QUERY_STRING} GLOBALS(=|\[|\%[0-9A-Z]{0,2}) [OR]
# Block out any script trying to modify a _REQUEST variable via URL
RewriteCond %{QUERY_STRING} _REQUEST(=|\[|\%[0-9A-Z]{0,2})
# Send all blocked request to homepage with 403 Forbidden error!
RewriteRule ^(.*)$ index.php [F,L]
#

#  Update Your Joomla! Directory (just / for root)
# RewriteBase /


########## Begin - Joomla! core SEF Section
#
RewriteCond %{REQUEST_FILENAME} !-f
RewriteCond %{REQUEST_FILENAME} !-d
```

```
RewriteCond %{REQUEST_URI} !^/index.php
RewriteCond %{REQUEST_URI} (/|\.php|\.html|\.htm|\.feed|\.pdf|\.raw|/
[^.]*)$  [NC]
RewriteRule (.*) index.php
RewriteRule .* - [E=HTTP_AUTHORIZATION:%{HTTP:Authorization},L]
#
########## End - Joomla! core SEF Section
```

FollowSymLinks set Off RewriteBase On

The following example has `FollowSymLinks` set to `Off` and `Rewritebase On`.

If you have your site in a subdirectory such as /Joomla or /website, you need to place that after the `Rewritebase /`, for example, `Rewritebase /website`.

```
##
# @version $Id: htaccess.txt 10492 2008-07-02 06:38:28Z ircmaxell $
# @package Joomla
# @copyright Copyright (C) 2005 - 2008 Open Source Matters. All rights
reserved.
# @license http://www.gnu.org/copyleft/gpl.html GNU/GPL
# Joomla! is Free Software
##


##  Can be commented out if causes errors, see notes above.
# Options +FollowSymLinks

#
#  mod_rewrite in use

RewriteEngine On

########## Begin - Rewrite rules to block out some common exploits
# Block out any script trying to set a mosConfig value through the URL
RewriteCond %{QUERY_STRING} mosConfig_[a-zA-Z_]{1,21}(=|\%3D) [OR]
# Block out any script trying to base64_encode crap to send via URL
RewriteCond %{QUERY_STRING} base64_encode.*\(.*\) [OR]
# Block out any script that includes a <script> tag in URL
RewriteCond %{QUERY_STRING} (\<|\%3C).*script.*(\>|\%3E) [NC,OR]
# Block out any script trying to set a PHP GLOBALS variable via URL
RewriteCond %{QUERY_STRING} GLOBALS(=|\[|\%[0-9A-Z]{0,2}) [OR]
# Block out any script trying to modify a _REQUEST variable via URL
RewriteCond %{QUERY_STRING} _REQUEST(=|\[|\%[0-9A-Z]{0,2})
# Send all blocked request to homepage with 403 Forbidden error!
```

```
RewriteRule ^(.*)$ index.php [F,L]
#


#  Update Your Joomla! Directory (just / for root)
RewriteBase /



########## Begin - Joomla! core SEF Section
#
RewriteCond %{REQUEST_FILENAME} !-f
RewriteCond %{REQUEST_FILENAME} !-d
RewriteCond %{REQUEST_URI} !^/index.php
RewriteCond %{REQUEST_URI} (/|\.php|\.html|\.htm|\.feed|\.pdf|\.raw|/
[^.]*)$  [NC]
RewriteRule (.*) index.php
RewriteRule .* - [E=HTTP_AUTHORIZATION:%{HTTP:Authorization},L]
#
########## End - Joomla! core SEF Section
```

Basic sh404SEF SEF basic .htaccess standard

The following is an example of the basic sh404SEF component's `.htaccess`
file, where you will need to check if you need `FollowSymLinks` set to `Off` and
`Rewritebase On`:

```
##
# @version $Id: htaccess.txt 10492 2008-07-02 06:38:28Z ircmaxell $
# @package Joomla
# @copyright Copyright (C) 2005 - 2008 Open Source Matters. All rights
reserved.
# @license http://www.gnu.org/copyleft/gpl.html GNU/GPL
# Joomla! is Free Software
##


## Can be commented out if causes errors, see notes above.
# Options +FollowSymLinks


#
#  mod_rewrite in use


RewriteEngine On


########## Begin - Rewrite rules to block out some common exploits
# Block out any script trying to set a mosConfig value through the URL
RewriteCond %{QUERY_STRING} mosConfig_[a-zA-Z_]{1,21}(=|\%3D) [OR]
```

```
# Block out any script trying to base64_encode crap to send via URL
RewriteCond %{QUERY_STRING} base64_encode.*\(.*\) [OR]
# Block out any script that includes a <script> tag in URL
RewriteCond %{QUERY_STRING} (\<|%3C).*script.*(\>|%3E) [NC,OR]
# Block out any script trying to set a PHP GLOBALS variable via URL
RewriteCond %{QUERY_STRING} GLOBALS(=|\[|\%[0-9A-Z]{0,2}) [OR]
# Block out any script trying to modify a _REQUEST variable via URL
RewriteCond %{QUERY_STRING} _REQUEST(=|\[|\%[0-9A-Z]{0,2})
# Send all blocked request to homepage with 403 Forbidden error!
RewriteRule ^(.*)$ index.php [F,L]
#


#  Update Your Joomla! Directory (just / for root)
RewriteBase /


########## Begin - 3rd Party SEF Section
############# Use this section if you are using a 3rd party (Non
Joomla! core) SEF extension - e.g. OpenSEF, 404_SEF, 404SEFx, SEF
Advance, etc
#
RewriteCond %{REQUEST_URI} ^(/component/option,com) [NC,OR] ##optional
- see notes##
RewriteCond %{REQUEST_URI} (/|\.htm|\.php|\.html|/[^.]*)$ [NC]
RewriteCond %{REQUEST_FILENAME} !-f
RewriteCond %{REQUEST_FILENAME} !-d
RewriteRule (.*) index.php
#
########## End - 3rd Party SEF Section
```

Index

Symbols

301 redirect
  about 291
  build up 291
  to new domain 291
301 redirect, activating
  from Joomla SEF to sh404SEF 159
  from non-sef URL 159
  from www/non-www 159
  Home page URL 160
  Log 404 errors option 160
.htaccess file
  301 redirects 291
  about 285, 288
  advantage 289
  basic rules 288
  basic sh404SEF component 296, 297
  common problems 289
  disadvantage 289
  extras 290
  FollowSymLinks 294-296
  problems, solving 289
  standard Joomla! .htaccess 292, 293

A

advanced configuration settings
  about 150
  available options 155, 156
  By component settings 161
  Delete META 151
  extended basics 154
  extra options 152
  Import/Export URLs 150
  language settings 156, 157
  Meta/SEO option settings, using 162
  META tags 151
  plugins, optimizing 155
  Plugins section 153, 154
  Purge Custom Redirects 151
  security 404 164
  sh404SEF Configuration 151, 152
  View/Edit 404 Logs 150
  View/Edit Custom Redirects 150
Alexa
  about 246
  Related Links 247
  Sites Linking In 247
Alexa web site
  statistics, providing 216- 218
articles
  better titles, writing 98
  confusion, avoiding 99
  consistency, maintaining 99
  keyword density 100
  keywords, inserting in title 98
  META tag description 99
  META tag keywords 99
  optimizing 96
  Session Settings value, modifying 96
  title, analyzing 97
  writing, in natural way 97
AWStats
  about 214
  advantages 215
  disadvantages 215
  using 214

B

baseline, statistics, setting up
  blocking cookie, creating 38
  Google Analytics, using 39, 40
  trackers, installing 34
  www.statcounter.com, using 34-38
basic sh404SEF component 296, 297
Bing, using
  sitemap.xml 66
  site verification 66
blocking cookie 38
blog
  about 243
  search services 245
Blogger
  about 249, 250
  setting up 249
blogging
  about 109
  comments 117
  MyBlog 135
  sepatare blog component, drawbacks 134
  sepatare blog component, MyBlog 135
  sepatare blog component, using 134
blogging, SEO
  advantages 110
  fresh content, creating 110
Blog layout 111
blog menu, Joomla! based blog
  creating, steps 114- 117
  Full Text, using instead of Intro Text feed 116
  link to the section, creating 114
  Parameters(Component) settings, changing 115
  separator, using 116
Blogpulse 246
blog writing time, minimizing
  articles, writing 256
  best articles, using 256
  bookmarking sites 256
bounce rate 232

C

cache 79
cache function, Joomla!

modules, checking 196
server settings, optimizing 196, 197
using 195
using, externally 197
Cache management tab
  using 158
categories
  naming 270
comments
  Alexa 246, 247
  Disqus 118
  examples 117
  importance 118
  posting 243
  posting areas, searching 244
  RSS Feeds 123
  visitors, interacting with 118
commercial template
  choosing 179
commercial tools, trade tools
  IBP 24
  KeywordDiscovery 27
  Keyword Elite 22
  SEO toolkit 27, 28
content
  404 page, using 276, 277
  fast writing 279
  HTML title, using 277
  meta tags, using 277
  writing 276-279
content analysis, Google Analytics 236
CSS
  easy file path, optimizing 203, 204
  files 198
  files, combining 202, 203
  files, optimizing 200, 201

D

different time span
  selecting 237
Disqus, comments
  about 118
  advantages 122
  disadvantages 122, 123
  downloading 121
  installing 121

service, configuring 119, 121
downloading
Joomlatwork SEF patch 72
sh404SEF 142

E

eXtensible Hyper Text Markup Language.
See **XHTML**

F

fluid width template
fast templates, using 185, 186
font changes, displaying 185
choosing 183
sample 184
FollowSymLinks 294-296
forum signatures 242
forums, using
incoming links, searching 242
free template
about 177
finding 178
limitation 179
free tools, trade tools
Google's AdWord 16
SEO Book Keyword tool 21
Wordtracker 19

G

global configuration, modifying
about 74, 75
HTML titles, using 80-82
menu HTML titles, creating 77, 78
metafields settings, options 76
new Joomlaatwork fields, using 80
page HTML titles, creating 79
Google
blog searching tool 110
Feedburner 110, 125
keyword, displaying 93
metadata, using 84
webmaster tools, using 279
Google Analytics
analyzing 226, 227
bounce rate 232

content analysis 236
keywords 235
number of pageviews 232
number of visitors 231
site overlay 237
static IP address visits, filtering 228
structure analysis 236
time, spent by visitor 232
traffic sources 234
traffic sources, options 235
visitors overview 230, 231
your visits, excluding from dynamic address 228, 229
Google Analytics, using 39
Google's AdSense 17
Google's AdWord, free tools
columns to display, choosing 16, 17
keywords, selecting 18, 19
use 16
Google's Feedburner, SEO
analyze tab 127
feed title, adjusting 126
feed URL 126
monitize tab 127
optimize tab 127
optimize tab settings, BrowserFriendly 127
optimize tab settings, SmartFeed 128
options, selecting 127-131
publicize tab 127
publicize tab settings, email subscriptions 129
publicize tab settings, FeedCount 130
publicize tab settings, NoIndex 131
publicize tab settings, PingShot 129, 130
RSS Feed replacement, with FeedBurner feed 131, 132
troubleshootize tab 127
Google Sites 248, 249
Google webmaster tools
HTML Suggestions 280
meta tag errors, helping out 280
preferred URL, setting up 280
results, analyzing 281, 283
using 279

H

headlines, using
  best options 100
  keywords, inserting into footers 102
  keywords, inserting into headers 102
  placeholders, creating 102
  web page, making more scanable 101
Home page meta settings, modifying
  about 164
  meta tags, adding on SEF component 166
  Robots tag 165
  URL, adding 168
HTML title
  about 80
  example 80
  using 81, 82
hubpage 251, 252

I

IBP, commercial tools
  about 24, 27
  ad groups, selecting 26
iBusinessPromoter. *See* **IBP, commercial tool**
Icerocket 246
ICL 141
IIS 288
images
  Alternative text, using 210
  caption text, using 210
  disadvantage 204
  improving, ways 204
  IrfanView 206
  Jasc Paint Shop Pro 8, using 205
  keywords used, for file naming 208
  on page size parameters, using 208, 209
  resizing 205
  right program, selecting 205- 207
  title tag, using 209
incoming link
  about 241
  disadvantage 241
  forums, using 242
  paid links 241, 242
installing

Joomlatwork SEF patch 73
Yslow 192, 193
International Information Services. *See* **IIS**
Internet Business Promotor. *See* **IBP, commercial tool**
Ion Cube Loader. *See* **ICL**

J

JavaScript
  about 198
  optimizing 197
  web site options, considering 199
Joomfish 2.0 156
Joomla!
  .htaccess file 285
  Blog layout 111
  cache function 195
  Joomla!robots.txt 285
  upgrading 88
Joomla! 1.5
  SEO 71
Joomla! 1.5 base installation
  SEF patch, installing 265
  SEO template, installing 267- 269
  setting up 265
  sh404SEF component, installing 265
Joomla! based blog
  blog menu, creating 114
  categories, selecting 112, 113
  limiting, category section 113
  section, structuring 111, 112
  setting up 111- 114
  term relevency, maintaining 113
Joomla! basic problems, solving
  E-mail icons 12
  global configuration meta tag settings 11
  meta generator tag 12
  PDF 11
  print format 11
  SEO Settings 10
Joomla! blogging 109
Joomla! robots.txt file, improving
  about 67, 68
  Google webmaster tools 69
  sitemap link, adding 68
Joomla! SEO

challenges 7
Joomla! statistics 239
Joomlatwork SEF 8
Joomlatwork SEF component
  distinct overview 89
Joomlatwork SEF patch
  about 72
  copy right field 89
  downloading 72
  generator meta name 88
  installing 73
  modifying 88
  uninstalling 88
  upgrading 88

K

KEI 25
keyword density, articles
  features 100
KeywordDiscovery, commercial tools 23, 27
Keyword Effectiveness Index. *See* **KEI**
Keyword Elite, commercial tools
  about 22
  advantage 23
  disadvantage 23
  new project, creating 22
  preferences option 23
keyword research
  basic research, conducting 14
  need for 13
keywords
  choosing 33
  displaying, in Google 93
  displaying, in Yahoo! 93
  selecting 91
  subject topic, selecting 92
  target keywords, searching 92
  writing 95
  writing with, importance 91
keywords, choosing
  amazon.com, using 33
  ask.com, using 28, 29
  baseline, statistics, setting up 34- 40
  examples 28
  Google Analytics, using 39, 40
  Google, using 31, 33

keyword packages 28
list 33
main keywords 33
related searches 29
www.statcounter.com, using 34- 37
yahoo.com, using 30, 31
Yahoo!, using 28
keywords, writing
  about 95
  content on page, structuring 95
  placing, in Article tittle 96
  placing, in first paragraph 96
  placing, in HTML title 96
  placing, in last paragraph 96
  placing, in meta tag description 96
  placing, in meta tag words 96

L

Latent Semantic Indexing. *See* **LSI**
link
  company name, using 259
  real contact information, providing 260
  real name, using 259
  requesting, techniques 257- 260
  topics, describing 259
linking empire, creating
  Blogger, using 249
  Google Sites, using 248, 249
  hubpage, using 251, 252
  services, using 247
  Squidoo, using 250
  WordPress, using 252
log files
  error, detecting 204
LSI 48
lynx 185

M

main keywords
  architects 33
  deck 34
  designers 34
  designs 33
  english garden 34
  garden 34
  gardeners 33, 34

greenhouses 34
ideas 33
japanese garden 34
jobs 33
landscape gardening 33
lightning 34
patio 34
plants 33
retaining wallls 34
software 33
supplies 34
tips 33
ware features 33

menus
Articles 270
images, using in blog layout 274
main menu 272, 273

menu structure, improving
better stucture, creating 51
items, restructuring 52- 54
separators, using 55
submenus, using 55

metadata fields, using
about 103
Copy right field 103
good meta tag description, HTML Title 104
good meta tag description, writing 104
Google settings 103
HTML Title field 103
keywords field, using 104, 106
Metadata Information tab 103
read more option, using 106
Robots meta tag 103
summary 106, 107

metafields settings
metadata 84
meta tag robots settings 83
show author meta tag 83
show joomla generator tag 83
show title meta tag 83

Meta/SEO option settings, using
Activate Meta Management, setting 162
change multiple h1 in h2 option 163
Insert h1 tags, option 163
Insert Title in read more...links, setting 163
outbound links symbol, inserting 163
Remove Joomla Generator tag, setting 162
Use table-less output option 163

MyBlog
additions 137
admin panel 135
general settings, configuring 137

N

niche
domain name, picking up 264
selecting 264

O

OctaGate service
color codes 191
using 190

ODP 87

Open Directory Project. *See* **ODP**

P

pages, improving
description tag, using 84
duplicate meta tag descriptions, avoiding 85
keywords, avoiding 85
keywords tag, using 85
metadata, using 84
metafields setting 83

PingShot
about 129
Newsgator 129
Ping-o-matic option 130

R

robots.txt
about 285
example 287
image standards, improving 287
making 285
rules, setting 285, 286
standard file 286

robots.txt file, using
Joomla! robots.txt file, improving 67
Search Engine Robots, putting to work 67

RSS Feeds, comments
about 123
activating 123
working with 123, 124

S

search engine results page (SERP) 140
Search Engine Optimization. *See* **SEO**
search engines, controlling
  Google settings 87
  index 86
  noarchive option 87
  noodp option 87
  nosnippe option 87
  Robots meta tag used 86
section
  category listing, creating 270
  naming 270
  structure 270
SEF components, options
  Artio JoomSEF 3 141
  SEF Advance 141
  sh404SEF 141
SEF URLs
  selecting 140
SEO
  about 71
  blogging 110
  Firefox 192
  Google's Feedburner 125
  speed 189
  usabilty, need for 181
SEO Book Keyword, free tools
  export to CSV 21
SEO site structure, creating
  categories, using 44, 45
  keyword list, using 47
  keywords, adding 46
  keyword, sorting 47
  keywords used, benefits 48
  ranking possibilities 48
  related topic, clustering 45
  sections, using 44, 45
SEO site structure, optimizing
  about 43
  categories, using 44

menu structure, improving 51
robots.txt file, using 66
sections, using 44
sitemap component, importance 56
sitemap, submitting to search engine 63
usability, enhancing for search engine 49
usability, enhancing for users 49
SEO strategy, setting up
  about 8, 9
  basic Joomla! problems, solving 9
  keyword research 13
  to-do list 8
SEO template
  points, looking out 172- 174
sh404SEF
  about 8
  404 (error) page 148
  choosing, need for 142
  configuring 143
  configuration options, enabled 145
  configuration options, file suffix 147
  configuration options, replacement charac-
    ter 146
  configuration options, replacement charac-
    ter list 146
  configuration options, selecting 144
  configuration options, strip characters 146
  configuration options, unique ID 147
  configuring, control panel 143
  configuring, plugin 144
  downloading 142
  features 142
  installing 143
  non-reachable URLs, preventing 169
  non-SEF URL, finding 149
  plugins tab, show section option 147, 148
  plugins tab, Use show category option 148
  plugins tab, Use Title Alias option 147
  SEF URLs, recreating 169
  slow loading times, overcoming 168
site analysis
  obtaining, from Google Analytics 218
  obtaining, from StatCounter 218
sitemap
  configuring 275
  installing 275
sitemap component, SEO site structure

configuring 57
installing 57
sitemap.xml file, using 56
Xmap, installing 57
Xmap, using 57
sitemap, submitting
site verification, Bing used 66
site verification, Google used 63, 64
site verification, Yahoo used 65
site overlay, Google Analytics 237
site verification, Google used
sitemap.xml link 65
uploading 64, 65
Squidoo
about 250
lens, creating 250
StatCounter
about 219
features 222- 226
graph 222
information 222
limitations 226
statistics 219, 220
static IP address visits, Google Analytics
filtering out 228
structure analysis, Google Analytics 236

T

Technorati
about 244, 245
blog, claiming 132, 133
blog settings, editing 134
template
searching, for site 171, 172
time span
changing 237, 238
trade tools
commercial tools 15, 22
free tools 15
traffice sources
options 235
traffice sources, Google Analytics
about 234
referring sites 235
search engines 235

U

usability, enhancing
for search engines 49
for users 49
improvements 49, 50
site, navigating through 49
uncategorized articles, placing 50
usabilty, SEO
headlines 182
site, customizing 182
typography, using 182

V

View/Edit 404 Logs 150
View/Edit Custom Redirects 150

W

W3C validation
about 175
code positioning 175, 176
tables, avoiding 176
tables, minimizing 177
Webalizer
about 212
benefits 213
issues 213
web site
different time span, selecting 237
Google Analytics, analyzing 226
Joomla! statistics 239
monitoring 212
monitoring, options 212
site analysis, from Google Analytics 218
site analysis, from StatCounter 218
StatCounter graph 222
StatCounter information 222
StatCounter stats 219
statistics 212
statistics, from AWStats 214
statistics, from Webalizer 212
statistics, getting free 216
web site, monitoring 212
website statistics
about 212
Alexa web site 216- 218

getting, free 216
WordPress
  about 252, 253
  blog, creating 254
  blogging 253
  downside 254
  free blogging services, using 255
  ranking 253
Wordtracker, free tools 20

X

XHTML 172
Xmap
  cache lifetime option 60
  configuring 58
  copy option 60
  delete and clean option 60
  installing 57
  linking, to sitemap 61, 62
  menus, adding to sitemap 60
  preference options 59
  search engine, sitemaps 62
  SET Default option 60
  using 57

Y

Yahoo, using
  keyword, displaying 93, 94
  site verification 65
Yslow
  installing 192, 193
  tools 194, 195

Thank you for buying
Joomla! 1.5 SEO

Packt Open Source Project Royalties

When we sell a book written on an Open Source project, we pay a royalty directly to that project. Therefore by purchasing Joomla! 1.5 SEO, Packt will have given some of the money received to the Joomla! project.

In the long term, we see ourselves and you—customers and readers of our books—as part of the Open Source ecosystem, providing sustainable revenue for the projects we publish on. Our aim at Packt is to establish publishing royalties as an essential part of the service and support a business model that sustains Open Source.

If you're working with an Open Source project that you would like us to publish on, and subsequently pay royalties to, please get in touch with us.

Writing for Packt

We welcome all inquiries from people who are interested in authoring. Book proposals should be sent to author@packtpub.com. If your book idea is still at an early stage and you would like to discuss it first before writing a formal book proposal, contact us; one of our commissioning editors will get in touch with you.

We're not just looking for published authors; if you have strong technical skills but no writing experience, our experienced editors can help you develop a writing career, or simply get some additional reward for your expertise.

About Packt Publishing

Packt, pronounced 'packed', published its first book "Mastering phpMyAdmin for Effective MySQL Management" in April 2004 and subsequently continued to specialize in publishing highly focused books on specific technologies and solutions.

Our books and publications share the experiences of your fellow IT professionals in adapting and customizing today's systems, applications, and frameworks. Our solution-based books give you the knowledge and power to customize the software and technologies you're using to get the job done. Packt books are more specific and less general than the IT books you have seen in the past. Our unique business model allows us to bring you more focused information, giving you more of what you need to know, and less of what you don't.

Packt is a modern, yet unique publishing company, which focuses on producing quality, cutting-edge books for communities of developers, administrators, and newbies alike. For more information, please visit our website: www.PacktPub.com.

PUBLISHING

Building Websites with Joomla!

ISBN: 978-1-904811-94-7   Paperback: 340 pages

This best selling book has now been updated for the latest Joomla 1.5 release

1. A step by step tutorial to getting your Joomla! CMS website up fast

2. Walk through each step in a friendly and accessible way

3. Customize and extend your Joomla! site

4. Get your Joomla! website up fast

Joomla! Cash

ISBN: 978-1-847191-40-3   Paperback: 180 pages

Money-making weapons for your Joomla! website

1. Learn to set up a cash-generating Joomla! website

2. Learn to implement a shopping cart on Joomla!

3. How to run an affiliate program from your site

4. Set up streams of income using Joomla!

5. Gain valuable search-engine ranking knowledge

Please check **www.PacktPub.com** for information on our titles

www.ingramcontent.com/pod-product-compliance
Lightning Source LLC
Chambersburg PA
CBHW080928060326
40690CB00042B/3204